WOMAN-CENTERED BRAZILIAN CINEMA

SUNY Series in Latin American Cinema
———————
Ignacio M. Sánchez Prado and Leslie L. Marsh, editors

WOMAN-CENTERED BRAZILIAN CINEMA

FILMMAKERS AND PROTAGONISTS OF THE TWENTY-FIRST CENTURY

EDITED BY

JACK A. DRAPER III AND CACILDA M. RÊGO

Cover credit: (From left to right) Maria Augusta Ramos, photo credit: Ana Paula Amorim; Paula Sacchetta, photo credit: Carine Wallauer; Petra Costa, photo credit: Diego Bresani; Mari Corrêa, photo credit: Thays Bittar; Yasmin Thayná, photo credit: Juh Almeida. Published by State University of New York Press, Albany

© 2022 State University of New York

All rights reserved

Printed in the United States of America

No part of this book may be used or reproduced in any manner whatsoever without written permission. No part of this book may be stored in a retrieval system or transmitted in any form or by any means including electronic, electrostatic, magnetic tape, mechanical, photocopying, recording, or otherwise without the prior permission in writing of the publisher.

For information, contact State University of New York Press, Albany, NY
www.sunypress.edu

Library of Congress Cataloging-in-Publication Data

Names: Draper, Jack A., III, 1976– editor. | Rêgo, Cacilda, editor.
Title: Woman-centered Brazilian cinema : filmmakers and protagonists of the twenty-first century / edited by Jack A. Draper III and Cacilda M. Rêgo.
Description: Albany : State University of New York Press, [2022] | Series: SUNY series in Latin American cinema | Includes bibliographical references and index.
Identifiers: LCCN 2022002209 | ISBN 9781438490250 (hardcover : alk. paper) | ISBN 9781438490267 (ebook) | ISBN 9781438490243 (pbk. : alk. paper)
Subjects: LCSH: Women in the motion picture industry—Brazil. | Women in motion pictures. | Motion pictures—Brazil—History.
Classification: LCC PN1993.5.B7 W66 2022 | DDC 791.430981—dc23/eng/20220505
LC record available at https://lccn.loc.gov/2022002209

10 9 8 7 6 5 4 3 2 1

*For the women workers of the Brazilian film industry—
past, present, and future.*

Contents

Introduction   1
   Jack A. Draper III and Cacilda M. Rêgo

Part 1
Breaking Ground/Making Space in the Industry

Chapter 1
Recognizing Women's Contributions to Brazilian Cinema   17
   Cacilda M. Rêgo

Chapter 2
Behind the Scenes: Brazilian Women Screenwriters in Film
and Television   47
   Leslie L. Marsh

Chapter 3
Resistance and Online Activism: Brazilian Women Filmmakers'
Initiatives (2014–2017)   71
   Daniela Verztman Bagdadi

Chapter 4
Interview with Maria Augusta Ramos   101
   Jack A. Draper III, Cacilda M. Rêgo, and
   Gustavo Procopio Furtado

Part 2
Politics of Public/Private Spaces

Chapter 5
From Tweets to the Streets: Women's Documentary Filmmaking and Brazil's Feminist Spring   115
Rebecca J. Atencio

Chapter 6
Motherhood and Making Kin in Contemporary Brazilian Cinema   139
Jack A. Draper III

Chapter 7
The Many Mirrors of Maria Augusta Ramos: Landscape, Institutions, and Everyday Lives in Contemporary Brazil   161
Paula Halperin

Chapter 8
Interview with Petra Costa   183
Jack A. Draper III

Part 3
Intersecting Identities

Chapter 9
Conditions for a Twenty-First-Century Black Woman Cinema in Brazil: The Politics and Aesthetics of Yasmin Thayná's Audiovisual Practice   197
María Mercedes Vázquez Vázquez

Chapter 10
Afro-Brazilian Women Creative Workers Speak: Juliana Vicente's Standpoint Cinema (Cinema of O *Lugar de Fala*)   217
Reighan Gillam

Chapter 11
Interview with Mari Corrêa   233
Gustavo Procopio Furtado

Chapter 12
Interview with Paula Sacchetta   251
    Rebecca J. Atencio

Contributors   267

Index   271

Introduction

Women have made their presence felt in cinema since the silent era, but the twenty-first century in Brazil represents a new era of greater prominence in all sectors of the national industry. Scholarship, however, has lagged behind this effervescence of artistic activity. The primary goal of this anthology is to start to fill that lacuna, casting a wide net in this first attempt in the English language to produce a collection of scholarship and interviews wholly focused on Brazilian women filmmakers and woman-centered film narratives. In addition to a consideration of the labor of women in the industry and the rich film oeuvres that women filmmakers have produced in recent decades, we propose the term *woman-centered cinema*. Woman-centered cinema is filmmaking that places diverse women protagonists at center stage and pays greater attention to common concerns of women in public and private life in Brazil. Often, though not always, woman-centered filmmaking takes a more critical or political, feminist stance on the unique situation of women. Their common experiences and struggles are explored, while films focusing on the intersections of women's gender with other aspects of their identities, such as race, class, sexuality, or political ideology, allow for an understanding of womanhood as an internally diverse category.

A normative approach to the category of woman would thus obscure more than it reveals, since we would not be considering in its totality the production of women's filmmaking in the current century nor what trajectories may lie ahead. Instead, we understand that universality, and by extension the universal category of woman, "has important and strategic use [in that] the assertion of universality can be proleptic and performative, conjuring a reality that does not yet exist and holding out the possibility for a convergence of cultural horizons that have not yet met"

(Butler 1999). Judith Butler posits this view of universality as one that "is defined as a future-oriented labor of cultural translation." This framework of the universal category of woman allows room for the diversity and evolution of womanhood as it is actually represented in the work of Brazilian filmmakers, acknowledging that the category is changing and cannot be fully captured in one anthology. However, we see the scholarship and interviews gathered here as an important beginning to such a project, exploring important connections between the film form and production of recent women's cinema in Brazil and the possible futures that may be born out of such connections.

Brazilian women's filmmaking demonstrates considerable psychological depths, including the "different voice," "different psychology," and "different experience of love, work and the family" of women with respect to the work of many male filmmakers (French 2018, 16). According to Kim Munro, women's filmmaking in general often features autobiographical narratives, which can serve a psychoanalytic function, or what Michael Renov calls "techno-analysis" (Munro 2018, 73). This characterization is confirmed by Kerreen Ely-Harper (2018), who notes that working through one's own personal trauma, and/or that inherited through the family from previous generations, is a common narrative thread in women's cinema. In woman-centered cinema in Brazil, in addition to explorations of personal psychology and the interpersonal relationships of a diverse array of women characters and subjects, one can also find a working-through of national trauma, from that experienced by the victims of the 1964–1985 military regime to the trauma of economic crisis and national political conflict and turmoil in recent years. Indeed, personal, intimate, and/or domestic narratives may well be intertwined with or reveal new aspects of national or international ones. This dialectic between the individual, private level and the national, public level is akin to that described by Deborah Shaw (2017, 147) in the work of Argentine director Lucrecia Martel, of whom she writes "[Martel] reveals (trans)national and trans-historical narratives and the power dynamics on which they rest through the micropolitics found in domestic spaces." Crucial issues impacting women, such as gendered violence, social class relations, employment, and intersections of race and gender experienced at the local level and in quotidian life but often linked with (inter)national struggles of feminism, are featured in many of the films analyzed in the pages that follow.

Related to some of these unique approaches to filmmaking of women in Brazil and elsewhere, and over the course of the scholarly conversations and filmmaker interviews involved in the editing of this volume, we discovered four general frameworks of cinematic expression and production that run throughout all chapters of this book to a greater or lesser degree. These frameworks, we contend, should provide fruitful avenues for further research on Brazilian women's filmmaking. First, we found attempts to interweave diverse voices in a filmmaking community characterized by collaboration, rather than the traditional approach in male-dominated cinema to focus on a master narrative and the vision of a dominant auteur figure. Second, we found common concerns about state film policy, including the need for policymakers and state officials to continue support for women filmmakers, as well as critical assessments of the current crisis in state film policy in Brazil, the latter often accompanied by cogent considerations of alternative sources of support for production and distribution, from state and municipal governments to new or established online streaming platforms. Third, we found a common emphasis on the importance of the so-called *lugar de fala*, or place of speaking, applied to both filmmakers themselves and the subjects and characters they represent, connected to cinematic theory and practice whose genealogy will be considered further below and in subsequent chapters. Fourth, we found an emphasis on the importance of women as witness-protagonists and the representation of their critical testimonies, in particular as subjects and voices within the documentary genre, as well as the (meta)cinematic testimonies of women filmmakers themselves on their place in their industry and society. The following paragraphs develop these four general frameworks in more detail and are followed by a more detailed overview of the book's structure.

In accordance with the first framework encompassed in this volume's scholarship and filmmaker interviews, women's filmmaking in Brazil demonstrates a *braided voice*, Trish FitzSimons's term for a more collaborative approach to film production as much as a hybrid approach to the formation of film narrative and style, interweaving multiple perspectives more than one master narrative (Munro 2018, 71). In fact, in her interview in this volume, filmmaker Petra Costa uses a similar language, referring to her process of knitting together diverse imagery and narratives with a voice-over in several of her films. For screenwriter and director Moara Passoni, who has also worked with Costa on several films, filmmaking involves collaboration in "a productive creative partnership [which] inspires, displaces, disturbs, provokes and enhances your voice" (Wissot 2020). Further, in her own analysis of Brazilian cinema, Lúcia Nagib (2017, 35) highlights Angela Martin's distinction between feminism and egocentrism; that is, the call to recognize and represent the personal as political is not merely a call for self-expression and thus is something more than a female auteurism.

In a related point, Nagib emphasizes that women filmmakers' films in Brazil often do not center around one dominant auteur figure but involve a process of collaboration, and this can involve partnerships not only between women but between women and men, or, to put it in less binary terms, between various genders. Nagib also emphasizes, importantly, the increasing influence of television production on cinema since the 1990s in Brazil. Because television is "a realm where teamwork is the rule," this development has "further undermin[ed] the auteurist approach" (2017, 37). She further argues that "because this collaborative tradition has not only continued but expanded in contemporary practices, female presence is felt everywhere," whether or not a film's director is a woman. The latter point is confirmed in various chapters and interviews of this study that reference screenwriting, editing, and producing roles that women have been prominently involved in, while Leslie L. Marsh's chapter focuses specifically on women screenwriters. The notion of a special emphasis on collaboration among women filmmakers also parallels developments in other parts of Latin America. For instance, Claudia Bossay and María-Paz Peirano (2017) develop the metaphor of the "common pot" in Chile, referencing the teamwork involved in making a meal with small contributions from a community of women and highlighting its similarity to collaborative production practices of women in that national cinema with a common scarcity of resources. Women's historically subaltern position in the field of cinema, they find, has helped "women feel more comfortable making documentary films in horizontal, collaborative and relatively inexpensive ways" (Bossay and Peirano 2017, 97). The same has often held true for women filmmakers in various genres in Brazil.

The second general framework to be found in the volume is the one most specifically related to film production, namely, the development of state film policy since the 1990s and the apparent crisis of the post-*retomada*/revival model for state support of the industry. While Cacilda M. Rêgo's chapter discusses this model in more detail, and the directors interviewed for this volume as well as various scholarly contributors generally praise its results for women filmmakers since the 1990s, most of the women filmmakers interviewed or analyzed herein also express serious concerns about the crisis of this model of public investment and partnership in the industry in the late teens of the twenty-first century. These concerns have only been made more acute by the demotion of the previously independent Ministry of Culture to the status of a subsecretariat within the Ministry of Tourism, under the right-wing government of Jair Bolsonaro (in power since 2019). Bolsonaro and his economic minister Paulo Guedes favor the neoliberal model of governance, whose disinvestment in cultural production, and cinema in particular, had resulted in a serious crisis in the early 1990s when a steep drop in production occurred in the Brazilian film industry. The research and filmmaker commentaries presented in this volume tend to agree that there is reason for serious concern about a resurgence of neoliberal policy even though alternative avenues for financing and distribution that have arisen since the 1990s, such as funding from state and municipal governments, international coproductions, and online streaming platforms, still provide hope for the future.

As a more diverse cross-section of women filmmakers has found space in the industry, in tandem with a more diverse audience making its own demands on filmmakers, the question of how well Brazilian cinema represents the true diversity of the Brazilian population has been increasingly foregrounded. In keeping with these developments, the third framework found throughout the book relates directly to filmic expression and the relevance of Black feminist Djamila Ribeiro's theory of the *lugar de fala* (place of speaking) in contemporary woman-centered cinema. As noted in several chapters in this volume including that of Reighan Gillam as well as Jack A. Draper III's interview of Petra Costa, Ribeiro's (2018) theory of the lugar de fala provides a revealing lens for understanding the contemporary politics of representation in Brazilian cinema. The notion of the lugar de fala draws from Kimberlé Crenshaw's (1989) theory of intersectionality, itself preceded by the related theory of the Combahee River Collective emphasizing the overlapping axes of oppression potentially faced by women based on differential racial, gender, class, or sexual orientation identities (Taylor 2017). Over the course of this volume, readers should appreciate that many artists among the generations of women filmmakers active since the 1990s have become increasingly conscientious of the importance of both examining their own place of speaking/enunciation in their works and supporting opportunities for filmmakers from historically oppressed or excluded groups to speak for or represent themselves on film. Further, in the context of Brazilian film studies scholarship, we recognize that an alternative analytical lens sometimes may be—and will continue to be—necessary to capture the places from which women filmmakers express themselves. This includes a greater focus on areas of the industry neglected by previous scholarship, such as screenwriting (Marsh's chapter), short films online (Vázquez's chapter), series (Gillam's chapter), or transmedia projects that extend beyond films into online platforms (Atencio's interview of Sacchetta).

The final framework of expression found throughout this volume revolves around the figure of the witness and the action of testimony. The filmmakers analyzed and interviewed in the volume, especially those of the documentary genre, produce works filled with testimonies of Brazilian women of the twentieth and twenty-first centuries on their experiences, desires, traumas, and struggles for justice and equality. Beyond these testimonies of cinematic subjects, the voices of Brazilian women filmmakers themselves in the interviews documented here and elsewhere, as well as in their own films, speak to historical and contemporary contributions and struggles of women in Brazilian cinema. Filmmaker Anna Muylaert, for one, whose work is discussed most extensively in Jack A. Draper III's chapter, has been one of the foremost critics of women's second-class-citizen status in Brazilian cinema. Many of the filmmakers discussed in this volume may well have had to overcome similar struggles as those described by Muylaert, such as "demeaning remarks from male colleagues, not receiving credit for her accomplishments, a perverse resistance to her (female) authority, and ongoing social barriers limiting women's access to financing" (Marsh 2017, 169). In an interview in *Primavera das mulheres / Women's Spring* (2017), director Isabel Nascimento Silva and screenwriter Antonia Pellegrino's television documentary on the burgeoning feminist and gender activist movement in Brazil, Muylaert expanded on her experience in the industry as a prominent, award-winning female director. Here, she stated that there is a glass ceiling for women in the industry. In her experience, it often takes much longer for a woman to bring a feature film to fruition because it is difficult for her to build and maintain support. She went so far as to say that it could take ten years for a woman from start to finish, while a man could easily go through the same process in one year. Muylaert said she broke through the glass ceiling individually, but at the cost of personal suffering and antagonism in a male-dominated industry. Muylaert's comments are backed up in Rebecca J. Atencio's interview of filmmaker Paula Sacchetta in this volume, in which Sacchetta describes the experience of a female director/ producer as a constant "battle" to have her authority taken seriously by men in the industry. Muylaert herself said she came to be perceived as a "dangerous woman" because she also brought public attention to the systemic discrimination against female filmmakers. However, she does feel that she was able to help achieve some broader progress, allowing for more opportunities for women in the industry.

These insights from one of the most successful female directors in recent decades are revealing of both the situation within which women still have to work in the industry and a certain opening of space and opportunities that were scarcer prior to the retomada (or revival) of Brazilian film in the 1990s. This progress is also discussed by Maria Augusta Ramos in her interview in this volume, in terms of the increasing involvement of female producers in the industry and their support for female filmmakers. In addition, Ramos highlights the supportive role women have played for female filmmakers by establishing themselves over the past decade in positions in the national film agency, Agência Nacional do Cinema (Ancine), and developing various programs and funding to support women in the industry. In her chapter, Cacilda M. Rêgo also emphasizes the advances women have achieved in the industry, while she recognizes past and current struggles to find recognition and compete on an equal playing field with male filmmakers. This volume thus makes a significant contribution to telling the often underrepresented tale of women's accomplishments since the turn of the century in cinema, all the more impressive in Brazil's still-patriarchal society.

Considering the structure of this volume more closely, the chapters are clustered under three central themes: (1) breaking ground and making space in the industry, (2) politics of public and private spaces, and (3) intersecting identities. The scholarship and interviews included in each section are strongly tied together by these themes, yet these clusters are by no means rigid, and the reader will find that these themes resonate throughout the book alongside the four general frameworks for women's filmmaking in Brazil outlined above. The first themed section broadly represents women filmmakers' efforts to find space to work in Brazilian cinema—not only in front of and behind the camera but also in professional organizations, in state institutes making film policy, and in a variety of online forums as well. The second section combines discussions and analysis of representations of private and public spaces in both documentary and fictional films, collectively demonstrating how the public and private realms mutually define and interpenetrate each other even as the distinctions between these spaces continue to be socially and politically relevant in the present, with deep roots in the colonial and postcolonial history of the racialized and gendered hierarchy of Brazilian society.

The third section includes chapters with the greatest focus on how the gender identity of women intersects with other important identities that differentiate women's experiences. In particular, the unique experiences of Black and Indigenous women, transgender women, and women of different generations are centered here. Again, it is notable that many of these themes cannot be isolated to the work of a particular filmmaker or group of filmmakers featured in this book. One example of this fluidity of themes throughout the volume is the discussion of Paula Sacchetta's work in a scholarly chapter in part 2, chapter 5 as well as an interview in part 3, chapter 12. While Sacchetta's work certainly focuses on the more universal feminist concern of violence against women in Brazilian society, the array of women's voices in her film *Faces of Harassment* (2016) represents, in her own words, "as diverse a range of experiences as possible." Similarly, while this volume focuses on certain filmmakers in one section or another, the reader will likely find that their works nevertheless dialogue with those of filmmakers in the other sections of the book.

Considering the sections more closely, part 1, Breaking Ground/Making Space in the Industry, begins with Cacilda M. Rêgo's look at the generation of women who were at the forefront of the cinematic revival of the 1990s. In chapter 1, "Recognizing Women's Contributions to Brazilian Cinema," she asserts that, with a few significant exceptions, the contributions of Brazilian women to national cinema are still under-recognized. Rêgo provides an overview of the limited extent to which these contributions have been analyzed in previous scholarship in Portuguese or English. Then, taking the cinematic revival of the 1990s as a point of departure, she offers an overview of the industry dynamics as a framework for a more nuanced understanding of women's participation in national cinema as well as the substantial challenges to their commercial success and to their recognition in a historically male-dominated field. Specifically, the chapter addresses the lack of attention given to Brazilian female directors. It also discusses how Globo Filmes, the production arm of Globo TV Network, has altered the landscape of the Brazilian film industry to the detriment of small and/or independent productions, which form the bulk of female-directed features. It shows, however, that industrial constraints (from access to funds for production to distribution and exhibition) have not curtailed artistic creativity—in fact, women have had a significant impact on documentary as well as on fictional cinema in recent years—nor have they (thanks to access to new platforms and formats) limited the reach of works by women, as exemplified by the growing number of new productions by a generation of younger (and especially Black) female filmmakers. Indeed, the increase in collective, grassroots, and popular filmmaking associated with video and new media technologies and the proliferation of film festivals, blogs and websites, and professional groups aimed at recognizing and promoting women's contributions to film culture have meant greater participation by women in filmmaking (28 percent in 2018) in twenty-first-century Brazil.

The following chapters in this volume take up different aspects of women's contributions to and participation in current film and media culture. Their common goal, within a wide divergence of methods and approaches, is to critically examine the creative work of women screenwriters, producers, and directors, especially those working in more marginal areas such as Black and/or nonmainstream cinema. Bringing to light the common areas of concern on the part of these women filmmakers, these chapters discuss how women have forged more visibility by seeking innovative ways of approaching filmmaking and creating new spaces that set their (and other marginalized) voices and visions in circulation beyond the traditional exhibition landscape of multiplexes, art houses, and film festivals. Together these chapters help illuminate several institutional questions—of production, distribution, exhibition, and outreach—and in so doing they not only fill a gap in the existing scholarship but extend the field beyond the framework of mainstream feminist film studies. Leslie L. Marsh in chapter 2, "Behind the Scenes: Brazilian Women Screenwriters in Film and Television," charts the current landscape of Brazilian cinema through a focus on the work of female screenwriters. As she argues, although there has been significant research in film studies celebrating female screenwriters and directors in Hollywood, there is yet very limited scholarship on this vital area of production associated with Brazilian women. Pointing to the necessity of further research on the creative work of female screenwriters, the chapter briefly maps the state of the profession of screenwriting in Brazil as it has evolved in recent decades, concentrating thereafter on issues of female screenwriters' authorship and agency and the different contexts (of film, television, and the new media) in which this creative practice by Brazilian women has emerged and thrived. Shifting the discussion to include important emerging women-led initiatives, chapter 3, "Resistance and Online Activism: Brazilian Women Filmmakers' Initiatives (2014–2017)," by Daniela Verztman Bagdadi, focuses on the political, social, and technological conditions that have enabled filmmaking by women to take place in the new millennium, such as the establishment of cine clubs, film festivals, and professional organizations, and the development of online groups across the country. As she concludes, although initiatives by women are not a new phenomenon in Brazil, these new contemporary groups have developed innovative and pioneering actions through their activism on Facebook. In chapter 4, "Interview with Maria Augusta Ramos," Jack A. Draper III, Cacilda M. Rêgo, and Gustavo Procopio Furtado address questions of belonging and non-belonging for the director (she lives between the Netherlands and Brazil), current women's production in Brazil, national trends, and how politics have informed her work. She also reflects on the democratization of production financing access (thanks to public incentives) as well as new media access, how women filmmakers are increasingly relying on the system of (transnational) coproductions, and the rising number of film productions by women that have been facilitated by Ancine in more recent years.

Part 2, Politics of Public/Private Spaces, begins with chapter 5, "From Tweets to the Streets: Women's Documentary Filmmaking and Brazil's Feminist Spring." Here, Rebecca J. Atencio remaps women filmmakers' engagement with gender-related protest movements, both online and in the streets, that have occurred in recent years. As Atencio argues, while largely associated with the social media and city streets, these protest movements—which became known as Brazil's Primavera Feminista (Feminist Spring)—were "amplified by the documentary filmmaking of emerging women directors, some of whom played an instrumental role in helping bridge the divide between the two spaces, virtual and physical." Taking two recently released documentary features—Paula Sacchetta's *Precisamos falar do assédio* (*Faces of Harassment*, 2016) and Amanda Kamanchek Lemos and Fernanda Frazão's *Chega de fiu fiu* (*Enough with Catcalling*, 2018)—Atencio points out the intrinsic links between filmmaking and social media and, ultimately, the power of their narratives in giving voice to women's agency on- and off-screen. In so doing, Atencio notes, they call for women's political engagement, summoning women to take action (against misogyny, racism, classism, and patriarchy) in the same tradition of feminist filmmaking in Brazil during the 1970s and 1980s. Drawing on Donna Haraway's notion of "making kin," chapter 6, "Motherhood and Making Kin in Contemporary Brazilian Cinema" by Jack A. Draper III, examines how Anna Muylaert's *Que horas ela volta* (*The Second Mother*, 2015) and Sandra Kogut's *Campo Grande* (2015) follow two different trajectories of women and children "making kin" in the multi-class context of domestic employers and workers in contemporary Brazil. As Draper argues, while "*The Second Mother* traces the process of the empowerment of a nanny in relation to her employers' family through the catalyst of her own biological daughter's influence, . . . an inverse process is established in *Campo Grande*, in which a middle-class mother must fill in for the absence of a former employee's daughter, looking after a poor boy and girl as they search for this woman, their biological mother." In chapter 7, "The Many Mirrors of Maria Augusta Ramos: Landscape, Institutions, and Everyday Lives in Contemporary Brazil," Paula Halperin concentrates her analysis on the documentary films by Maria Augusta Ramos, including her highly acclaimed and more recent award-winning film *O processo* (*The Trial*, 2018). Viewed in conjunction, Halperin argues, Ramos's works are built around distinctive structures and spaces within which the characters' stories and experiences are framed. In her words, Ramos's "work explores menial aspects of daily life, but through character building, dramatization, and mise-en-scène, she transforms the common and simple details into an unusual and complex portrayal of contemporary Brazil." In chapter 8, "Interview with Petra Costa," Jack A. Draper III, in conversation with Petra Costa, discusses her documentary practice in the context of Brazilian society today. Costa, who belongs to a generation of filmmakers who released their first films in the 2000s, initiated her career with a poignant rendering of her grandparents' relationship in the short *Olhos de ressaca* (*Undertow Eyes*, 2009). A decade later she came to international prominence following her Oscar-nominated documentary feature *Democracia em vertigem* (*The Edge of Democracy*, 2019), in which she casts a critical eye on the social and political crisis that swept Brazil starting with the June protests of 2013, ultimately leading to President Dilma Rousseff's impeachment in 2016 and paving the way to Jair Bolsonaro's presidency (2019–).

Chapter 9, "Conditions for a Twenty-First-Century Black Woman Cinema in Brazil: The Politics and Aesthetics of Yasmin Thayná's Audiovisual Practice," begins part 3, Intersecting Identities, and deals with filmic and cultural representation by Black women directors. Taking Yasmin Thayná's short film *Kbela* (2015) as a case study, María Mercedes Vázquez Vázquez brings to light the complicated status of Black female identities and subjectivities through cinematic practice. By so doing, she problematizes what constitutes the defining aesthetics (and politics) of films made by Black women, doubly marginalized in Brazilian society, and their role as political and social agents. In her words,

Although Thayná's filmmaking career is short, her work is proof of the positive effects of left-wing cultural policies for the advancement of diversity, and the impact of her work is a sign of a new sensibility in Brazilian filmmaking and society at large toward race and gender. Besides this, Thayná is not only a filmmaker but also a cultural activist and intellectual who seeks to understand cultural processes regarding the Black presence in Brazil's audiovisual industries and therefore deserves close attention.

Chapter 10, "Afro-Brazilian Women Creative Workers Speak: Juliana Vicente's Standpoint Cinema (Cinema of *O Lugar de Fala*)" by Reighan Gillam, establishes a dialogue with Vázquez Vázquez's discussion of gender and race representation in filmmaking by women of color. Informed by Djamila Ribeiro's notion of lugar de fala (place of speaking, or standpoint) as a form of empowerment for women in front of and behind the camera, Gillam reflects on the *Afronta!* (*Face it!*) video series by Juliana Vicente. As she writes,

> These short videos in the *Afronta!* series constitute short life stories, narratives, or testimonies about one's life and work, and they voice the life experiences of a particular group of young Black female workers in the cultural industries. By recording their statements, editing the content, and presenting the videos together, Vicente brings into view a group of cultural workers who have little representation in Brazil and in ways that Black women are rarely seen: young Black women who work in the culture industries and pursue their interests through music, style, acting, filmmaking, and dance.

In chapter 11, "Interview with Mari Corrêa," Gustavo Procopio Furtado brings to light the interconnection between gender, self-representation, and filmmaking in Indigenous communities in an interview with Mari Corrêa who, although relatively unknown in film circles in Brazil, has produced remarkable work in the area of documentary filmmaking with Indigenous people. In closing the volume, chapter 12, "Interview with Paula Sacchetta" by Rebecca J. Atencio, contributes to our understanding of the various "faces of harassment"—the spoken (and, often, the unspoken) violence suffered by women within both the private/domestic and public spheres—eloquently captured by Sacchetta in her documentary feature

Faces of Harassment. Identifying herself as a feminist filmmaker, Sacchetta explains that her film, in both its subject and form, was inspired by and conceived in the context of increasing participation of women filmmakers in gender-related protests and/or initiatives that emerged in Brazil (and elsewhere), and she explains how she became committed to creating a film around the personal stories of women in order to expose the systemic violence against them in the public and private arenas.

Works Cited

Bossay, Claudia, and María-Paz Peirano. 2017. "*Parando la olla documental*: Women and Contemporary Chilean Documentary Film." In *Latin American Women Filmmakers: Production, Politics, Poetics*, edited by Deborah Martin and Deborah Shaw, 74–104. London: IB Tauris.

Butler, Judith. 1999. *Gender Trouble: Feminism and the Subversion of Identity*. 2nd ed. New York: Routledge. Audiobook.

Crenshaw, Kimberlé. 1989. "Demarginalizing the Intersection of Race and Sex: A Black Feminist Critique of Antidiscrimination Doctrine, Feminist Theory and Antiracist Politics." *University of Chicago Legal Forum* 1 (8): 139–67.

Ely-Harper, Kerreen. 2018. "Record Keeping: Family Memories on Film—Rea Tajiri's *History and Memory: For Akiko and Takashig* and *Wisdom Gone Wild*." In *Female Agency and Documentary Strategies: Subjectivities, Identity and Activism*, edited by Boel Ulfsdotter and Anna Backman Rogers, 84–99. Edinburgh: Edinburgh University Press.

French, Lisa. 2018. "Women in the Director's Chair: The Female Gaze in Documentary Film." In *Female Authorship and the Documentary Image: Theory, Practice and Aesthetics*, edited by Boel Ulfsdotter and Anna Backman Rogers, 9–21. Edinburgh: Edinburgh University Press.

Marsh, Leslie L. 2017. "Women's Filmmaking and Comedy in Brazil: Anna Muylaert's *Durval Discos* (2002) and *É proibido fumar* (2009)." In *Latin American Women Filmmakers: Production, Politics, Poetics*, edited by Deborah Martin and Deborah Shaw, 164–85. London: IB Tauris.

Nagib, Lúcia. 2017. "Beyond Difference: Female Participation in the Brazilian Film Revival of the 1990s." In *Latin American Women Filmmakers: Production, Politics, Poetics*, edited by Deborah Martin and Deborah Shaw, 32–50. London: IB Tauris.

Martin, Deborah, and Deborah Shaw, eds. 2017. *Latin American Women Filmmakers: Production, Politics, Poetics*. London: IB Tauris.

Munro, Kim. 2018. "Hybrid Practices and Voice-Making in Contemporary Female Documentary Film." In *Female Agency and Documentary Strategies: Subjectivities, Identity and Activism*, edited by Boel Ulfsdotter and Anna Backman Rogers, 70–83. Edinburgh: Edinburgh University Press.

Ribeiro, Djamila. 2018. *Quem tem medo do feminismo negro?* Rio de Janeiro: Companhia das Letras.

Shaw, Deborah. 2017. "Intimacy and Distance—Domestic Servants in Latin American Women's Cinema: *La mujer sin cabeza* and *El niño pez/The fish child*." In *Latin American Women Filmmakers: Production, Politics, Poetics*, edited by Deborah Martin and Deborah Shaw, 134–63. London: IB Tauris.

Taylor, Keeanga-Yamahtta. 2017. *How We Get Free: Black Feminism and the Combahee River Collective.* Chicago: Haymarket Books.

Ulfsdotter, Boel, and Anna Backman Rogers. 2018. *Female Agency and Documentary Strategies: Subjectivities, Identity and Activism.* Edinburgh: Edinburgh University Press.

———. 2018. *Female Authorship and the Documentary Image: Theory, Practice and Aesthetics.* Edinburgh: Edinburgh University Press.

Wissot, Lauren. 2020. "'An Attempt to See Anorexia from a Perspective That Goes Beyond that of the Spectacle': Moara Passoni on Her CPH:DOX Debut *Ecstasy*." *Filmmaker Magazine*, March 26, 2020. https://filmmakermagazine.com/109431-a-film-only-with-voiceover-and-empty-spaces-mirroring-the-process-of-becoming-anorexic-moara-passoni-on-her-cphdox-debut-ecstasy/#.X6x1T8hKi71.

PART 1
BREAKING GROUND/MAKING SPACE IN THE INDUSTRY

Chapter 1

Recognizing Women's Contributions to Brazilian Cinema

CACILDA M. RÊGO

In the early 1990s, the Brazilian film industry faced the deepest crisis of its history resulting from a rash of neoliberal measures implemented by President Fernando Collor de Mello (1990–1992). Aimed at addressing Brazil's fiscal problems, these measures were as swift as they were controversial: in addition to dismantling cultural institutions, including the Brazilian film enterprise Empresa Brasileira de Filmes (Embrafilme) that funded Brazilian cinema, Collor de Mello abolished Law 7.505/86 of 1986, known as Lei Sarney (Sarney Law), which provided a tax benefit for private investments in cultural projects, thus doing away with all state support for the film industry. As a result, national production, which had exceeded one hundred films a year during Embrafilme's heyday (1969–1985), sharply declined and, consequently, "practically vanished from the internal exhibition market, not to mention its total disappearance from the external market" (Moisés 2003, 7). However, the film industry reversed this trend and gained steam and rebounded from the ashes, following the institution of three important measures: the promulgation of the Federal Law for Culture Incentive (Law 8.313/91), most commonly known as Lei Rouanet (Rouanet Law), in 1991, which allows for individuals and private firms to invest a share of their income tax rates in cultural projects where there is no prospect of financial return; the creation of the Prêmio Resgate do Cinema Brasileiro (Brazilian Cinema Rescue Award) in late 1992, which redistributed the assets of Embrafilme; and the publication of Law 8.586/93 in 1993, also known as Lei do Audiovisual (Audiovisual Law), which confers tax exemptions for individuals and firms investing in national film production. The so-called industry rebound initiated a period of *retomada* (revival) of national film production that lasted from 1995 until 1998. Catapulted by the commercially successful historic comedy *Carlota Joaquina, Princesa do Brasil (Carlota Joaquina, Princess of Brazil*, 1995) by actress-turned-director Carla Camurati, this period of revival produced seventy-six films, nineteen of which were either directed or codirected by women (Ancine 2019).

Credited as being at the forefront of the retomada were filmmakers such as Tizuka Yamazaki, Lúcia Murat, and Ana Maria Magalhães who were already established and relatively well known, as well as Tata Amaral, Anna Muylaert, Laís Bodanzky, and Eliana Caffé who, like Carla Camurati, had transitioned from documentary and short to feature-length films and were not yet prominent. Among the seventeen new and veteran women filmmakers, some of them, such as Tata Amaral and Eliana Caffé, gained international attention at their debuts in the field of feature-length films. Others, such as Carla Camurati and Sandra Werneck, had rare commercial successes for first-time directors (Labaki 1998, 19). Yet only a few, such as Tata Amaral, Lúcia Murat, Tizuka Yamazaki, and Anna Muylaert, have been able to maintain a steady output and thus establish themselves as career filmmakers; the majority of them have been able to direct only one or two films since the retomada (Ancine 2019). Either way, it can be said that one of the most striking phenomena in recent Brazilian cinema is, admittedly, the number and range of films made by women since the retomada: out of 1,741 films released between 1995 and 2018, 360 features, or nearly 21 percent, were directed or codirected by women (Ancine 2019). The year 2018, in particular, was important in consolidating the commercial success and promise of women's cinema in Brazil with fifty-two (out of a total of 185) films, or 28 percent, made by both established and emerging female directors (Ancine 2019). This is not a small feat considering that until the retomada there had been comparatively fewer Brazilian women in directorial positions and that their films were (and still are) either sporadically or inadequately distributed and exhibited in commercial venues. Therefore, it has become possible to argue that from the mid-1990s onward, and especially in the new millennium, women's filmmaking has grown dramatically in both volume and quality of production, with an unprecedented number of feature-length, documentary, and animation features, several of which have received national and international awards and, consequently, increased press and social media coverage in Brazil. A case in point is the extensive media exposure received by Petra Costa's documentary *Democracia em vertigem* (*The Edge of Democracy*, 2019) after its nomination for the 2020 Academy Awards under the Best Documentary Feature category. At the same time, this boom in production by women does not speak to the unfortunate consequences of Globo Filmes' dominance of the domestic market and, thus, the inability of "independent" films, under which category the bulk of women-directed features fall, to compete with Globo productions. Nor does this boom speak to the challenges faced by women directors breaking into a (until recently) male-dominated field, nor to the lack of recognition of the work of emerging directors, nor to the limited access to big budgets as well as the (still) often inadequate distribution and exhibition of their films, to name only a few of the difficulties women directors often face when making films (Ancine 2019).

It is my contention in this chapter that in a field where women have increasingly taken prominent roles behind the screen as directors, producers, associate producers, screenwriters, cinematographers, editors, and so on, the contributions of Brazilian women to national cinema are still under-recognized. Granted, the contributions of women to Brazilian cinema become more noteworthy when one considers the trajectories and practices that have shaped individual films and informed developments in the industry over time. In the following pages, therefore, I offer a concise overview of the industry dynamics as a framework for a more nuanced understanding of women's actual participation in and contributions to national cinema as well as the substantial challenges to their commercial and critical success and to their recognition in a historically male-dominated field. This chapter starts with a discussion of the lack of attention (and status) given to Brazilian women directors within both academia and film industry. It then analyzes how the entrance of Globo Filmes has changed the landscape of film production in the 2000s to the detriment of independent productions, which form the bulk of women-directed features. It is followed by a concise discussion of women's authorship in film, and some of the women-led initiatives currently in place, which are specifically aimed at recognizing and promoting women's contributions to cinema culture in twenty-first-century Brazil. It concludes with a brief overview of the current trends in the film industry and the reasons why the gradual dismantling of the national film agency (Agência Nacional do Cinema [Ancine]) by the current government poses a particular threat to women filmmakers, who often depend on state support to produce, distribute, and exhibit their films.

Invisible Women

As Patricia Torres San Martín (2013, 29) notes, "The participation of Latin American women in cinema is an invisible, hidden and incomplete history, which needs to be written, disseminated and linked to current film practices." Prior to the 1980s, she argues, "The study of women's contribution to history and culture, seemed an implausible task. Accounts about women in film highlighted their participation in front of rather than behind the camera" (30). In "When Women Film," Elice Munerato and Maria Helena Darcy de Oliveira (1982a, 340) discuss women's contributions to filmmaking in Brazil from the 1930s to the late 1970s and, likewise, conclude that "the history of Brazilian women's participation in the cinema is no exception to the rule: they have often performed *in front* of the camera, but they have rarely worked *behind* it [italics in original]." Furthermore, many of the films by women directors are still difficult to obtain, and the small number of viewers able to see them further contributes to the lack of attention given to them in film criticism. As Parvati Nair and Julián Daniel Gutiérrez-Albilla (2013, 5) argue, in Brazil as elsewhere in Latin America, "The exhibition of films directed by women remains [largely] circumscribed to film festivals . . . , thereby contributing to the ghettoization or compartmentalization of films directed by women and ultimately women themselves." Also, in addition to the many lost films made by women from the earliest period of Brazilian cinema, a disturbing number of films have been lost in more recent years (see Ramos and Miranda 2000; Silva Neto, 2002). Moreover, many of the films directed by women are often available only in limited numbers of copies during brief cinema runs or film festivals, and only a few of these—that is, those especially made by Globo Filmes, the production arm of Globo TV Network—find their way onto video; even fewer are available on commercial and cable television or on Internet streaming platforms such as YouTube, Vimeo, Hulu, and Netflix, among others currently available in Brazil. Many of these films do not find any sort of distribution—a fact suggesting that, despite existing quotas for national film's exhibition in both theatrical and television markets, women still face difficulties making their films known to a wider public in the post-retomada years (Ancine 2019) and, consequently, "in establishing solid career trajectories" (Benamou and Marsh 2013, 65).

Furthermore, as Stephanie Dennison (2020, 57) points out, despite the increasing number of women filmmakers or women working in the film industry, there is still a relative absence of women in academic studies about Brazilian cinema—published either in English or Portuguese—when compared with their male peers. Granted, scholarly works on Brazilian cinema are still largely devoted to the work of male directors, some including very few or no women at all. Be that as it may, such an absence has been explained away as a reflection of the timid presence of women filmmakers in national production until the mid-1990s. As Peter Rist (1996, 192) notes, "Only twenty Brazilian films had been directed by women before Tisuka Yamazaki began shooting *Gaijin* in 1979, and none [had] been as ambitious . . . or received as much critical acclaim: *Gaijin* won five awards, including Best Film at the 1980 [Havana] film festival." It is perhaps worth noting that, although some fifty films were directed by women between 1979 and 1994 (the last year covered by Rist's book and, coincidentally, the year prior to the beginning of the retomada period), only four female-directed films—Yamazaki's *Gaijin*, Ana Carolina's *Mar de rosas* (*Sea of roses*, 1977), Tata Amaral's *A hora da estrela* (*The Hour of the Star*, 1985), and Mirella Martinelli's *Opressão* (*Oppression*, 1993)—are examined as token representations of Brazilian cinema for that same period (see Ramos and Miranda 2000 for a list of female-directed films in the period).

Although there is as yet very limited scholarship on the subject of women's filmmaking in Brazil, films made by Brazilian women have started to attract some critical attention, not in the least in the literature devoted to Latin American women's filmmaking in general, and Brazilian cinema in particular. Notable among them are Parvati Nair and Julián Daniel Gutiérrez-Albilla's *Hispanic and Lusophone Women Filmmakers: Theory, Practice and Difference* (2013), Traci Roberts-Camps's *Latin American Women Filmmakers: Social and Cultural Perspectives* (2017), and Deborah Martin and Deborah Shaw's *Latin American Women Filmmakers: Production, Politics, Poetics* (2017), each containing two essays on Brazilian women directors and their respective films. Lúcia Nagib's *O Cinema da Retomada* (2002) includes interviews by several women directors who participated in the retomada, while Randal Johnson and Robert Stam's *Brazilian Cinema* (1982) and, more recently, Stephanie Dennison's *Remapping Brazilian Film Culture in the Twenty-First Century*

(2020) each offer a chapter on Brazilian women's cinema. However, books entirely focused on Brazilian women filmmakers are still rare. Examples include Elice Munerato and Maria Helena Darcy de Oliveira's *Musas da matinê* (1982b), the first catalog published on the subject, later followed by Heloisa Buarque de Hollanda's *Quase catálogo: Realizadoras de cinema no Brasil (1930/1988)* (1989), Ana Pessoa's *Carmen Santos* (2002), Leslie L. Marsh's *Brazilian Women's Filmmakers: From Dictatorship to Democracy* (2012), Karla Holanda and Marina Cavalcanti Tedesco's *Feminino e plural: Mulheres no cinema brasileiro* (2017), and the edited volume by Luiza Lusvarghi and Camila Vieira da Silva, *Mulheres atrás das câmaras: As cineastas brasileiras de 1930 a 2018* (2019).

Aside from the glaring absence of women in published scholarly works, Paula Alves, José Eustáquio, and Denise Britz do Nascimento (2011, 373) also note their absence in film rankings, observing, for instance, that only five features directed by Brazilian women appear in a critic's list of the top-290 foreign and national films (out of a total of 2000) released in Brazil between 2005 and 2008: Betse de Paula's *Celeste & Estrela* (2005); Lúcia Murat's *Quase dois irmãos* (*Almost Brothers*, 2005); Mara Mourão's *Doutores da alegria—o filme* (*Doctors of Joy*, 2005); Laís Bodanzky's *Chega de saudade* (*The Ballroom*, 2008); Cristina Leal's *Iluminados* (2008, literally translated as "the shining"); and Daniela Thomas's *Linha de passe* (*Passing line*, 2008), which was the only codirected project, by Walter Salles, in the group. Pointing to this example as an illustration of the limited opportunities for women to carry out film projects in an industry where decisions about resources, such as funding for postproduction and distribution, are predominantly made by men, and state financial support is still limited, Roberts-Camps (2017, xv) concludes that "even with the rise of female directors [in Brazil and elsewhere in Latin America] in [the] last decades, their work is [still] not being recognized by those in charge of creating the parameters of 'good films.'" Equally pernicious is the omission of women's names in projects codirected by high-profile male directors. A case in point, as Dennison (2020, 61) notes, was the dropping of Kátia Lund's name from both the credits of *Cidade de Deus* (*City of God*, 2002), "purportedly to enable the film to compete at the Oscars (under the name of Fernando Meirelles), where co-direction is not recognized," and the spin-off television series, *Cidade dos homens* (*City of Men*), broadcasted by Globo TV Network between 2002 and 2005. That women's roles in codirected projects by famous male filmmakers—as has been the case, for example, of Kátia Lund/Fernando Meirelles, Kátia Lund/

João Moreira Salles, Daniela Thomas/Walter Salles, and Cris D'Amato/ Daniel Filho, among others—"is not always acknowledged" (Dennison 2020, 61) not only suggests that "women filmmakers are still culturally undervalued on the basis of their gender" (Nair and Gutiérrez-Albilla 2013, 5) but also reflects "the perhaps unconscious process of privileging solo directors both within academia and within the film industry, itself a reflection of a certain obsession on the part of film studies academics, film critics and funders with an *auteurist* filmmaking [read, male] tradition" (Dennison 2020, 61).

Against All Odds

As seen above, the mid-1990s represents the beginning of a new era in women's participation in Brazilian film culture, thus contributing to the diverse and enormously vibrant cinematic production that has emerged in the country since the retomada. As Lúcia Nagib (2017, 33) notes, "Among the 90 filmmakers active between 1994 and 1998, 17 were women, that is, nearly 19 percent, a significant rise compared with the less than 4 percent female presence in the pre-Collor years." Going beyond the figures provided by Nagib, recent data published by Ancine (2019) show that a total of nineteen films (seventeen fiction and two documentary features), or 25 percent of the national production, were directed or codirected by women between 1995 and 1998, the year in which the retomada (officially) came to an end. The total jumped to ninety-six films (fifty-seven fiction and thirty-nine documentary features), that is, 17.5 percent of the national production, between 1999 and 2009 and to 245 films (102 fiction, 139 documentary, and four animation features), or nearly 22 percent of the national production, between 2010 and 2018, the last year for which official figures are available (Ancine 2019).

Be that as it may, despite the drastic increase in the numbers of women working in key behind-the-scene roles as directors (some 250 women have made their debuts in the past two decades alone, per the list published by Ancine for 1995–2018), executive producers, assistant producers, screenwriters, cinematographers, and editors, women are still a small part of the film industry. In fact, even though there are more women making film today than ever before, the numbers can be deceiving. As mentioned above, most have only managed to produce one or two films (see Ancine 2019). As well, despite the fact that several women directors have been able to maintain a steady output (with three or more films), and despite the emergence of new directors on the scene from the year 2000 onward, there is still a (relative) paucity of women filmmakers currently working in feature-length fiction. Thus, although historically high, with a total of 168 for 2000–2018, the number of feature-length fiction films made by women is still small compared with the number of those made by their male peers, which totaled 578 for the same period. In fact, since the retomada there has been a noticeable decline in feature-length fiction films and a sharp increase in documentary films made by women. For instance, of the nineteen films made by women between 1995 and 1998, only two were documentary films. This number increases to forty-six between 1999 and 2010 and to 139 between 2011 and 2018. The increase is particularly noticeable starting in 2008, when four fiction and eight documentary features made by women were released. By 2012, the numbers were seven fiction and seventeen documentary features, going up steadily onto the following years, reaching eleven fiction and twenty documentary features in 2017 and twenty-four fiction and twenty-seven documentary features in 2018, respectively. In 2016 alone, women were responsible for 29.5 percent of all documentary features released in the theatrical market, and for only 15.5 percent of all fiction features (Observatório Brasileiro do Cinema e do Audiovisual [OCA] 2018, 4). While it is perhaps too early to say that these numbers indicate a dominant trend, one cannot help but notice that women directors have increasingly favored this genre in recent years. In this regard, it is perhaps worth recalling that Brazilian women filmmakers have, at least since the 1960s, moved seamlessly from short to documentary and feature-length films, as well as to other modes of audiovisual production, including video and television. However, the question remains whether their choices are simply governed by practical considerations or personal preferences, or both. It is worth noting that in spite of the increase in production and viewership, the documentary, as Gustavo Furtado (2019, 3) notes, "is far from a mainstream cultural form": "The documentary-viewing public remains too small to allow production to thrive without the continued support of the state"—a situation also true for Brazilian fiction films given their inadequate distribution in the domestic market in post-1990s Brazil. As he puts it, the dependence of Brazilian cinema "on the state condemns Brazilian film production to cycles of booms and bust[s] tied to the increase or decrease in governmental support" (3). In the last analysis, it is very probable that as state support for production continues to dwindle under the current government, women filmmakers will find themselves scaling down the scope and vision of their projects when presented with the alternative of making no film at all, or else, as some are increasingly doing, wholly embracing mainstream commercial cinema by joining Globo Filmes or turning to international coproductions, or both, as illustrated by Sandra Kogut's most recent works. Data for 2018 show, for instance, that twenty international coproductions were released that year in the domestic market, ten of which were either directed or codirected by women—an unprecedented amount for international coproduced projects, especially by women, when compared with previous years (Ancine 2019; see also Guerini 2019; De La Fuente 2017; Meleiro 2013).[1] Among them were seven fiction and three documentary features, including Lúcia Murat's *Praça Paris* (*Paris Square*, 2018), Caroline Leone's *Pela janela* (*A Window to Rosália*, 2018), Ana Katz's *Sueño Florianópolis* (*Florianópolis Dream*, 2018), and Maria Augusta Ramos's *O processo (The Trial*, 2018). Addressing the trial that resulted in President Dilma Rousseff's (2010–2016) impeachment, Ramos's documentary was one of the twenty most-watched films in 2018, reaching close to sixty-six thousand spectators (translated into a box office revenue of R$915.174,00 or US$228,793.50 in 2020 dollars). A considerable number, no doubt, yet one that lags behind the box office receipts of more commercial films for that year (Ancine 2018, 21).[2]

More significant, though, are the growing numbers of documentary and fiction films either directed or codirected by women, which are made in association with Globo Filmes.[3] Created in late 1998 with the goals of "strengthening the Brazilian audiovisual industry" and "increasing the synergy between cinema and TV" (Globo Filmes n.d.), Globo Filmes has since become one of the most important national film producers, with resources, star-power, and technical know-how guaranteed by Globo TV Network and its *padrão de qualidade* (standard of quality) (see Hamburger 2017 for further discussion). In this capacity, Globo Filmes has produced and/or coproduced 296 films between 1998 and 2019, including several landmark films such as Fernando Meirelles and Kátia Lund's *Cidade de Deus* (*City of God*, 2002), Hector Babenco's *Carandiru* (2003), and José Padilha's *Tropa de elite* (*Elite Squad*, 2007) and its sequel *Tropa de elite 2* (*Elite Squad 2*, 2010) which, having attracted 10.7 million viewers to movie theaters, became one of the most commercially successful films in the history of Brazilian cinema. Yet when one scans Globo Filmes' filmography, one cannot help but notice that there is still a relative dearth of films directed by women: of the 296 films released by Globo Filmes between 1998 and 2019, only seventy-four (one animation, fifty-five fiction, and eighteen documentary features), or 20 percent, have been directed or codirected by women. These include Flávia Moraes's *Acquaria* (2003), the first female-directed film coproduced by Globo Filmes; Sandra Werneck's *Cazuza: O tempo não pára* (*Cazuza: Time Doesn't Stop*, 2005, codirected by Walter Carvalho), Tata Amaral's *Antônia* (2006), an award-winning hip-hop drama that became a Globo TV series (2006–2007); Monique Gardenberg's *Ó pai ó* (2007, which can be roughly translated as "look at this"), which also became a Globo TV series (2008–2009); Tisuka Yamazaki's *Xuxa em o mistério da feiurinha* (*Xuxa and the mystery of the little ugly princess*, 2009); Chris D'Amato's *SOS: Mulheres ao mar* (*SOS: Women to the sea*, 2014) and its sequel, *SOS: Mulheres ao mar 2* (*SOS: Women to the sea 2*, 2017); and Susana Garcia's *Minha vida em Marte* (*My life on Mars*, 2018) and *Minha mãe é uma peça 3* (*My mother is a character 3*, 2019), among others.

Forming a trilogy with André Pellenz's *Minha mãe é uma peça* (2013) and César Rodrigues's *Minha mãe é uma peça 2* (2016), Garcia's *Minha mãe é uma peça 3* reached 11.5 million spectators, becoming the most commercially successful film in the history of Brazilian cinema in terms of box office receipts.[4] It is still necessary, however, to contextualize Garcia's achievement within the local filmmaking landscape. Comedy is the most popular genre among cinemagoers in Brazil and thus, as Dennison (2020, 35) notes, more likely to bring exceptionally good box office returns. This is evident particularly with Globo's light comedy productions—popularly known as *globochanchadas*—which, aside from having guaranteed distribution in the domestic film market, also reach millions more spectators on television and other ancillary markets after their theatrical releases. Figures for 1995 through 2017 show that all twenty top-grossing films for the period had the participation of Globo Filmes. Of those, fourteen were light comedies aimed primarily at a young audience (Ancine 2019; see also Johnson 2005; Guerini 2017; Dennison 2020 for further discussion).

Without adequate space to examine in-depth the production practices of Globo Filmes, suffice it to say that a number of factors have contributed to the commercial success of the great majority of films associated with the Globo brand.[5] First, undoubtedly, has been Globo's strategy to forge partnerships with members of the Motion Picture Association such as Paramount, Sony, Fox, Universal Pictures, and Warner Bros. as producer partners and distributors (Johnson 2005, 24). Second, although under the 1993 Audiovisual Law Globo Filmes is not considered an independent producer[6]—a sine qua non condition to participate directly in the tax incentive schemes for film production—Globo works around this law by forging partnerships with local independent producers who are allowed to raise funds under the law. In so doing, Globo Filmes guarantees the production capital and distribution resources needed to boost films with its signature of "quality" and, thus, maintains its stronghold in the national market (Donoghue 2011, 55). Third, while the inclusion of television stars in Globo Filmes productions does not necessarily translate into box office success for a film project, films with nationally recognized stars have been the most successful among cinemagoers in Brazil. Given that actors contracted by the Globo TV Network cannot work in film projects made by other production firms, Globo Filmes gains a commercial edge in the domestic market by utilizing Globo TV's stars in all of its productions. Fourth, even though top-grossing films do not necessarily equate with artistically and/or culturally significant works, films made by Globo Filmes have effectively attracted the larger, young television audiences to movie theaters on par with those drawn by Hollywood blockbusters (Johnson 2005; Rêgo 2008, 2011a, 2011b; Donoghue 2011). Fifth, Globo TV Network has increasingly used the strategy of media convergence to promote its productions, giving individuals without access to movie theaters the opportunity to watch its films through different platforms and technologies such as free-to-air as well as cable and satellite television, DVD (digital versatile disc), and the Internet. Globo even has its own OTT ("over the top" video-on-demand platform) service for delivery on devices such as cell phones, significantly broadening the visibility of its films beyond the traditional theatrical market. Lastly, Globo Filmes has also increasingly relied on character-driven franchises, especially in its comedy series. As Courtney Brannon Donoghue (2011, 61) notes, Globo Filmes franchises "rely heavily on pre-sold characters that [are] spun off into a lucrative, multi-annual film franchise" across multiple platforms.

All of this brings us back to Garcia's *Minha mãe é uma peça 3* as it provides a good contrastive example to "non-Globo" films, that is, films that are not (co)produced by Globo Filmes, which, as mentioned above, form the bulk of productions directed by women. Written (in collaboration with Susana Garcia and Fil Braz) and featuring well-known late television and theater actor Paulo Gustavo (1978–2021), the film—which is based on his play of the same name—follows the life of Dona Hermínia (Paulo Gustavo), a (drag) fictional character inspired by Gustavo's real mother, her son Juliano (Rodrigo Pandolfo), and her daughter Marcelina (Mariana Xavier) over the years. It was produced by Midgal and Globo Filmes in association with Paramount and Universal Pictures and released simultaneously in 1,456 multiplex cinemas throughout Brazil on December 26, 2019, by two of the nation's major distributors: Downtown and Paris Films. Populated by stars of Globo TV's soap operas and series, the franchise was being made into a television series to be shown exclusively by Globoplay, a subscription video-on-demand channel owned by Globo TV Network, at the time of Gustavo's untimely death in 2021. In sum, for better or worse, Garcia's film contrasts with the great majority of films by (particularly young, emerging) women directors not associated with Globo Filmes. But to what extent has Globo's clout in the market impacted Brazilian cinema in general and, particularly, national independent (or "non-Globo") filmmaking, the category encompassing the majority of women-made films?

One may try to answer this question by recalling that while widely welcomed at first, Globo's entrance into film has yielded harsh criticism from industry professionals. One apparent reason for this is the built-in feature of Globo's productions, namely the self-styled standard of quality that only Globo can afford, thus making other national productions pale in comparison. Given Globo's financial and technological resources, it is able to churn out super-productions (by Brazilian standards) and spend more money on stars, sets, special effects, and publicity than any independent producer in the country. In order to take advantage of Globo's resources, a growing number of independent producers have established coproduction partnerships with Globo Filmes, turning out films and television serials that they could not afford on their own (Rêgo 2011b, 43). Consequently, Globo Filmes (and thus Globo TV) has gained significant influence and control over the production of its independent partners. In addition to this, Globo Filmes has also been criticized for its alleged monopoly of the film industry by effectually maintaining control over production, distribution, exhibition, and marketing of its productions. As Roberto Pinheiro Machado (2018, 414) notes, using the extended reach of Globo TV's Network, Globo Filmes can—unlike the great majority of national independent producers—influence a film's advertising campaign without any extra expense by simply having the participation of actors and directors in its high-audience talk shows, "thus providing them with important media exposure that in turn can be charged back on to 'independent' partners as advertising air time." Further criticism of Globo's supremacy in the film industry refers to both the commercial aesthetic favored by its productions (and to which Brazilian audiences are accustomed) and its partnership with US majors, which provides film financing, film exhibition spaces (normally multiplex cinemas in the country's largest cities), and guaranteed national and international film distribution in both theatrical and ancillary markets. As noted elsewhere (Rêgo 2011b, 207), "without the benefit of such a cozy relationship with US majors, the great majority of 'independent' producers find, in spite of (or, perhaps, because of) current film policies, numerous distribution and exhibition difficulties that almost certainly condemn their films to commercial failures from the outset." Data published by Ancine (2019) for box office performance and distribution of Brazilian films during the 1995–2018 period show that enormous distortions exist in the market for national films. For instance, notwithstanding the fact that some Globo Filmes productions have enjoyed good box office success, the vast majority of local films (*circa* 85 percent of the total of national production and nearly all of the films made by women) released in the period have failed to either attract significant numbers of spectators or secure distribution in the commercial circuit (Ancine 2019). This situation is aggravated by the lack of adequate support (a glaring flaw of the 1993 Audiovisual Law) for marketing, distribution, and exhibition of national films and the fact that, despite existing quotas for local productions,[7] exhibitors (the great majority of which are foreign) can at any time replace a film that produces low box office receipts with (most likely a foreign) one that will generate bigger profit. Examples of this practice, too many to cite, are given by the female filmmakers interviewed by Nagib (2002) when discussing some of the hurdles they faced to showcase their work in the years after the retomada boom (see also Rêgo 2011a, 42; Benamou and Marsh 2013, 65–66).

Created in 2001 with the goal of fostering, regulating, and monitoring the Brazilian audiovisual industry, Ancine has been ineffective in curbing Globo Filmes' monopolistic behavior, for which Ancine has been severely criticized. Further criticism of the agency regards its bureaucratization of film production, which results in either slowing or hindering the conclusion of projects by small and independent producers (R. Machado 2018, 414). Consequently, the fact remains that film "projects that do not receive Globo Filmes' favor tend to face extreme difficulty in reaching a larger public" (414). In this context, as Benamou and Marsh (2013, 65) argue, "Women's careers as directors are more likely to be tripped up by an incentive system that focuses on production to the detriment of adequate distribution and exhibition." However, Globo Filmes' alleged monopoly of the film industry notwithstanding, what currently worries film industry professionals is the future of Ancine and, thus, the future of the film industry itself under the current administration.

A Creative Endeavor Called "Shared Authorship"

Given the intrinsic collaborative nature of filmmaking, women around the world have often worked in key behind-the-scene roles in tandem with (but also independent from) their male peers since the early years of the industry. Thus, Brazilian women have not been alone in this endeavor. Certainly, Brazilian women have historically participated in film culture behind the scenes as directors and/or codirectors, screenwriters, cinematographers, production executives, editors, and so on, either in solo- or duo-led projects (usually with other male directors), thereby contributing to both mainstream commercial and art cinemas since at least the 1930s. And yet, as discussed earlier, women's creative work has been largely obscured and/or misrecognized, especially in collaborative filmmaking. Speaking of the lack of status of women in what concerns film authorship, Shelley Cobb (2015, 1) argues that "*auteurism* is still an exclusionary model of authorship" which, "because of its masculine connotations, has [not] been readily available for women filmmakers." Hence, to Cobb, to speak of women's film authorship "requires the recognition of the status of the woman author, or, more to the polemic point, her lack of status":

> The rhetoric around women filmmakers and the analysis of their authorial identities necessarily has to contend with their exceptionalism; in other words, because there are relatively few female filmmakers, they cannot be talked about, reviewed, analyzed, or appreciated in the same way as male filmmakers. This is in part due to the masculinized discourse and image of the auteur as well as to the conspicuousness of the few, well-known women film directors. Their conspicuousness functions to make manifest the gendered nature of authorship. (Cobb 2015, 5)

In what concerns women's authorship in film, in "Beyond Difference: Female Participation in the Brazilian Film Revival of the 1990s," Nagib (2017) suggests a novel critical paradigm with which to interpret women's production in the post-retomada context: one that stretches the boundaries of the field to theorize the authorial position of women filmmakers beyond the dominant "woman author in the text" approach utilized in feminist film criticism. Arguing that "authorship, since the Retomada period is . . . diluted and diffused," she proposes instead an approach that takes into consideration the woman filmmaker as one more collaborator in the already collaborative art of filmmaking. In so doing, she puts forward the notion of collaborative (male/female) authorship across all forms of creative work (director, writer, producer, etc.), which is forged by the rules and relationships (either personal and professional or both) present in the main production context in which they work. Hence, in her aim to analyze the trends that propelled the rise of women's filmmaking from the mid-1990s on, she rejects the "exceptional woman" approach alluded to by Cobb and instead makes the argument that "the most decisive contribution brought about by the rise of women in Brazilian filmmaking has been the spread of teamwork and shared authorship, as opposed to a mere aspiration to the auteur pantheon, as determined by a notoriously male-oriented tradition" (Nagib 2017, 32). Thus, rather than focusing on any individual "exceptional woman" director (or directors) that participated in the retomada, Nagib discusses the phenomenon of shared or coauthorship, highlighting some of the collaborative work between female and male directors that have emerged since the 1990s, for example, that of Daniela Thomas and Walter Salles, whose *Terra estrangeira (Foreign Land*, 1995) is said to be one of the foundational features of the revival. In so doing, she brings attention not only to other female-male working partnerships, such as those of director Sérgio Rezende and producer Mariza Leão, directors Bia Lessa and Dany Roland, director Sandra Werneck and sound engineer Silvio Da Rin, but to the rise of a new generation of female editors—"a task curiously excelled by women worldwide," and producers—"a realm normally dominated by men"—which have helped to foster contemporary film culture in Brazil (Nagib 2017, 36). In sum, to Nagib, the very collaborative nature of filmmaking undermines the auteurist approach to works directed by women: "female presence," she argues, "is everywhere, even when a female director's signature is not appended to the film's credit" (36).

Whether or not one agrees with Nagib, her assessment of the current state of women's filmmaking in Brazil is provocative and suggests the importance of understanding women's authorial position "beyond differences."[8] Yet, when one looks at the films and women filmmakers currently working in Brazil, as well as the conditions that either enable or limit their production and recognition, one cannot help but notice that, as seen above, they are often overshadowed by the notoriety accorded their male peers. As in the case of Kátia Lund and Daniela Thomas, Brazilian women directors, particularly those who made their first features after 2000, are much less known internationally than their peers. Unlike Lund, Fernando Meirelles, for example, is well-known for several international productions: *The Constant Gardener* (2005), *Blindness* (2008), *360* (2011), and *The Two Popes* (2019), and, unlike Thomas, Walter Salles is also internationally known for *High Art* (1991), *The Motorcycle Diaries* (2004), *Dark Water* (2005), and *On the Road* (2012). Both Lund and Thomas receive far less support and/or recognition for their achievements at home, generally taking the back seat in shared or coauthored projects by high-profile male peers. Not coincidentally, Brazilian women directors have sought to establish their position of authority in the field in other significant and practical ways.

Of Recent Initiatives Supporting Women's Creative Work in Film

In "The Brazilian Film Industry Has a Gender Issue, But Also a Race One," Luisa Pécora (2017) reminds us that, as in many parts of the world, discussions on gender equality in the film industry have gained increased momentum in Brazil in the last two years, following the global anti–sexual harassment #MeToo movement and Hollywood's Time's Up campaign. In her words:

> After all, in the last two years the Brazilian film industry has experienced a much-needed awakening when it comes to debating gender equality in entertainment, and while the road ahead is long, the feeling is that there is so much going on. There are more women speaking out, more movie fans willing to listen, more online sharing that leads to mainstream media coverage, and more festivals, seminars and other events dedicated to female filmmakers. Perhaps more importantly, women in Brazil are getting organized, they are gathering themselves and finding support in [the] form of collectives, film societies and even Facebook groups. (Pécora 2017, n.p.)

Still, according to Pécora, this growing movement has yet to lead to substantial transformations, given that despite "all the significant changes that Brazil has faced in the last half a century in film production, economy and politics, the cinematic industry remains largely male and white" (n.p.). Thus, she writes, "These last two years have left a very clear message in Brazil: to talk about women in film is to talk about *Black* women in film. Or, in other words, it is to talk about the *absence* of Black women" (and I would add Indigenous and LGBTQ+ women) in key production roles (n.p., italics in original).⁹

In fact, like Indigenous and LGBTQ+ women, Black women have long been under-represented on and behind Brazil's cinema screens (see Dennison 2020). According to a study by the Group for Multidisciplinary Studies of Affirmative Action, Black women appeared in only two out of every ten features released between 2002 and 2012 despite making up close to 52 percent of the country's female population. When they did appear in films, Black actresses only accounted for 4.4 percent of the main characters. During that same period none of the 218 top-grossing national features employed a Black female director or screenwriter (Viola 2016). Moreover, in 2018, OCA (2018, 4) published a report on the diversity (or lack thereof) of the Brazilian film industry, concluding that only 13 percent of the top-grossing films released between 1995 and 2016 were directed by women, none of whom were Black. Taking the year of 2016 as an example, the report shows that 19.7 percent of all fiction features released in the theatrical market were directed by women (none by Black, LGBTQ+, or Indigenous), and 2.1 percent were directed by male Black directors (OCA 2018, 9). However, it is accurate to say that film production by women has since risen (reaching, as noted above, 28 percent in 2018), in part due to innovations made possible by access to more affordable means of making films in several platforms and formats, including cell phones. All in all, recent technological innovations have created the possibility for new projects, especially for younger female directors who focus on themes such as race and ethnicity, LGBTQ+, and Indigenous communities.

More specifically, increases in funding for small film projects during the presidency of Dilma Rousseff, and access to cheap digital technologies, have encouraged the emergence of a new generation of Black female filmmakers such as Sabrina Fidalgo, Everlane Moraes, Viviana Ferreira, and Yasmin Thayná (creator of the site Afroflix, which streams films and other audiovisual content made with at least one Black individual in an artistic or technical role) and a wave of short, medium, and feature-length documentaries dealing with issues of gender and race in Brazilian society in more recent years.[10] And yet, for these Black women directors, making (largely alternative and/or noncommercial) films is not an easy enterprise as they still have to fight prejudices held against women in power. In Fidalgo's own account,

> The director is the one who gives the final word on set, everything has to be done the way they want. [But as a female director] you have to keep repeating yourself, the male actors do not do as you say, at first. They want to argue and show you that they are right and you, wrong. (Viola 2016, n.p.)

Proving that the landscape in the 2000s is not so different from the 1940s, when Gilda de Abreu found filmmaking "extremely difficult" (Munerato and Oliveira 1982a, 343) due to the reluctance of male crew members to take orders from a woman, Fidalgo decided to make her last two short features, *Rainha* (*Queen*, 2016) and *Alfazema* (*Lavender*, 2019), with a mostly female crew.

In any case, in the face of the (relatively) low numbers of women who get to make films in Brazil and the potential exclusion of those films from the canonical auteur pantheon that still haunts film studies (and the industry alike), there is an indisputable need for women to claim cultural legitimacy through authorizing themselves in various other ways. Thus, beginning in 2015, while still working in collaboration with their male peers, women in Brazilian film have attempted to counter their lack of status and, hence, visibility and recognition by promoting numerous initiatives, including collectives, group discussions, grassroots and professional organizations, film clubs and seminars, platforms, and screenwriting workshops, as well as shows and festivals aimed at enhancing women's contribution to the audiovisual. Their final aim is to make their work more visible in Brazil and abroad.[11] In 2015, for example, Luisa Pécora created Mulher no Cinema (Woman in Cinema), a website containing news, interviews, videos, reviews, and scholarly works about women in Brazilian and international film industries (Pécora 2017). This led to other important initiatives, such as the online platform NGO Mulheres no Audiovisual (Black Women in the Brazilian Audiovisual). Inspired by Netflix, this platform provides video streaming services aimed at showcasing women's productions while also providing information on the history of women in film and promoting the participation of new women filmmakers in national productions. Other important initiatives include the Facebook group Mulheres do Audiovisual Brasileiro (Women of Audiovisual Brazil); the scholarly group Academia das Musas (Academy of Muses) formed by academics dedicated to the research, debate, and diffusion of works directed by women; and the Festival Internacional de Cinema de Realizadoras (International Film Festival of Women Directors), among numerous other important initiatives launched in the past few years (see Santos and Tedesco, 2017; see also Marsh's and Verztman Bagdadi's chapters in this volume).

Concluding Remarks

As noted elsewhere, the Brazilian film industry has gone through ups and downs, and yet it has succeeded in maintaining a continuous, albeit uneven, production of films even under the most challenging conditions (Rêgo 2011a). In this chapter, I have shown that the industry rose from the ashes in the mid-1990s, after a downturn that reached its nadir with the extinction of Embrafilme in 1990. The so-called industry rebound initiated a period that was marked by the institution of fiscal incentive mechanisms largely provided by the Rouanet and Audiovisual laws. Together they provided a substantial increase in available funds for film production and have been regarded as essential for its upturn from the mid-1990s onward.

In what concerns women's cinema in the twenty-first century, the films and filmmakers that appeared since 2000 have not all received the same amount of attention, nor have they been equally productive. Some directors have made several films and others have directed only one or two as of 2019. Each year OCA publishes a report listing the numbers of films released in the domestic market and their respective directors. Women in this role accounted for about 19 percent between 1994 and 1998, down to 17.5 percent between 1999 and 2009, and back up to nearly 22 percent between 2010 and 2018. While small, this is a significant increase considering that, despite the growth in the number of releases during the period, the share of national films in the domestic market (14.8 percent as of 2018, thus comparatively unchanged from 2009) did not keep the same pace, and that, historically, releases of films by female directors have been considerably smaller than those by their male peers (Ancine 2018, 12). Beginning around 2008, documentary features by women have increasingly stood out, as illustrated by works of Lúcia Murat, Tetê Amaral,

Paula Gaitán, Maria Augusta Ramos, Sandra Kogut, and Marlene França among others. Indeed, as Patricia White (2015, 8) notes,

> The fiction features by women . . . are by no means the only, or even the most obvious, sites in which women's cinema and feminist film culture thrive today. With the advent of digital filmmaking, women's work in documentary is more vital, varied and widespread than ever; short film, web-based media, gallery-based fine art, television and popular cinema all represent significant areas of women's production within multiple and national and global media fields.

The surge in documentary production occurring in Brazil from the mid-1990s onward, and especially in the twenty-first century, seems to confirm that. According to Furtado (2019, 3), the rise in documentary features since the retomada was made possible by several factors, including the implementation of public funding laws for production (especially the 1993 Audiovisual Law); the emergence of affordable technology such as portable video cameras; the recognition of the documentary genre as an artistic form of expression and critical reflection on a par with fiction; the advent of a film culture that consists of film festivals, receptive audiences, specialized publications, and blogs; the increased professionalization of filmmakers working in the field; and the increased distribution and exhibition of documentary films in movie theaters and television.

And yet, despite creating a more propitious atmosphere for national film production, public funding laws, especially the Audiovisual Law of 1993, have also proved to be little more than missed opportunities to significantly change prevailing distribution and exhibition practices or the hegemonic presence of foreign films in the domestic market. And, as Globo Filmes franchises continue to dominate film consumption for local productions, the situation is unlikely to change. Unfortunately, while providing (ever so limited) financial support to national productions, the Audiovisual Law has ultimately led independent local productions to face competition from not only the Hollywood films but also Globo films, pitting independent directors against directors whose productions are oiled by the Globo machine.

As for the Rouanet Law, it has been mired in controversy since its inception. As R. Machado (2018, 411) points out, since the law does "not discriminate among art forms, it ended up including gospel music, fashion shows, and circus" as well as films. Misunderstood by many Brazilians, the law has been criticized for promoting "everything" but "art"; vying for its funds, cultural producers also criticize the mechanism of the law that transfers decisions over the type of cultural products to support to private firms.

The fact remains that despite the increased output of films by women, the vast majority of these films find little to no distribution in the commercial (and still the most profitable) circuit. The difficulty of reaching a large public is, as the numbers reported by Ancine show, quite evident for independent productions, especially those made by female directors. As discussed elsewhere (Rêgo 2011a), the hurdles faced by filmmakers are many, starting as early as the initial stages of seeking out private funders for a project and continuing through the filming process on to postproduction and distribution—a situation that has been aggravated by the closure of Petrobras Film Distributor (Petrobras Distribuidora) in 2019. This also meant the end of Petrobras's financial support to several film festivals, where the great majority of films made by women circulate. To this, one can add the dwindling financial support of other public institutions for film production. Like Petrobras, the National Bank for Economic and Social Development (BNDES, Banco Nacional de Desenvolvimento Econômico e Social) has also cut funds for the sector. Both Petrobras and the BNDES are federal public companies and until 2019 represented about 70 percent of all investments in film production made via the tax incentive scheme provided by law (Bittencourt 2019). Additionally, the new funding policies for production and distribution of national features set in place by BNDES tend to privilege those whose content complies with the government's ideology. Women-directed films, especially those revolving around feminist and political themes, are most likely to be targets of these new funding policies. And here I add, quoting Roberts-Camps (2017, xii), "Now, imagine if you are a female director dealing with all of the above with the added challenges of patriarchal notions of the workplace and hesitations about women's abilities to carry film projects."

Moreover, once he was sworn into office in January 2019, Jair Bolsonaro enacted a series of measures that sparked concerns in the local film community. He dismantled the Ministry of Culture, replacing it with the Ministry of Citizenship, which would encompass sports, communications, social policy, and culture. In November 2019 the newly created Special Secretariat for Culture was transferred to the Ministry of Tourism, under which the audiovisual industry currently functions. Since then, there have been several attempts at either censoring cultural projects—whether they are publicly or privately funded—or suspending state support for cultural productions that do not conform to the Christian faith-based discourse that the government seeks to promote, and which currently drives public cultural policy in Brazil (Foggin 2020).

Ancine has been the main target of Bolsonaro's bile against culture in general and Brazilian cinema in particular. While claiming that he is not censoring culture but "curating" it in line with his religious beliefs, Bolsonaro has also threatened to close Ancine if it continues to support films whose themes revolve around women, Black and Indigenous people, and the LGBTQ+ community. In his words, "Ancine should accept filters" or face "privatization or closure" (A. Machado 2019, n.p.; see also Magalhães 2019; Bittencourt 2019).

The agency is protected by law, and in order to dismantle it the government needs to take radical measures to reduce its autonomy. Consequently, Bolsonaro has already taken several steps in this direction. After removing Christian de Castro as the agency's president (and replacing him with the more conservative Evangelical pastor Edilasio Barra), Bolsonaro signed a decree slashing public funding for the audiovisual industry by 43 percent, thus further eroding state financial support for national film production. According to the Institute of Economic Research at the University of São Paulo, about 70 percent of movies produced in Brazil rely on public funding. It remains to be seen how the film industry will maintain its current output (of 185 films in 2018) under the existing budgetary and political constraints. Without state financial support, women directors will likely find it even more difficult to produce and distribute their films. In sum, the threats to the future of Ancine and, consequently, of the film industry itself, come as other sources of public funds (both at federal and state levels) and private-sector funds are either cut or removed altogether, leaving film professionals, particularly independent producers, to wonder what is yet to come.

Turning back to the main subject of this chapter, I wish to recall, quoting Cobb, that the lack of status and recognition for women in cinema has become an increasingly pressing issue in the mainstream media in recent years, especially during the award season when "articles are written lamenting the numbers of women directors nominated for awards and the major festivals get rightly taken down for not including many films by women in their programs" (Cobb 2015, 2–3). As I write this conclusion, the 92nd Academy Awards is about to begin. With not a single woman nominated for the Best Director category, the Best Documentary Feature category this year has become the first to achieve parity since the #OscarSoWhite hashtag took off in 2015: four of the five documentary features nominated for the award are either directed or codirected by women, including Costa's *The Edge of Democracy*. Originally showcased in the 2019 Sundance Festival and later released by Netflix, the documentary, which is narrated in the first person, follows Brazilian politics from Rousseff's impeachment in 2016 to the imprisonment of former President Luiz Inácio "Lula" da Silva in mid-2018 to the election of Bolsonaro at the end of that year. *The Edge of Democracy* has caused much controversy in Brazil and has been accused of being a propaganda tool for the Workers' Party (Partido dos Trabalhadores), to which both Rousseff and Lula belong. Its nomination for the Oscars drew the ire of Bolsonaro's followers and right-wing politicians and from Bolsonaro himself, who, attempting to discredit it, called the film "a fiction."[12] Petra Costa, after all, is not taking home the Oscar statuette, but I hope that with her nomination she will pave the way for more Brazilian productions directed by women to be appreciated, and that Brazilian women will be recognized for their creative work behind the screen in the context of twenty-first-century Brazil.

Notes

1. Brazil released on average four to six international coproductions between 1995 and 2009 totaling seventy-nine for the period, only a handful of which were directed by a woman, among them Sandra Kogut's *Um passaporte Húngaro* (*A Hungarian passport*, 2001); Julia Murat's *Peso da massa, leveza do pão* (*Weight of the dough, lightness of the bread*, 2009), and Mariana Viñoles's *Exilados* (*Exiles*, 2009) (Meleiro 2013). They were followed by Beatriz Seiger's *O sonho Bollywoodiano* (*Bollywood Dream*, 2010), which was the first coproduction between India and Brazil. The average numbers of international coproductions climbed to thirteen from 2011 to 2016 (Hopewell 2019), totaling 117 for the 2005–2016 period (Ancine 2019). However, data published by Ancine (2019) for the period between 1995 and 2017 do not identify international coproductions by women during those years.

2. Three of the most-watched films listed by Ancine for 2018 were associated with Globo Filmes, including Susana Garcia's *Minha vida em Marte* (*My life on Mars*). While Ramos's documentary was distributed by Vitrine Filmes and shown in fifty-eight movie theaters nationwide, Garcia's film was distributed by Downtown/Paris Distributors and shown in 925 movie theaters nationwide to close to one million spectators, which translated into a box office revenue of R$14.715.902,00 (US$3,677,975.50 in 2020 dollars) (Ancine 2018).

3. Having not produced or coproduced a film directed by a woman until 2003, Globo Filmes released an average of one film per year by a female director between 2003 and 2006 (with none released in 2005), two films per year between 2007 and 2013, and four to six films per year between 2014 and 2016. The numbers considerably rose to thirteen films in 2017, seventeen films in 2018, and sixteen films in 2019. Unlike the great majority of national films, films produced or coproduced by Globo have been adapted for and exhibited on television and are also available on DVD.

4. Garcia's film had a bigger box office return than the two first franchises combined, which was of R$173.798,33 (US$43,449.50 in 2020 dollars) by its third-week run (Anonymous 2020a; Anonymous 2020b). Together, the trilogy sold over 25 million tickets as of February of 2020 and is currently available in different digital platforms.

5. As noted elsewhere (see Rêgo 2008, 2011a), although some Globo Filmes productions have enjoyed excellent box office performances, others have failed to attract significant numbers of viewers.

6. According to the 1993 Audiovisual Law, in order to be eligible to receive funds from the tax exemption scheme, the producer must be "independent," that is, without any direct association with a mass communication enterprise, which is not the case of Globo Filmes. Ironically, however, for film industry insiders, the term *independent* has become synonymous with films, filmmakers, and production firms not associated with Globo Filmes (R. Machado 2018, 414).

7. Established in 2016 by Ancine, the current quota for national films is not mandatory. It establishes that movie theaters with one screen must show local productions for a minimum of twenty-eight days and at least three different titles per year. However, despite the increased numbers of local productions being released in the past few years, admissions by foreign films still dominate. One reason for this is that the exhibition sector is predominantly owned by foreign firms (Ancine 2019, 5).

8. While Nagib's argument is particularly productive for thinking about film authorship and the cultural politics of gender, it also offers a less stable frame through which to view the creative work of women. The working notion of "filmmaking as collaboration" seems to be a double-edged sword; one that might inevitably serve to erase and/or minimize the significance of women filmmakers' participation in shared or coauthored projects. Thus, while sympathetic to her desire to challenge the traditional notion of authorship as a male, individualistic, creative practice, it is my contention that one cannot speak of coauthorship without acknowledging that any woman working in the cultural field does so within the parameters set largely by men, both on the level of discourse and material resources.

9. Adélia Sampaio's *Amor maldito* (*Damned Love*, 1984) was the first feature-length film directed by an Afro-Brazilian woman. She has made numerous contributions to film as producer, production manager, art and cast director, and

screenwriter for projects by both male and female directors. However, there is practically no mention of her work in published volumes about Brazilian cinema. See Mercedes Vázquez Vázquez's and Reighan Gillam's chapters in this volume for a more detailed discussion of contemporary Brazilian Black cinema.

9. See Mercedes Vázquez Vázquez's chapter in this volume for further discussion.

10. In 2013, the Secretariat of Audiovisual Activities of the Ministry of Culture, together with the Secretariat of Women's Policies of the Presidency of the Republic of Brazil, created the Carmen Santos Cinema Award with the goal of giving increased visibility to the work of women's directors and technicians and promoting equal opportunities for them in the audiovisual industry, with special attention to Indigenous women, Afro-Brazilian women, and women from vulnerable groups (UNESCO n.d.; Anonymous 2018).

11. For more on Petra Costa and *The Edge of Democracy*, see Jack A. Draper III's interview with her in this volume.

Works Cited

Alves, Paula, José Eustáquio Alves, and Denise Britz do Nascimento Silva. 2011. "Mulheres no cinema Brasileiro" [Women in Brazilian cinema]. *Revista Caderno Espaço Feminino* 24, no. 2, 365–94.

Ancine. 2019. "Listagem dos filmes brasileiros lançados 1995–2018" [List of films released 1995–2018]. https://oca.ancine.gov.br/cinema.

Ancine. 2018. "Anuário estatístico do cinema brasileiro 2018" [Annual report of Brazilian cinema 2018]. https://oca.ancine.gov.br/cinema.

Anonymous. 2018. "TV Brasil estreia obras do prêmio Carmen Santos de cinema de mulheres" [TV Brazil shows films awarded with the Carmen Santos Prize]. *Revista de Cinema*, April 21, 2018. http://revistadecinema.com.br/2018/04/tv-brasil-estreia-obras-do-premio-carmen-santos-de-cinema-de-mulheres/.

Anonymous. 2020a. "'Minha mãe é uma peça 3' foi assistido por mais 9,3 mi de espectadores" ['My Mother is a Character 3' was seen by 9.3 million spectators]. *Correio Braziliense*, January 20, 2020. https://www.correio braziliense.com.br/app/noticia/diversao-e-arte/2020/01/24/interna_diversao_arte,822727/minha-mae-e-uma-peca-3-foi-assistido-por-mais-9-3-mi-de-espectadores.shtml.

Anonymous. 2020b. "'Minha mãe é uma peça 3' bate recorde na estreia" ['My Mother is a Character 3' reaches record attendance at its premier]. *Jornal de Brasília*, January 1, 2020. http://jornaldebrasilia.com.br/clicla-brasilia/cinema-clicla-brasilia/minha-mãe-e-uma-peca-3-bate-recorde-na-estreia/.

Benamou, Catherine L., and Leslie L. Marsh. 2013. "Women Filmmakers and Citizenship in Brazil, from *Bossa Nova* to the *Retomada*." In *Hispanic and*

Lusophone Women Filmmakers: Theory, Practice and Difference, edited by Parvati Nair and Julián Daniel Gutiérrez-Albilla, 54–71. Manchester: Manchester University Press.

Bittencourt, Ela. 2019. "Brazil's Film Sector Up in Arms Over Jair Bolsonaro's Censorship Threat." *The Hollywood Report*, July 22, 2019. https://www.hollywoodreporter.com/news/brazils-president-jair-bolsonaro-threatens-increase-film-censorship-1226219.

Buarque de Hollanda, Heloisa, ed. 1989. *Realizadoras de cinema no Brasil (1930/1988)* [Women filmmakers in Brazil, 1930/1988]. Rio de Janeiro: CIEC.

Cobb, Shelley. 2015. *Adaptation, Authorship, and Contemporary Women Filmmakers*. London: Palgrave Macmillan.

De La Fuente, Anna Marie. 2017. "Co-Productions on the Rise in Brazil." *Variety*, May 18, 2017. https://variety.com/2017/film/global/co-productions-brazil-1202434200/.

Dennison, Stephanie. 2020. *Remapping Brazilian Film Culture in the Twenty-First Century*. London: Routledge.

Donoghue, Courtney Brannon. 2011. "Globo Filmes, Sony, and Franchise Film-Making: Transnational Industry in the Brazilian Pós-Retomada." In *New Trends in Argentine and Brazilian Cinema*, edited by Cacilda Rêgo and Carolina Rocha, 51–66. Bristol, UK: Intellect.

Foggin, Sophie. 2020. "Why Bolsonaro is 'Curating' Brazil's Culture." *Latin American Reports*, January 29, 2020. https://latinamericareports.com/why-bolsonaro-is-curating-brazil's-culture/4174/.

Furtado, Gustavo Procopio. 2019. *Documentary Filmmaking in Contemporary Brazil: Cinematic Archives of the Present*. Oxford: Oxford University Press.

Globo Filmes. n.d. "Globo Filmes. O cinema que fala a sua língua" [Globo Filmes: The cinema that speaks your language]. Accessed January 24, 2020. https://globofilmes.globo.com/quem_somos/.

Guerini, Elaine. 2017. "The Highest-Grossing Brazilian Films of Last 20 Years Revealed." *Screen Daily*, August 16, 2017. https://www.screendaily.com/news/the-highest-grossing-brazilian-films-of-last-20-years-revealed/5120882.article.

———. 2019. "Does Brazil's New Government Threaten its Growing Co-Production Industry?" *Screen Daily*, February 7, 2019. https://www.screendaily.com/features/does-brazils-new-government-threaten-its-growing-co-production-industry/5136688.article.

Hamburger, Esther. 2017. "Brazilian Film and Television in Times of Intermedia Diversification." In *A Companion to Latin American Cinema*, edited by Maria M. Delgado, Stephen M. Hart, and Randal Johnson, 375–91. West Sussex, UK: Wiley Blackwell.

Holanda, Karla, and Marina Cavalcanti Tedesco, eds. 2017. *Feminino e Plural: Mulheres no Cinema Brasileiro* [Feminine and plural: Brazilian cinema]. São Paulo: Papirus.

Hopewell, John. 2019. "In Brazil, Co-Productions and OTT Provide Stability in Tumultuous Time." *Variety*, February 7, 2019. https://variety.com/2019/film/features/in-brazil-co-productions-and-ott-provide-stability-in-a-tumultuous-time-1203131695/.

Johnson, Randal. 2005. "TV Globo, the MPA and Contemporary Brazilian Cinema." In *Latin American Cinema: Essays on Modernity, Gender and National Identity*, edited by Lisa Shaw and Stephanie Dennison, 11–38. North Carolina: McFarland.

Johnson, Randal, and Robert Stam. 1982. *Brazilian Cinema*. East Brunswick, NJ: Associated University Presses.

Labaki, Amir. 1998. *O Cinema Brasileiro—The Films from Brazil*. São Paulo: Publifolha.

Lusvarhi, Luiza, and Camila Vieira da. 2019. *Mulheres atrás das câmaras: As cineastas brasileiras de 1930 a 2018* [Women behind the cameras: Brazilian directors from 1930 to 2018]. São Paulo: Estação Liberdade.

Machado, Adriano. 2019. "Bolsonaro Removes Director of Cinema Agency." *Plataforma*, August 31, 2019. https://www.plataformamedia.com/en-uk/news/politics/bolsonaro-removes-the-director-of-the-brazilian-cinema-agency-11255242.html.

Machado, Roberto Pinheiro. 2018. *Brazilian History: Culture, Society, Politics 1500–2010*. Newcastle upon Tyne, UK: Cambridge Scholars.

Magalhães, Letícia. 2019. "How is the Brazilian Film Industry Threatened by Bolsonaro?" *Cine Suffragette*, August 20, 2019. https://medium.com/cinesuffragette/how-is-the-brazilian-film-industry-threatened-by-bolsonaro-78595c82083f.

Marsh, Leslie L. 2012. *Brazilian Women's Filmmaking: From Dictatorship to Democracy*. Urbana: University of Illinois Press.

Martin, Deborah, and Deborah Shaw. 2017. *Latin American Women Filmmakers: Production, Politics, Poetics*. London: IB Taurus.

Meleiro, Alessandra. 2013. "Finance and Co-productions in Brazil." In *Contemporary Hispanic Cinema: Interrogating the Transnational in Spanish and Latin American Film*, edited by Stephanie Dennison, 181–204. Suffolk, UK: Tamesis.

Moisés, José Álvaro. 2003. "A New Policy for Brazilian Cinema." In *The New Brazilian Cinema*, edited by Lúcia Nagib, 3–22. London: IB Taurus.

Munerato, Elice, and Maria Helena Darcy de Oliveira. 1982a. "When Women Film." In *Brazilian Cinema*, edited by Randal Johnson and Robert Stam, 340–50. East Brunswick, NJ: Associated University Presses.

Munerato, Elice, and Maria Helena Darcy de Oliveira. 1982b. *As musas da matinê* [The cinema's muses]. Rio de Janeiro: Rioarte.

Nair, Parvati, and Julián Daniel Gutiérrez-Albilla, eds. 2013. *Hispanic and Lusophone Women Filmmakers: Theory, Practice and Difference*. Manchester: Manchester University Press.

———. 2013. "Introduction." In *Hispanic and Lusophone Women Filmmakers: Theory, Practice and Difference*, edited by Nair Parvati and Julián Gutiérrez-Albilla, 1–11. Manchester: Manchester University Press.

Nagib, Lúcia. 2003. "Introduction." In *The New Brazilian Cinema*, edited by Lúcia Nagib, xvii–xxvi. London: IB Taurus.

———. 2017. "Beyond Difference: Female Participation in the Brazilian Film Revival of the 1990s." In *Latin American Women Filmmakers: Production, Politics, Poetics*, edited by Deborah Martin and Deborah Shaw, 31–47. London: IB Taurus.

Observatório Brasileiro do Cinema e do Audiovisual (OCA). 2018. "Informe mercado: Diversidade de gênero e raça nos longas-metragens brasileiros lançados em salas de exibição em 2016" [Market report: Gender and race diversity in Brazilian films released in 2016]. https://oca.ancine.gov.br/sites/default/files/repositorio/pdf/informe_diversidade_2016.pdf.

Pécora, Luisa. 2017. "The Brazilian Film Industry Has a Gender Issue, but Also a Race One." *Her Film Project*, October 12, 2017. http://www.herfilmproject.com/news/the-brazilian-film-industry-has-a-gender-issue-but-also-a-race-one.

Pessoa, Ana. 2002. *Carmen Santos: O cinema dos anos 20* [Carmen Santos: Cinema in the 1920s]. Rio de Janeiro: Aeroplano.

———. n.d. "Por trás das cameras" [Behind the cameras]. Rio de Janeiro: Fundação Casa de Rui Barbosa. http://www.casaruibarbosa.gov.br/dados/DOC/artigos/o-z/FCRB_AnaPessoa_Por_tras_cameras.pdf.

Ramos, Fernão, and Luiz Felipe Miranda, eds. 2000. *Enciclopédia do cinema brasileiro* [Encyclopedia of Brazilian cinema]. São Paulo: SENAC.

Rêgo, Cacilda. 2008. "Rede Globo: A TV que virou estrela de cinema" [Globo TV: The television that became a film star]. *Studies in Latin American Popular Culture* (27), 182–90.

———. 2011a. "The Fall and Rise of Brazilian Cinema." In *New Trends in Argentine and Brazilian Cinema*, edited by Cacilda Rêgo and Carolina Rocha, 35–49. Bristol, UK: Intellect.

———. 2011b. "Brazilian Cinema Since 1990." *Review: Literature and Arts of the Americas*, Issue 83 (44) 2: 204–11.

Rist, Peter. 1996. "Gaijin, caminhos da liberdade." In *South American Cinema: A Critical Filmography*, edited by Timothy Barnard and Peter Rist, 192–94. Austin: University of Texas Press.

Roberts-Camps, Traci. 2017. *Latin American Women Filmmakers: Social and Cultural Perspectives*. Albuquerque: University of New Mexico Press.

San Martín, Patricia Torres. 2013. "Lost and Invisible: A History of Latin American Women Filmmakers." In *Hispanic and Lusophone Women Filmmakers: Theory, Practice and Difference*, edited by Parvati Nair and Julián Daniel Gutiérrez-Albilla, 29–41. Manchester: Manchester University Press.

Santos, Érica Ramos Sarmet dos, and Marina Cavalcanti Tedesco. 2017. "Feminist Initiatives and Actions in Contemporary Brazilian Audiovisual." *Revista Estudos Feministas* (25) 3: 1373–89.

Silva Neto, Antônio Leão da. 2002. *Dicionário de filmes brasileiros* [Dictionary of Brazilian films]. São Paulo: Futuro Mundo Gráfica & Editora.

UNESCO. 2016. "Enhancing Gender in Brazilian Audiovisual." https://en.unesco.org/creativity/policy-monitoring-platform/edital-carmen-santos-cinema-de.

Viola, Kamille. 2016."Brazil's New Wave of Filmmakers Tackles Racism." *The Women and Girls Deeply Archives*, July 19, 2016. http://www.newsdeeply.com/womenandgirls/articles/2016/07/19/brazils-new-wave-of-filmmakers-tackles-racism.

White, Patricia. 2015. *Women's Cinema, World Cinema*. Durham, NC: Duke University Press.

Chapter 2

Behind the Scenes

Brazilian Women Screenwriters in Film and Television

Leslie L. Marsh

In 2018, the Brazilian national film agency Ancine (Agência Nacional do Cinema) published a landmark study of gender and race in feature-length films released in 2016. The report's findings supported what many had suspected but, with numerical data, the stark inequality and lack of diversity in the audiovisual sector was confirmed. Despite a limited sample size of works released in one calendar year, the study showed that women directed 19.7 percent of films and wrote the screenplays for 16.2 percent.[1] Notably, the study indicates that no Black woman directed or wrote a film released that year (OCA 2018). The study generally supported prior findings by Ancine, which started publishing data on gender and film directors in 2015.[2] Fortunately, women's participation in the audiovisual sector is changing and becoming more diverse albeit quite slowly. If we think further about diversity and structural inequalities in contemporary Brazil, we must acknowledge the years of activism by women and Black Brazilians. Efforts to improve diversity and equality can also be traced in part to affirmative action policies advanced since the 1990s (Htun 2004). During the Luiz Inácio Lula da Silva administration, cultural policies actively sought to cultivate ideas of a "new Brazil" that was more inclusive and diverse (Marsh 2016, 3024–25; Marsh 2021).

Studies conducted by Ancine help develop a historiography of women's participation in Brazilian audiovisual production, but they do not capture a complete story. Similarly, scholars of Brazilian cinema who have studied women's participation in audiovisual production and examined the representation of gender have tended to focus on directors. This is the case with my own book, *Brazilian Women's Filmmaking: From Dictatorship to Democracy* (2012), where I focus primarily on directors. In most instances, however, this generation of women frequently produced, directed, and wrote their films. Yet, film and media production is most often a collective practice and enterprise. Directors and actors most often receive the greatest accolades for their work, but a team of artists, producers, and technicians is vital to audiovisual productions and shapes what viewers see on screens. From a more inclusive perspective, writing is fundamental to filmmaking. Scholars of Hollywood cinema have developed several important studies of women screenwriters (Smyth 2016; Welch and Beauchamp 2018; Cobb 2014) yet there are few works that focus on Brazilian (or Latin American, more generally) women screenwriters.[3] Official government agencies have broadened their scope when studying women's participation in the audiovisual sector—accounting for directors, screenwriters, producers, cinematographers, and art directors—in an effort to capture a more accurate view of the field and develop inclusive policies. Similarly, this essay places screenwriting at the center of analysis to assess how Brazilian women artists are "breaking ground" in audiovisual production.

There are advantages to focusing on screenwriting. Reflections by writers on their craft bring forth issues related to shifts in the audiovisual industry and the creative practices of film and media. That is, a focus on writers expands a view of contemporary audiovisual production and acknowledges ways women participate in shaping ideas about Brazilian culture and society. Like other members of an audiovisual production, screenwriters participate in a particular artistic context that shapes their creative practice. Screenwriters have a "mental camera" that captures and describes environments and characters. Additionally, production budgets can shape or limit a screenwriter's imagination. For instance, narratives with multiple characters and locations are far more expensive than dramas taking place in fewer, more defined spaces. Scripts are written works that inspire additional creative activity. Indeed, the word *realizador*, a synonym in Portuguese for director, suggests the activity of "making real or come to fruition" the ideas presented by a screenwriter. Scripts are subject to interpretation and undergo change not unlike a theatrical play, which manages to retain more prestige than screenplays. Taking into consideration some of the unique aspects of screenwriting, this chapter first briefly maps the state of the profession of screenwriting in Brazil as it has evolved over the past several decades. The second part of this chapter considers issues related to female screenwriters' authorship and agency, which involves their reflections on their roles as screenwriters and emerging opportunities in Brazilian audiovisual production.

State of the Script

Brazilian cinema has tended to celebrate *cinema de autor* (auteur cinema), reflecting in part the influence of Brazil's celebrated Cinema Novo directors who wrote and directed acclaimed works in the mid-twentieth century. In the case of auteur cinema, the director's vision of a project presumably guides the overall production from start to finish. More generally, directors are far more celebrated than writers or others who play fundamental roles in film production (e.g., editors or art directors). Given an emphasis on auteur cinema, the screenwriter in Brazilian cinema has not been a historically celebrated role.

In his reflections on the state of screenwriting in the Brazilian audiovisual landscape, Chico Matoso believes scripts and screenwriters are generally less valued in Brazilian film production relative to production practices found in the United States. That is, he finds that in Brazil the screenwriter is not included as much and therefore cannot respond to questions regarding the writer's intent and other concerns that may arise during production. By contrast, Matoso asserts that the script is more valued in serial programs (such as the *novela*), where he sees a stronger tradition of including the screenwriter in the production process on set (O2 Filmes 2017a). As will be discussed in this chapter, women screenwriters differ in opinion about their role on set.

Formation in the Profession

Although less celebrated (historically) in Brazilian filmmaking, screenwriting as an artistic practice and profession has undergone significant transformation in recent years. Training to become a screenwriter and entering the profession has evolved considerably. Reflecting an auteurist approach to filmmaking, many women directors who began developing consistent careers in the 1970s and 1980s also wrote the scripts for their works (Marsh 2012, 16–21, 34–36). Similarly, many women screenwriters, whose careers began in the 1980s to the mid-1990s, reveal they learned to write scripts by writing, revising their work, and learning from people around them.

The professionalization of screenwriting began to advance significantly in the mid-1990s, coinciding with the "revival" (*retomada*) of Brazilian filmmaking. Following the closure of Brazil's film agency at the time (Embrafilme) and the dramatic reduction in film production in the early 1990s, filmmakers returned to their craft taking advantage of new incentive laws and facing a new market-oriented landscape (Rêgo 2011; Meleiro 2010). The revival of cinema in the 1990s was also stimulated by the international success of *Central do Brasil* (*Central Station*, 1998), which won the Sundance screenwriting award in 1996 and went on to become an international success. Carla Esmeralda, who had worked in Embrafilme, developed a collaboration with the Sundance Institute to organize and offer screenwriting labs in Brazil.[4] Esmeralda played an important role in helping develop screenwriting as a profession and practice in Brazil.

Several women have been selected to participate in Sundance writing labs. In 1998, Elena Soarez, Anna Muylaert, and Lúcia Murat were among the first women writers who benefited from the Sundance Institute's support. (Notably, the Sundance Screenwriters Lab included writer and director Suzana Amaral, who directed the acclaimed *A hora da estrela* [*Hour of the Star*, 1985], as a leader for the workshop.) While Lúcia Murat's script for the feature film *Brava gente brasileira* (*Brave New Land*, 2000) was selected for the lab in 1998, Anna Muylaert participated in the workshop with the script for *Durval Discos* (*Durval Records*, 2002) and Elena Soarez was selected to develop her first film script *Eu, tu, eles* (*Me, You, Them*, 2000).[5] Soarez, who is now a veteran screenwriter for film and television, acknowledges that there had not been a strong tradition of developing screenwriters in Brazil and that most are self-taught (Grillo 1998). Although she states that she struggled for four years to write *Me, You, Them*, Soarez has now become a consultant on scripts for the Sundance Institute, participating in workshops in the United States, India, and the Middle East. Similarly, Anna Muylaert has continued her involvement with the Sundance Institute as a consultant, leading screenwriting workshops and master classes. Echoing Soarez, Melanie Dimantas, coauthor of the script for *Carlota Joaquina, princesa do Brasil* (*Carlota Joaquina, Princess of Brazil*, 1995)—a film frequently credited with starting the revival of Brazilian cinema in the mid-1990s—asserts that workshops like those offered by Sundance and those subsequently organized by Carla Esmeralda have changed the landscape for screenwriting in Brazil. Like many other screenwriters—past and present, male and female—Dimantas did not study cinema. Indeed, there has been a tendency for screenwriters in Brazil to pursue degrees in social sciences (i.e., anthropology, sociology, etc.). Dimantas notes that training workshops offered in recent years have allowed screenwriters to make professional connections and develop their technique (Dimantas 2018).

Formation of the Profession

If screenwriting in Brazil evolved due to new production practices and international support from the Sundance Institute, the work of screenwriters has also changed significantly due to the gradual development of a professional, national support network over the past twenty years. For example, in 2000, screenwriters for television formed the Associação de Roteiristas de TV (Association for Television Screenwriters). Then, a group of writers working in cinema formed the group Autores de Cinema (Cinema Authors) in 2006. Both organizations have since united to become the Associação Brasileira de Autores Roteiristas (Brazilian Association of Screenwriters), whose work includes defending the rights of screenwriters, advocating for improved compensation, and supporting the professional development of screenwriters.

Indeed, the professionalization of screenwriting in Brazil and the creation of opportunities for new voices to enter the industry has benefited from a range of private and public initiatives. Adopted in 2011, Law 12.485/11 (or Brazil's "pay TV law") required pay television to include more Brazilian content per week. The measure is generally seen as invigorating the independent Brazilian television sector and, subsequently, stimulating demand for scripts. The law took effect at a time when cultural policies emphasized development of the creative economy in Brazil. Consistent with these industry changes, the first edition of the Rio Content Market took place in 2011. Known as Rio2C, the event has become the largest in Latin America, focusing on entertainment and innovation. The event includes lectures, workshops, and pitching sessions with industry leaders. Notably, the 2016 edition of Rio2C gathered executives from Amazon Studios, Hulu, and Netflix, who looked to invest in international, original projects and highlight the work of female creators. The effort to be more inclusive is laudable but, as Carol Rodrigues observes, the entrance fee to attend Rio2C has been prohibitive for newcomers to pitch their projects to industry executives and further emphasizes structural barriers to achieving greater diversity in Brazilian audiovisual production (Rodrigues 2018).

Following her work with the Sundance Institute, Carla Esmeralda developed the Laboratório Novas Histórias (New Stories Laboratory) in 2011, a project undertaken in collaboration with SESC (Serviço Social do Comércio [Social Service of Commerce]) and SENAC (Serviço Nacional de Aprendizagem Comercial [National Commercial Apprenticeship Service]) of São Paulo as part of an initiative to develop scripts and screenwriting as a profession in Brazil. The New Stories program includes applications from newcomers as well as those who have written or directed no more than one feature-length film. Several women screenwriters (and writer-directors) have benefited from the Novas Histórias program, including Anna Muylaert (*Que horas ela volta? / The Second Mother*, 2015), Juliana Rojas (*As boas maneiras / Good Manners*, 2017), Beatriz Manela (*O rastro / The Trace We Leave Behind*, 2017), and Caroline Leone (*Pela janela / A Window to Rosália*, 2018) to name a few.

Festivals dedicated specifically to screenwriting have further assisted new writers and contributed to the professionalization of screenwriting. The first edition of the Festival de Roteiro Audiovisual de Porto Alegre (Porto Alegre Screenplay Festival [FRAPA]) took place in 2013. In a short time, the festival has become the largest event in Latin America focused on screenwriting for television and film, offering workshops, debates, and opportunities to pitch projects to industry professionals. In addition, other notable festivals dedicated to screenwriting include GUIÕES (Festival do Roteiro de Língua Portuguesa [Portuguese Language Screenplay Festival]), which focuses on stimulating the production of content in Portuguese in Lusophone countries, and ROTA (Festival de Roteiro Audiovisual [ROTA Screenplay Festival]), which invites submissions primarily from beginning screenwriters.[6] Specific to women, the Cabíria Festival was inaugurated in 2015 with the goal to encourage debates about gender, diversity, and representation in all facets of audiovisual production as well as stimulate the quantitative and qualitative participation of women in front of and behind the cameras. Led by Marília Nogueira and Vânia Matos, the festival awards the Cabíria Prêmio de Roteiro (Cabíria Script Prize) to recognize women screenwriters in feature-length fiction films, serial programs, and children's content. The professional development of women screenwriters in television also benefits from the Prêmio Diadorim (Diadorim Award), offered by the Associação de Mulheres no Audiovisual (Association of Women in the Audiovisual Sector) in partnership with the Imprensa Mahon (Mahon Press).[7] These awards offer women screenwriters small amounts of funding and clearly recognize their talent, but they also stimulate interest in their work more generally. These awards and additional training opportunities may also increase opportunities for new funding from other agencies, such as those offered by the Special Secretariat for Culture, formerly the Ministry of Culture, which offered a series of grants in 2018 with quotas for projects developed or directed by women.

A New Generation

A younger generation of women screenwriters entered an industry that has transformed significantly. They have also benefited from academic opportunities created in recent years. Gabriela Amaral Almeida, who participated in a Sundance Screenwriters Lab in 2014 with the script for *A sombra do pai* (*The Father's Shadow*, 2018), began developing her interest in film production in academic programs. (Her development of horror is discussed below.) Almeida completed a degree in communication at the Federal University of Bahia, where she specialized in literature and cinema of horror, writing a thesis on American writer Stephen King. Almeida then spent two years in Cuba at the Escuela Internacional de Cine y TV (International School of Film and TV [EICTV]) in San Antonio de los Baños, where she focused on becoming a screenwriter. Notwithstanding the expansion of academic programs in the last two decades, Carol Rodrigues was dissuaded from studying cinema in college and chose, like a surprising number of other screenwriters, to pursue social sciences. She eventually completed a short course on cinema at the University of São Paulo where she focused on directing and editing. Later, she took additional courses on screenwriting and participated in a writing group that helped her further master the craft, modeling a tendency of "learning by doing" that previous generations had followed. Rodrigues, who has written for film, television, web series, and Netflix, has become an outspoken advocate for greater diversity of voices in the Brazilian audiovisual industry and especially for LGBTQ+ and Black representation. For those who did not attend university programs, workshops and seminars affiliated with festivals and other organizations (such as those described above) remain a vital opportunity for training. Mirna Nogueira reveals that she took vacation time from work to attend a screenwriting workshop offered at the Mostra de Filme de Tiradentes (Tiradentes Film Festival) (O2 Filmes 2017g). Lastly, starting in 2018, SESC in Rio de Janeiro initiated the program SESC Argumenta, a project intended to contribute to the development of screenwriters. Structured similarly to other screenwriting labs, the SESC Argumenta program focuses on writers at an early stage in their careers.

Independent of festivals, several new training programs, websites, and podcasts offer additional support to screenwriters and those interested in screenwriting. Industry professionals José Carvalho and Viviane Valim Carvalho founded Roteiraria, a private school and agency that offers courses on screenwriting. The VAV Vitrine Audiovisual (VAV Audiovisual Showcase) is a digital networking platform for screenwriters and other audiovisual professionals. Both of these agencies are ultimately for-profit organizations, and participation is limited to those who can afford their services. However, other free resources have been developed recently. Screenwriters Filippo Cordeiro and Bruno Bloch founded the podcast *Primeiro tratamento* (First Treatment), where they interview contemporary screenwriters who discuss the craft of writing and their industry experiences.[8] Lastly, the website Tertúlia Narrativa (Narrative Community) is a project initiated by Marcos Hinke and Jaqueline Souza, who is one of several young Black women entering the audiovisual industry. The website makes available screenplays from world cinema, information about opportunities for screenwriters, and practical advice on developing and pitching a project.

Authorship and Agency

The founding of a new national film agency, Ancine, in 2001 marked the beginning of a new phase in Brazilian cinema. Not only did the agency aim to regulate and stimulate the industry, but it also inaugurated a shift in production practices that sought to be on par with international standards.[9] Commercial viability and success were emphasized, and there was new pressure for creative storytelling and screenwriting. A gradual shift in production practices took place at this time from a *cinema de autor* to a *cinema de produtor*. That is, auteur cinema came into tension with producer-driven films. In turn, the practice of screenwriting changed to one that asked writers to be aware of different working relationships with directors and different production circumstances. Mirna Nogueira, who is among the new generation of women screenwriters, has written for television as well as film, including the comedy *Carrossel: o filme* (*Carrossel, the Film*, 2015), the documentary *Aqualoucos* (*Aquacrazy*, 2017), and the action crime drama *O doutrinador* (*The Awakener*, 2018). She asserts that writers for different productions—whether commercial or independent—need to be cognizant of different working relationships, differentiating between collaborating with a production team hired by a producer and working with a director who has developed a project (O2 Filmes 2017g).

Excluding those women who have written, produced, and directed their own films, women screenwriters vary in their relationships with directors and producers and, subsequently, how they see their role as writers. In some instances, women writers have worked consistently with one or more collaborators (whether intimate or creative partner). For instance, Laís Bodanzky has worked on numerous occasions with Luiz Bolognesi, her ex-husband and business associate. Melanie Dimantas collaborated regularly with Carla Camurati on feature films, including *Carlota Joaquina* (1995) and *Copacabana* (2001). For her part, Anna Muylaert has been consulted on many scripts at the request of fellow screenwriters and directors, including Elena Soarez when she was developing the series *Filhos do carnaval* (*Sons of Carnival*) for HBO.[10]

Shifts in production methods and opportunities have impacted the way writers generally engage with projects. For Julia Rezende, learning to become a screenwriter was integral to becoming a director. Daughter of esteemed director Sérgio Rezende and producer Mariza Leão, Julia Rezende shares that when she decided to get into directing, she felt that she also needed to know how to write. She adds that prior to her entrance into the field, there wasn't as strong a presence of a *cinema de produtor* and that filmmaking was much more defined as "*diretor-autor* (i.e., auteur cinema)" (Rezende 2019). Changes in production have also impacted how writers produce scripts. Elena Soarez observes a shift from the start of her career when the director was the "owner" of the production to practices that are now more collaborative (O2 Filmes 2017f). What Soarez observes is an increasing emphasis on producer-driven cinema that deemphasizes the creative work as belonging to an individual artist. Her reflections are also informed by new opportunities for screenwriting for series, especially subscription video-on-demand (SVOD) programs for companies such as Netflix, which Carol Rodrigues asserts employ an "American model" of creating scripts in a *sala de roteiro* (a writers' room). Scholars of women's screenwriting in Brazil need to recognize individual as well as collaborative and collective work. If screenwriters have been generally overlooked in studies of Brazilian film and media, the contributions of women screenwriters tend to be elided further when their work does not fit into existing paradigms celebrating individual success.

A Role on the Set?

The relationship the writer has to the director and producer, as well as the type of production, tends to shape how she sees her role in the production. Although individuals and their creative work tend to be celebrated, most women screenwriters underscore the importance of *desapego* (letting go) of the texts they have written and express little desire to participate in the production on set. Writer-director Julia Rezende does not believe the writer needs to be on set as the set is the place of execution and not creation (Rezende 2019). Elena Soarez states she does not feel like she belongs on the set and that her work takes place beforehand (Soarez 2018). Synthesizing their perspectives, Gabriela Amaral Almeida asserts that the screenwriter's role is fundamental in audiovisual production, but screenwriters need to understand that the film is not the script; it is more like a musical score. Almeida further explains her perspective, noting that the script is a hybrid form that anticipates the director. A good script should provide all the conditions for the director to become the narrator of the script and interpret it technically (Almeida 2019). This is not the case in all production contexts. Melanie Dimantas echoes a lack of interest in being on set (generally) due to some disappointments with how her screenplay is brought to life, yet she underscores that she had a close collaboration with director Carla Camuratti with whom she *decupava* (sequenced) all the scenes of their films, taking on a more interpretive role in film production (Dimantas 2018).

Views on Writing

When screenwriters reflect on the visual nature of their work, they offer additional insights into tendencies in Brazilian cinema as well as their agency as artists. Both Adriana Falcão and Elena Soarez observe that Brazilian cinema has historically relied significantly on dialogue and not on images. Falcão believes that dialogue was underdeveloped in the past, and she spent years collaborating with others to learn how to improve this aspect of her writing. Although she sees people writing better dialogue now, she also believes more people are thinking of contemporary cinema in Brazil that does not depend so much on dialogue. As examples, she offers the case of Daniel Filho's *Se eu fosse você* (*If I Were You*, 2006) whose narrative needed significant dialogue. By contrast, Selton Mello's *O palhaço* (*The Clown*, 2011) includes very little. In addition to less scripted dialogue, she observes more improvisation that she dates to Globo TV's *Avenida Brasil* (*Brazil Avenue*, 2012) (Falcão 2018). Soarez corroborates Falcão's observations regarding the tendency to not rely enough on images in Brazilian cinema, suggesting that this is an influence of American and British modes of conveying narrative information in more subtle ways (Soarez 2018). Perhaps owing to an evolution in screenwriting in Brazilian cinema that Soarez and Falcão outline, Gabriela Amaral Almeida defines her work in terms of a *dramaturgo visual* (visual dramatist) and asserts that screenwriters need to think about their work as being visualized (Almeida 2019).

If they are aware of unique tendencies in Brazilian cinema, they are equally cognizant of their agency and responsibility in creating narratives. Writer-director Laís Bodanzky, who notes recent quantitative studies that reveal the relatively low numbers of women in Brazilian audiovisual production, recognizes that cinema is a powerful medium to shape understanding. For that reason, she calls on screenwriters to be active citizens that are aware of politics and the ideological dimensions of what they present (O2 Filmes 2017d). In this way, she seems to further the views of other screenwriters such as Carol Rodrigues and Anna Muylaert who advocate for going beyond the visual by disrupting expectations and stereotypes (O2 Filmes 2017e; Rodrigues 2018). Indeed, screenwriters like Gabriela Amaral Almeida and Carol Rodrigues see their perspectives as offering important contributions to contemporary narratives. Almeida, who asserts that "*tudo foi contado*" ("everything has been told"), feels it is necessary to be personally engaged in the writing process and the stories she tells. In doing so she aims to address her own fears and make new discoveries. For her, this is the fundamental way that she can contribute to contemporary narrative (Almeida 2019). Rodrigues, who is an outspoken critic of racial and gender inequality in Brazilian audiovisual, asserts that her goal is to represent the world and challenge stereotypes (Rodrigues 2018).

FILM, TELEVISION, STREAMING?

Divisions between working in film and television began to erode significantly in the late 1980s and early 1990s. Prior to the rebirth of cinema in the mid-1990s, those who had worked in the film industry survived professionally in television and advertising. Notably, the company O2 Filmes, which produced *Cidade de Deus* (*City of God*, 2002), *Lixo extraordinário* (*Waste Land*, 2011), and several series for television, has sustained a strong profile in advertising.

Women screenwriters have frequently worked in both film and television. An important exception is Glória Perez, an established screenwriter for novelas who has worked for the Globo Network since her debut in 1984. Perez is known for featuring strong female characters and for the practice of social merchandising, a type of education-entertainment in which social issues are raised, including topics such as bone marrow transplants, human trafficking, and AIDS prevention (Rosas-Moreno 2014, 2017). More common are career trajectories like those of Elena Soarez, Anna Muylaert, Julia Rezende, Ludmila Naves, Maria Camargo, and Juliana Rojas who have scripted works for the big and small screen. The introduction of SVOD services such as Netflix in 2011 has presented a new area of work for women screenwriters. Notably, Brazil is Netflix's second-largest foreign market behind the United Kingdom (Gruenwedel 2019). The series *3%* (2016–) was the first production for Netflix made entirely in Brazil and included writers Carol Rodrigues and Juliana Rojas. Elena Soarez and Sofia Maldonado have also written for the series *O mecanismo* (*The Mechanism*, 2018–) created by José Padilha for Netflix.

While each venue represents different challenges and opportunities for women's participation, the choice for women screenwriters to pursue careers in television versus film is more complicated than a question of taking advantage of opportunities that arise. First, in television, screenwriters and scripts generally tend to be more valued and writers are consulted on scripts and are more likely to participate in the production on set. Second, the financial realities of writing for cinema may encourage women writers to pursue careers in television or, more recently, series for SVOD. Adriana Falcão has written scripts for the commercially successful films *If I Were You* (2006) and *If I Were You 2* (2009)[11] and several television series, including *Mister Brau* (2017) and *A fórmula* (*The Formula*, 2017). Based on her experience, Falcão asserts that she does not believe there is a market for screenwriters in Brazil. She offers that, even considering the most money she has ever earned for a screenplay, the pay is not sufficient to live on after dividing the funds amongst her collaborators and by the months (or years) it takes to complete the project. Ironically, she is aware that others earn more to write for film. By contrast, Falcão reveals that she can write for the Globo Network and be able to pay her bills and support her family (Falcão 2018). Similarly, Melanie Dimantas, who has written extensively for television and film,[12] reveals that she has taken on different types of projects as a matter of survival and opportunities to develop a varied career (Dimantas 2018). That is, the decision whether to write for film, television, or streamed content is sometimes a financial one before it's an artistic one.

The economic and technical evolution of cinema has resulted in a dichotomy between franchise or blockbuster films and low(er)-budget, independent artistic cinema. Carol Rodrigues, who has written for web series and Netflix's *3%*, as well as written and directed short films such as *A felicidade delas* (*Their Happiness*, 2019), finds more opportunities in series. Rodrigues observes that the film industry has increasingly invested in major franchise films with astronomical budgets and that this practice is leading to the disappearance of *cinema média* (literally "middle cinema," or films produced with a modest budget). Independent films with small budgets continue to exist, but she believes that middle cinema is being reformulated for television. What is more, she finds more inventiveness for characters and situations and opportunities for more diversity in middle cinema (Rodrigues 2018). Notably, SVOD has opened up new arenas for screenwriting in Brazil in terms of genre. While science fiction, fantasy, and horror do not have a strong history in Brazilian cinema, these genres have been widely developed in SVOD series for Netflix, including the dystopian thriller *3%* and the more recent science fiction *Onisciente* (*Omniscient*, 2020–), written by a team that includes a new generation of women screenwriters: Ludmila Naves, Thais Fujinaga, and Maria Shu.

Black Women's Voices in Brazilian Audiovisual

The 2018 Ancine study on race and diversity in Brazilian cinema reports that no Black woman wrote or directed a feature-length film in 2016 (Ancine 2018, 9–11). Fortunately, this situation is changing.[13] What is more, the report does not fully capture the presence of Black women's voices in Brazilian audiovisual production or their efforts to promote greater social inclusion in the sector. An increasing presence of Black talent and discussion of race has emerged from years of activism and policy changes. Carol Rodrigues believes affirmative action policies that were developed for universities have led to a questioning of racial disparity in Brazilian society more generally (Rodrigues 2018). What is more, affirmative action policies have afforded Black Brazilians access to historically elite universities where cinema programs are housed, and these policies have also led to the regional expansion of cinema programs such as those in the northeastern state of Bahia. Such expansion of opportunities outside traditional centers—Rio de Janeiro, Brasília, or São Paulo—for training have further contributed to an increase in Black participation in Brazilian audiovisual production.

Not captured in the Ancine report are the accomplishments of a new generation of young Black women emerging from film collectives and university programs who have written as well as directed short films and contributed to other audiovisual productions. Their works circulate largely outside commercial venues (for now). The works of Black women screenwriters and writer-directors have challenged the historic invisibility of Black bodies on Brazilian screens. They frequently do so by rejecting white, Eurocentric perspectives and emphasize African cultural heritage such as that found in the short film *Kbela* (2015) by Yasmin Thayná, a writer, director, and outspoken advocate of Black representation.

While a limited series of official policies have helped to dismantle structural barriers to diverse participation, Black women writers who have been able to enter audiovisual production have taken initiatives themselves to further advance social inclusion and diversity in Brazilian audiovisual production. Their work as writers frequently overlaps with their work as directors and advocates for greater diversity. For example, Viviane Ferreira, whose film *O dia de Jerusa* (*Jerusa's Day*, 2014) was screened at the Cannes Film Festival, cofounded the Associação de Profissionais do Audiovisual Negro (Association of Black Audiovisual Professionals) in 2016 to unify and advocate on behalf of Black artists. Writer, director, and producer Juliana Vicente founded the production company Preta Portê that promotes Black representation on screen.[14] Carol Rodrigues established the website Mulheres Negras no Audiovisual Brasileiro (Black Women in Brazilian Audiovisual). Black Brazilian women have also developed collaborations that challenge prevailing paradigms of authorship, emphasizing individual work and seeking to further advance the participation of Black women (and men) in audiovisual production. Collectives such as Tela Preta (Black Screen), founded by women enrolled at a film studies program at the Universidade Federal do Recôncavo in Cachoeira, Bahia, have helped foster Black women's development in audiovisual production.[15]

In the case of women artists who have been historically excluded from film production, scholars must look at other arenas where Black women have participated. Writing has often been an important practice and departure point for creating new opportunities. Of particular interest is how Black Brazilian women are occupying new spaces online and in television, in both fiction and nonfiction formats. Two notable efforts include the web series *Empoderadas* (*Empowered women*) and the collaborative channel Afroflix founded by Yasmin Thayná. The Afroflix platform features Brazilian audiovisual works—films, series, web series, videos, video blogs—that either feature or are produced, written, directed by Black artists. The web series *Empoderadas* was founded by screenwriter Renata Martins, who most recently wrote for Rede Globo's *Malhação, viva a diferença* (*Slander, long live difference*, 2017–2018, 213 episodes). The web series led by Martins is a particularly important example of Black activism and self-determination. The project aims to expand the representation and participation of Black women in all facets of audiovisual production—in front of and behind the camera. Thus far, the series has completed three seasons, with the third showcasing Black and Indigenous women of Brazil. After its first season, the series evolved to become an "edu-communicative" project that helps train women and provides an opportunity for women to develop their résumés to be eligible for future opportunities. According to Carol Rodrigues, who has participated in writing and directing episodes of *Empoderadas*, the initiative has become an important audiovisual training site for Black women as well as part of a broader *disputa do imaginário* (struggle over a popular imaginary) of race and gender in Brazil (Rodrigues 2018). Both initiatives highlighted here aim to further Black women's participation as writers and producers of audiovisual content while streaming new consciousness of race, gender, and class.

Women Screenwriters and Genre Cinema

The increased commercialization of Brazilian cinema has coincided with the development of film genres in recent years, with comedy making a prominent reappearance. That said, Brazilian cinema has a consistent history of film comedy ranging from the *chanchadas* (light comedies) of the 1930s and 1940s to more recent box office successes, sometimes disparagingly referred to as *globochanchadas* given that many are coproduced by Globo Filmes. With important exceptions, women screenwriters (and directors) have had a limited presence in this area of Brazilian cinema. Historically, films by the comedy troupe Os Trapalhões are among the top-grossing films of Brazilian history.[16] Pioneering writer-director Tereza Trautman cowrote the screenplay for *Os saltimbancos trapalhões* (*The bumbling acrobats*, 1981) and veteran writer Yoya Wursch cowrote the script for *Os heróis trapalhões: Uma aventura na selva* (*The bumbling heroes: An adventure in the forest*, 1988). More recently, women writers have gained a footing in Brazilian film comedy.

Film comedy can be too easily dismissed as lowbrow entertainment. Yet in the case of women writers in the genre, it is key to consider how their narratives intervene in debates about gender, class, and social change. Indeed, a number of film comedies by women writer-directors offer contemporary critiques of Brazilian society and culture (Marsh 2017a, 2017b). Screenplays by Julia Rezende (*Meu passado me condena / My past condemns me*, 2013), Adriana Falcão (*Se eu fosse você / If I Were You*), or Cris D'Amato (*SOS: Mulheres ao mar / SOS: Women to the sea*, 2014) are as light-hearted as they are critical of contemporary understandings of gender and women's roles in Brazilian society.

The work of Anna Muylaert is particularly notable in this regard. Muylaert spent nearly twenty years developing the script for her film *Que horas ela volta?* (*The Second Mother*, 2015) that captured the changes of the "Lula years" when the young protagonist, Jéssica, daughter of a live-in domestic worker played by Regina Casé, arrives in São Paulo to go to university.[17] Muylaert describes her work as a process that undergoes an evolution, evident in the extended time taken to complete the script for *Que horas ela volta?* (O2 Filmes 2017b). After including dialogue and other nuances to the narrative, Muylaert explains that she engages in a process of disruption whereby she purposefully aims to disrupt expectations and stereotypes, rethinking characters roles and actions. Muylaert explains that in developing characters and scenes, she is always *procurando vida* (looking for life) and not beauty or perfection in her scenes, but rather that the scene appears alive (O2 Filmes 2017c). This defying of expectations comes through not only in characters of *Que horas ela volta?* but also in the dark humor of her films *Durval Discos* (*Durval Records*, 2002) and *É proibido fumar* (*Smoke Gets in Your Eyes*, 2009). In both films, Muylaert's narratives offer feminist critiques of urban development and gender.

Science Fiction, Fantasy, and Horror

Genres other than comedy have gained strength in recent years, including science fiction, fantasy, and horror. Ludmila Naves has written for the

Netflix science fiction series *Onisciente* (*Omniscient*, 2020–) and was the head writer for the horror series *Terrores urbanos* (*Urban Horrors*, 2018) for TV Record. Alongside Elena Soarez and Carol Rodrigues, Juliana Rojas wrote for the Netflix series *3%*. Rojas, who has developed a varied career in television and film in a short time, wrote and directed several short horror and fantasy films before writing the screenplays for the feature-length horror and fantasy film *Trabalho cansa* (*Hard Labor*, 2011) and *As boas maneiras* (*Good Manners*, 2017), which she also codirected with Marco Dutra. She also wrote and directed *Sinfonia da necrópole* (*Necropolis Symphony*, 2014), which blends elements of horror, musical, romance, and comedy.

Until more recently, horror was not a common genre in Brazilian cinema. The most well-known figure in horror has been José Mojica Marins, who directed numerous low-budget productions in the 1960s and 1970s. He is also known for the character Coffin Joe (Zé do Caixão), who appeared in *A meia noite levarei a sua alma* (*At Midnight I'll Take Your Soul*, 1964), considered Brazil's first horror film. Gabriela Amaral Almeida, a notable new voice in a wave of horror films that critics assert are led by a new generation of women writers and directors, has reflected on the presence of women in the film industry as well as the emergence of horror and genre cinema in recent years. Following her participation in a Sundance writing lab in 2014, Almeida debuted as director and cowriter with Luana Demange of the horror thriller *O animal cordial* (*Friendly Beast*, 2017), followed by the fantasy horror tale *A sombra do pai* (*The Father's Shadow*, 2018).

Reflecting on her own development of horror, Almeida offers insight into the expansion of genre cinema led by a new generation of screenwriters. In her case, she claims she grew up watching Hollywood genre films on broadcast television in the 1980s and 1990s and renting films from stores whose collections consisted primarily of genre films. However, Almeida sees horror in Brazil as more akin to independent or alternative film in the United States than franchise horror films (Almeida 2019). She has further observed that the genre has been underappreciated partly because horror has an inherently disruptive nature and responds to moments of transition when societies are forced to adapt to change (Argemon 2019). Regarding the assertion that women are particularly present in horror, Almeida rejects notions of a "feminine sensibility" in filmmaking and observes more concretely that there are hierarchies in cinema (Argemon 2019). Simply stated, horror has not been (thus far) dominated by men in the industry, and this opening has created an opportunity for women artists.

Documentary

Documentary film is a form in which women have historically seen slightly more success than fiction film. This may be in part due to the concentration of funding in the hands of their male counterparts and the fact that documentary filmmaking is generally less expensive. Returning to the findings from the 2018 study of race and gender in Brazilian cinema, women appear to have a stronger presence in documentary filmmaking, where they direct over 29 percent of films and write 25 percent of documentary scripts (Ancine 2018, 9, 11). However, there is a lack of racial diversity in documentary film as over 95 percent of documentary films from the period under study were written by white Brazilians (11). Again, this report does not capture the work of women producing works to stream online as is the case with several collaborations described above.

Two stars of Brazilian documentary film are Maria Augusta Ramos and Petra Costa.[18] Ramos, who moved to the Netherlands to study film in the 1990s, has explored the criminal justice system in *Justiça* (*Justice*, 2004) and *Juízo* (*Judgment*, 2007),[19] in which she reveals a judicial system that works against Brazil's young, poor, and Black citizens. She has further explored the fractures of the Brazilian political system in her documentary on the impeachment of Dilma Rousseff, *O processo* (*The Trial*, 2018). Like Ramos, Petra Costa focused on the impeachment of Rousseff in *Democracia em vertigem* (*The Edge of Democracy*, 2019), available on Netflix and nominated for an Oscar for Best Documentary in 2020. As with several of Costa's previous documentaries, she mixes the personal with the political, acknowledging her own privileged socioeconomic status while questioning the intersection of class and politics in Brazilian society.

Concluding Remarks

The study of women's screenwriting in Brazil prompts considering how scholars frame studies of contemporary Brazilian audiovisual production. While an auteurist approach to women's audiovisual production appropriately describes the work of some women writers (and writer-directors), film and media production is rarely an autonomous endeavor, and celebration of the independent artist may potentially conform to racist or patriarchal paradigms. Collective and collaborative writing practices must be acknowledged. Unlike screenwriters who are frequently hired to write for others, academics choose who, how, and what they write about. Just as it is important to recognize the importance of screenwriting generally, issues of authorship and agency need to be framed in ways that do not impede the study of screenwriting in Brazil, women screenwriters, and women's participation in contemporary audiovisual production. Screenwriting is a vital area of film and media production. For several established women directors, screenwriting has been an important part of their artistic practice. Screenwriting has also been a departure point for a new generation of Brazilian women artists who advocate for greater diversity and inclusion in front of the camera and behind the scenes.

Notes

1. Studies show that the number of women directors between 2014 and 2018 has fluctuated between a low of 10 percent to a high of 22 percent (see Rêgo's chapter in this volume for further discussion). Similar numbers are reported for screenwriters, ranging between a low of 11 percent (2017) and 22 percent (2018) of films released (Ancine 2019, 12–13).

2. See the report "Anuário estatístico do cinema brasileiro" published by Ancine in 2015 and subsequent annual statistical reports available online at https://oca.ancine.gov.br/publicacoes. See also specific reports on women's participation in the Brazilian audiovisual industry, including the 2019 report "Participação feminina na produção audiovisual brasileira (2018)" available at https://oca.ancine.gov.br/sites/default/files/repositorio/pdf/participacao_feminina_na_producao_audiovisual_brasileira_2018_0.pdf.

3. A notable exception is the work of Jack A. Draper III on veteran screenwriter Elena Soarez. See Draper's essay "Reimagining Rosinha with Andrucha Waddington and Elena Soarez: Nature, Woman and Sexuality in the Brazilian Northeast from Popular Music to Cinema" (Draper 2011, 243–56). Regarding Mexican cinema, see the valuable text by María Teresa DePaoli, *The Story of the Mexican Screenplay: A Study of the Invisible Art Form and Interviews with Women Screenwriters* (New York: Peter Lang, 2014).

4. Esmeralda worked in collaboration with the Sundance Institute to develop screenwriting labs from 1996 to 2002.

5. Both Muylaert and Murat wrote the screenplays and directed the films.

6. The GUIÕES and ROTA festivals began in 2015 and 2017, respectively.

7. The network Mulheres do Audiovisual Brasil was formed in 2016 with the goal to advance gender policies in the Brazilian audiovisual market. For more

on the association, see https://mulheresaudiovisual.com. The Imprensa Mahon is a YouTube channel that provides advice and commentary on audiovisual production. For more information, see https://www.youtube.com/watch?v=tFiamNvIHoI.

8. The series of interviews is also an exceedingly valuable resource for scholars of screenwriting in Brazil.

9. See Rêgo's chapter in this volume for further discussion.

10. The series ran on HBO for two seasons in 2006 and 2009.

11. Notably, the film *If I Were You 2* (2009) places seventh among the most-seen Brazilian films.

12. A few of the many films Dimantas has written screenplays for include *Carlota Joaquina, princesa do Brasil* (*Carlota Joaquina, Princess of Brazil*, 1995), *Copacabana* (2001), *O outro lado da rua* (*The Other Side of the Street*, 2004), and *Olhos azuis* (*Blue Eyes*, 2009).

13. Sabrina Rosa, the first Black woman to direct a feature film since Adélia Sampaio's film *Amor maldito* (*Damned love*, 1984), codirected *Vamos fazer um brinde* (*Let's make a toast*) with Cavi Borges in 2011. In 2017, Black filmmaker Glenda Nicácio codirected *Café com canela* (*Coffee with cinnamon*) with Ary Rosa. Rosa and Nicácio have since codirected the feature-length films *Ilha* (*Island*, 2018) and *Até o fim* (*To the End*, 2020).

14. See Mercedes Vázquez Vázquez's and Reighan Gillam's chapters in this volume for more on Yasmin Thayná and Juliana Vicente, respectively.

15. The film program in Cachoeira was created in 2008 and reflects the expansion of educational opportunities outside the historically elite universities located in the southeast.

16. Roughly translated as "the bumbling ones," Os Trapalhões was a comedy group and television show on the Globo Network (1977–1993). The group acted in numerous feature-length film comedies, which are among the films with the greatest viewership in Brazilian history.

17. See Jack A. Draper III's chapter in this volume for more on *The Second Mother*.

18. For more on Ramos and Costa in this volume, see the respective interviews with each director/screenwriter, as well as Paula Halperin's chapter on Ramos.

19. The word *juízo* in Portuguese is generally translated as "judgment" in English.

Works Cited

Almeida, Gabriela Amaral. "Episode 107: Gabriela Amaral Almedia." Produced by Bruno Bloch and Filippo Cordeiro. *Primeiro tratamento*, December 18, 2019. Podcast, 41:22. https://www.primeirotratamento.com.br/2019/12/18/primeiro-tratamento-gabriela-amaral-almeida-ep-107-roteiro/.

Ancine. 2019. "Participação feminina na produção audiovisual brasileira (2018)." Brasília: Observatório Brasileiro de Cinema e do Audiovisual (OCA), Agência Nacional do Cinema.

Argemon, Rafael. 2019. "'O terror decodifica ansiedades que estão no ar,' diz diretora de 'A Sombra do Pai.'" *Huffpost Brasil*, May 5, 2019. https://www.huffpostbrasil.com/entry/a-sombra-do-pai_br_5ccb2fe3e4b0e4d7572f979b.

Cobb, Shelley. 2014. *Adaptation, Authorship, and Contemporary Women Filmmakers*. Houndmills, Basingstoke, Hampshire: Palgrave Macmillan.

Dimantas, Melanie. "Episode 44: Melanie Dimantas." Produced by Bruno Bloch and Filippo Cordeiro. *Primero tratamento*, September 12, 2018. Podcast, 1:33:45. https://www.primeirotratamento.com.br/2018/09/12/primeiro-tratamento-melanie-dimantas-ep-44-roteiro/.

Draper III, Jack A. 2011. "Reimagining Rosinha with Andrucha Waddington and Elena Soarez: Nature, Woman and Sexuality in the Brazilian Northeast from Popular Music to Cinema." In *New Trends in Argentine and Brazilian Cinema*, edited by Cacilda Rêgo and Carolina Rocha, 243–56. Bristol: Intellect.

Falcão, Adriana. "Episode 38: Adriana Falcão." Produced by Bruno Bloch and Filippo Cordeiro. *Primeiro tratamento*, August 1, 2018. Podcast, 1:22:14. https://www.primeirotratamento.com.br/2018/08/01/primeiro-tratamento-adriana-falcao-ep38-roteiro/.

Grillo, Cristina. 1998. "Sundance faz laboratório de roteiros no Rio." *Folha de São Paulo*, June 2, 1998. Ilustrada. https://www1.folha.uol.com.br/fsp/ilustrad/fq02069821.htm.

Gruenwedel, Erik. 2019. "Bye Bye Brazil? Not for Netflix." *Media Play News*, February 21, 2019.

Htun, Mala. 2004. "From 'Racial Democracy' to Affirmative Action: Changing State Policy on Race in Brazil." *Latin American Research Review* 39 (1): 60–89. doi: 10.2307/1555383.

Marsh, Leslie L. 2012. *Brazilian Women's Filmmaking: From Dictatorship to Democracy*. Urbana: University of Illinois Press.

———. 2016. "Branding Brazil through Cultural Policy: Rio de Janeiro as Creative, Audiovisual City." *International Journal of Communication* 10: 3022–41.

———. 2017a. "Women's Filmmaking and Comedy in Brazil: Anna Muylaert's *Durval discos* (2002) and *É proibido fumar* (2009)." In *Latin American Women Filmmakers: Production, Politics, Poetics*, edited by Deborah Martin and Deborah Shaw, 149–71. London and New York: IB Tauris.

———. 2017b. "Women, Gender and Romantic Comedy in Brazil: Love on the High Seas in *Meu passado me condena* (2013) and *S.O.S. mulheres ao mar* (2014)." *Feminist Media Histories* 3 (2): 98–120.

———. 2021. *Branding Brazil: Transforming Citizenship on Screen*. New Brunswick, NJ: Rutgers University Press.

Meleiro, Alessandra. 2010. *Cinema e mercado*. São Paulo, Brazil: Iniciativa Cultural.

Observatório Brasileiro do Cinema e do Audiovisual (OCA). 2018. "Informe mercado: Diversidade de gênero e raça nos longas-metragens brasileiros lançados em salas de exibição em 2016" [Market report: Gender and race diversity in Brazilian films released in 2016]. https://oca.ancine.gov.br/sites/default/files/repositorio/pdf/informe_diversidade_2016.pdf.

O2 Filmes. 2017a. "Roteiristas #17—Chico Matoso / A importância do roteirista." https://www.youtube.com/watch?v=m0BeD_ige00&list=PL49Z075YcDVsegpwSxZIjNHgHRXPifLEE&index=17.

———. 2017b. "Roteiristas #18—Anna Muylaert / Processo criativo." https://www.youtube.com/watch?v=eNpR1xgWwQs&list=PL49Z075YcDVsegpwSxZIjNHgHRXPifLEE&index=18.

———. 2017c. "Roteiristas #22—Anna Muylaert / Método de trabalho." https://www.youtube.com/watch?v=8B3TbR937p4&list=PL49Z075YcDVsegpwSxZIjNHgHRXPifLEE&index=22.

———. 2017d. "Roteiristas #28—Laís Bodanzky / Dica para iniciantes." https://www.youtube.com/watch?v=spHN4XvZ4e4&list=PL49Z075YcDVsegpwSxZIjNHgHRXPifLEE&index=28.

———. 2017e. "Roteiristas #46—Anna Muylaert / A função do cinema." https://www.youtube.com/watch?v=BzMnSfe4wxs&list=PL49Z075YcDVsegpwSxZIjNHgHRXPifLEE&index=47&t=0s.

———. 2017f. "Roteiristas #50—Elena Soares / Parceria com diretor." https://www.youtube.com/watch?v=YdpiZqC78w8&list=PL49Z075YcDVsegpwSxZIjNHgHRXPifLEE&index=50&t=0s.

———. 2017g. "Roteiristas #63—Mirna Nogueira / Parceria com diretor." https://www.youtube.com/watch?v=SSYJ91slLzw&list=PL49Z075YcDVsegpwSxZIjNHgHRXPifLEE&index=62.

Rêgo, Cacilda. 2011. "The Fall and Rise of Brazilian Cinema." In *New Trends in Argentine and Brazilian Cinema*, edited by Cacilda Rêgo and Carolina Rocha, 35–49. Bristol, UK: Intellect.

Rezende, Julia. "Episode 69: Julia Rezende." Produced by Bruno Bloch and Filippo Cordeiro. *Primeiro tratamento*, March 20, 2019. Podcast, 1:07:22. https://www.primeirotratamento.com.br/2019/03/20/primeiro-tratamento-julia-rezende-ep-69-roteiro/.

Rodrigues, Carol. "Episode 27: Carol Rodrigues." Produced by Bruno Bloch and Filippo Cordeiro. *Primeiro tratamento*, May 9, 2018. Podcast, 1:12:01. https://www.primeirotratamento.com.br/2018/05/09/primeiro-tratamento-carol-rodrigues-ep27-roteiro/.

Rosas-Moreno, Tania Cantrell. 2014. *News and Novela in Brazilian Media: Fact, Fiction, and National Identity*. Lanham, MD: Lexington Books.

———. 2017. "Brazilian Telenovelas and Social Merchandising." *ReVista (Cambridge)* 17 (1): 50–53, 66.
Smyth, J. E. 2016. "A Woman at the Center of Hollywood's Wars: Screenwriter Mary C. McCall Jr." *Cinéaste* 41 (3): 18–23.
Soarez, Elena. "Episode 26: Elena Soarez." Produced by Bruno Bloch and Filippo Cordeiro. *Primeiro tratamento*, May 2, 2018. Podcast, 1:19:51. https://www.primeirotratamento.com.br/2018/05/02/primeiro-tratamento-elena-soarez-ep26-roteiro/.
Welch, Rosanne, and Cari Beauchamp. 2018. *When Women Wrote Hollywood: Essays on Female Screenwriters in the Early Film Industry.*

Chapter 3

Resistance and Online Activism

Brazilian Women Filmmakers' Initiatives (2014–2017)

DANIELA VERZTMAN BAGDADI

The Brazilian film industry is characterized by a landscape of inequality that deeply affects women filmmakers across the country. According to Ancine (2018), Brazil's national film agency, 142 feature films were released in commercial venues in 2016. Among them, 75.4 percent were directed by white men, 19.7 percent by white women, and 2.1 percent by Black men. No Black woman occupied the director's chair or wrote a screenplay for these films.[1] The Observatório Brasileiro do Cinema e do Audiovisual (OCA, 2016) also revealed a substantial disparity among professionals in the field. In 2014, women represented 21 percent of screenwriters, 41 percent of producers, and 8 percent of cinematographers. This gap is even bigger when considering women of color. The Grupo de Estudos Multidisciplinares da Ação Afirmativa (Group for Multidisciplinary Studies of Affirmative Action) revealed that no Black woman directed or wrote the screenplay of any top-grossing film released between 1995 and 2016 (Candido et al. 2017). It is clear that inequality in the film industry highly affects women and especially women of color. Despite its importance, research on Indigenous and LGBTQ+ communities remains scarce to this day.

Women's unequal participation in the Brazilian film industry is not an isolated case. Scholarly work on the topic has shed light on its international disposition as well as its structural and systemic nature. From a historical perspective, Annette Förster (1997) has argued that the focus of film historians on specific figures, such as George Méliès and the Lumière brothers, ended up marginalizing the work of important early women filmmakers such as Alice Guy Blaché. In the specific case of Brazil, Leslie L. Marsh (2012, 13) states that "a considerable amount of historiographical work on Brazilian cinema has been undertaken, but it has overlooked or only tangentially included women's participation." Considering working conditions for women in the international market today, a study from 2014 in eleven countries demonstrated that women's struggles include fewer work opportunities, scarce leadership positions, and limited time on screen (Smith, Mac Choueiti, and Pieper 2014).

In 2014 Brazilian women filmmakers began to intensively campaign for more opportunities under the umbrella of their newly founded initiatives. In three years they have created one hundred film collectives, cinema clubs, film festivals, online forums, events, and awards focusing on women filmmakers. Their foundation is contemporary to the Arab Spring and Feminist Spring, the Brazilian protests of 2013, and other social justice movements around the world. Similar to their counterparts (Castells 2015), Brazilian women filmmakers have battled against their limited presence in the media and in the public sphere by voicing their criticism and struggles through social media platforms. This is highly relevant in the case of Brazil because

> the Brazilian mainstream media are controlled by fewer than ten families, including the Marinhos of *Globo Organisation*, who retain a total of 80% of the nation's media content. Despite the growth of professionalism and balance in the newsroom since the 1990s in the context of the country's re-democratization, the Brazilian media, represented mainly by the newspapers *O Globo*, *Folha de São Paulo*, the magazines *Veja* and *Isto É* and *TV Globo*, still struggle with partisan practices and are not sufficiently plural. (Matos 2017, 429)

In this context, decision-making processes around the production and circulation of content falls into the hands of a small number of companies, which are neither diverse nor inclusive. When the public sphere and the film industry fail to provide visibility and opportunities to women filmmakers, social media can be excellent channels of counter-discourse for them to voice their demands and to challenge dominant narratives.

This chapter investigates the emergence of one hundred initiatives created by Brazilian women filmmakers between January 2014 and August 2017 while analyzing their online activism on Facebook. Accordingly, this analysis seeks to answer the following questions: In which context did these initiatives emerge? What are the social media practices of Brazilian women filmmakers, and how do those practices impact the movement? I argue that it is not possible to address this movement without a thorough investigation of its social media presence. Not only have initiatives gained strength through social media channels, but also new modes of sociability and participation in the film industry were formed through these platforms.

This analysis provides details that range from a complete list of initiatives and their regional distribution to quantitative data of social media practices. Interviews with several professionals were also performed for this work. This chapter is divided into four sections. After this introduction, the following section provides an overview of the initiatives by Brazilian women filmmakers and explains the social and political context from which they emerged. The next section investigates their social media practices, followed by the conclusion. It is important to note that the category of filmmakers used in this analysis also includes film critics and film festival directors.

Initiatives by Brazilian Women Filmmakers: An Assessment

The initiatives addressed in this chapter emerged in a turbulent period for democratic and women's rights in Brazil. In 2015, the country ranked fifth in gender-based violence cases worldwide (Francheschini 2015). In that year, ongoing conservative legislative agendas were set in motion and could have resulted in restrictions to several constitutional rights, including women's access to "morning-after pills, the possibility of abortion in case of rape, not to mention the law project [or bill] *PL 6583/2013*" that could reduce the concept of family to households of only a man, a woman, and their children (Verztman Bagdadi 2016). Moreover, many evangelical politicians started to campaign against feminism and gender equality across the country. In 2015, for example, the city council of Campinas passed an official motion against the work of Simone de Beauvoir to avoid the dissemination of what they called "gender ideology" (Redação Pragmatismo 2015). Two years later, councilmen from the city of Belo Horizonte approved a local decree that prohibited the use of the word "gender" in official publications (Ernesto 2017), and, while attending a seminar on democracy in São Paulo, Judith Butler and her partner were harassed at the airport of Congonhas by a group of anti-feminist protestors (Finco 2017). In addition to these events, the first elected female president, Dilma Rousseff, was impeached in 2016. Her impeachment was followed by the dissolution of the Ministério das Comunicações (Ministry of Communications) (Pereira 2016) and the Ministério dos Direitos Humanos (Ministry of Human Rights), later replaced by the Ministério da Mulher, da Família, e dos Direitos Humanos (Ministry of Women, Racial Equality, Youth and Human Rights) (Biblioteca 2016). The near-extinction of the Ministério da Cultura (Ministry of Culture) was followed by reactions by groups of artists and filmmakers across Brazil. The movements Reage, Artista! (Artists, react!) and Cinema Brasileiro pela Democracia (Brazilian cinema for democracy) are two examples of groups that gained momentum in this period. Additionally, other social justice and women's rights movements around the world (e.g., the Brazilian protests [2013], the Brazilian Feminist Spring (2015), the International Women's March [2017], the women's protest at the Cannes Film Festival [2015], the #AskHerMore campaign [2015], and the #MeToo movement [2016/2017]) further motivated women to speak up more intensely against discrimination and injustice. As noted by Carolina Matos (2017), women's political mobilization grew considerably throughout Brazil.

The initiatives examined in this chapter are included in this process. Filmmakers have not only actively participated in those protests but also built dialogues with various movements across Brazil. Maria Cardozo (2017), film director, founder, and cocurator of the Festival Internacional de Cinema de Realizadoras (FINCAR) (International Women Filmmakers Festival) explains that the initiative interacts with many social justice movements, including Ocupe Estelita (Occupy Estelita). The latter stood against gentrification and condemned the eviction of poor families in the city of Recife. According to Cardozo, art should not be separated from politics. Iasmin Alvarez (2017), filmmaker and creator of the women's film festival Mostra das Minas (Women's Film Exhibition) adds to this statement by noting that "it is very important [for our movement] to go beyond filmmaking, to go beyond discussing the role of women in the industry. It is important to discuss the role of women in society as a whole" (Iasmin Alvarez, Skype interview with author, February 14, 2017).

A highly relevant topic for Brazilian social justice movements is racism and the legacy of the country's near four hundred years of slavery. As noted by Grada Kilomba (2010, 40), "the experienced reality of racism, the subjective encounters, experiences, struggles, knowledge, understanding and feelings of Black people with respect to racism, as well as the psychic scars racism causes, have been largely neglected." Franciele Campos (2017), filmmaker and cofounder of the film collective Cartel Adélias (Adélia's Cartel), explains that impact of racism and inequality on Brazilian women filmmakers must be discussed in more depth in film circles across the country:

> I come from a favela of 30,000 inhabitants (Manguinhos), located in the northern part of the city of Rio de Janeiro. I have had the privilege to transcend its borders to study. The social logic in which our society is structured, educates us—poor women and women of color—to work as maids for the upper classes. . . . The majority of us at Adélia's Cartel is Black and poor. And we are poor women interacting in bourgeois spaces. This is already a violent movement for us because all doors are closed, especially when you are Black. Every woman is affected by patriarchy but it's even worse when we also consider racism. (Franciele Campos, WhatsApp interview with author, October 1, 2017)

As noted by Kimberlé Crenshaw (1989, 149), Black women "experience double-discrimination—the combined effects of practices which discriminate on the basis of race, and on the basis of sex." Although not a focus of this chapter, it is important to keep this topic in mind and remember that women filmmakers experience different realities across Brazil. Differences in access to work, education, and technology are directly connected to the intersection of inequalities in regard to gender, class, and race.

Brazilian women filmmakers' initiatives are diverse. They can be divided into five categories: film collectives, cinema clubs, women's film festivals, events, and awards. Moreover, several online discussion forums and groups on Facebook were created with the goal of boosting connectivity and dialogue among women. The one hundred initiatives created between 2014 and 2017 appear in table 3.1.

Considering their regional distribution, a total of eleven initiatives were created in the south, forty-two in the southeast, eleven in the central-west, and ten in the northeast. No initiatives were founded in the northern states of Acre, Amapá, Amazonas, Pará, Rondônia, Roraima, and

Table 3.1

	Film Collectives	Cinema Clubs	Women's film festivals and smaller screenings	Events	Awards	Facebook Groups
1	Coletivo Vermelha (Red Collective)	Cinemaclube Delas (Women's Cinema Club)	FINCAR (Festival Internacional de Cinema de Realizadoras) (FINCAR—International Women Filmmakers Festival)	I Colóquio Brasileiro de Cinema de Autoria Feminina (First Brazilian Colloquium of Cinema of Female Authorship)	Prêmio Vermelha (Red Award)	Mulheres do Audiovisual Brasil (Women in the Audiovisual Industry in Brazil)
2	Coletivo Mangaba (Mangaba Collective)	Cineclube NovasMusas (Cinema Club New Muses)	Mostra das Minas (Women's Film Exhibition)	I Encontro de Cineastas e Produtoras Negras (First Meet-up of Black Filmmakers and Producers)	Prêmio Cabíria de Roteiro (Cabiria Screenwriting Award)'	Mulheres Negras no Audiovisual (Black Women in the Audiovisual Industry)
3	Babu Coletivo (Babu Collective)	Cineclube das Outras (Others' Cinema Club)	Mostra Ela na Tela (Film Festival Her on Screen)	Ciclo de Cinema: Mulheres em Tela. Um debate feminista (Film Circle Women on Screen: a feminist debate)		Minas do Cinema RJ (Women in Film in the State of Rio de Janeiro)

4	Coletivo Carne e Osso (Flesh and Bones Collective)	Cineclube Aranha (Spider's Cinema Club)	Curta as Minas (Women's Short Film Exhibition)	UFFilme + Quase Catálogo—Sessão: Mulheres Diretoras UFF's Cinema and Almost Catalogue Cinema Club: Women Directors Session)	Bechdelles
5	We are Magnólias	Cineclube Academia das Musas (Academy of Muses Cinema Club)	Mostra Elas (Her Exhibition)	Mostra com Mulheres—VII Cachoeira Doc (Exhibition with Women—VII Cachoeira Doc)	MUFA—Mulheres Filmmakers e do Audiovisual (MUFA—Women in Film and in the Audiovisual Industry)
6	Feministas de Quinta (Quinta Feminists)	Cineclube Quase Catálogo (Almost Catalogue Cinema Club)	Mostra Lugar de Mulher é no Cinema (Film Exhibition—Her place is making movies)	CachoeiraDoc—Com Mulheres—8ª Semana dos Realizadores (CachoeiraDoc Festival—With Women—8th Filmmakers' Week)	Mulheres do Audiovisual São Paulo (Women in the Audiovisual Industry in the State of São Paulo)
7	Coletivo Malva (Malva Collective)	Facção Feminista Cineclube (Feminist Faction Cinema Club)	Mostra de Cinema Audiovisual Feminino Conceição Hyppolito (Conceição Hyppolito's Women's Film Exhibition)	Estado Crítico—Residência Crítica de Cinema—III Fronteira (Critical State—Film Critics Residency—III Fronteira Film Festival)	Mulheres do Audiovisual Baiano (Women in the Audiovisual Industry in the State of Bahia)

continued on next page

Table 3.1 (Continued)

	Film Collectives	Cinema Clubs	Women's film festivals and smaller screenings	Events	Awards	Facebook Groups
8	Somos mais que 30 (We are more than 30)	Cineclube Mulheres Audiovisual (Women in the Audiovisual Industry Cinema Club)	Mostra Mulheres em Cena (Film Exhibition Women on Stage)	Mostra Mulheres no Cinema—23º Festival de Cinema de Vitória (Women in Film Exhibition—23rd Vitória Film Festival)		Mulheres do Audiovisual Ceará (Women in the Audiovisual Industry in the State of Ceará)
9	Cartel Adélias (Adélia's Cartel)	Cineclube Feminista (Coletivo de Mulheres Matilde Magrassi) (Feminist Cinema Club of the Women's Collective Matilde Magrassi)	1ª Mostra Mulheres e Cinema (First Film Exibition Women and Film)	Mostra Mulheres Atrás das Câmeras—11º Festival de Cinema Latino—Americano de São Paulo (Women Behind the Camera Exhibition) 11th Latin American Film Festival of São Paulo		Mulheres do Audiovisual—Curitiba (Women in the Audiovisual Industry in Curitiba)
10	MulherEspelhos (Mirror Women)	Cineclube Adélia Sampaio (Adélia Sampaio's Cinema Club)	Mulheres gritam Ação, Todas as Mulheres no Cinema (Women scream action, All women in the Film industry)	Mostra Feminino Plural—27ª Festival Internacional de Curtas Metragens de São Paulo (Female Plural Exhibition—27th International Festival of Short Films of São Paulo)		Mulheres no Audiovisual no Rio Grande do Sul (Women in the Audiovisual Industry in the State of Rio Grande do Sul)

11	Mulheres no Audiovisual PE (Women in the Audiovisual Industry in Pernambuco)	Mostra Directoras (Women Film Directors' Exhibition)	Seminário Internacional Mulheres no Audiovisual (Ancine) (Ancine's International Women in the Audiovisual Industry Seminar)	Mulheres Profissionais do Audiovisual (Female Professionals in the Audiovisual Industry)
12	DAFB (Collective of Women Cinematographers)	Mostra Subjetivas UFpel (UFpel's subjective film exhibition)	Mulher e Relações de Gênero—Cineclube de Março (Women and Gender Relations—Março Cinema Club)	Mulheres do Audiovisual—Brasília (Women in the Audiovisual Industry in Brasilia)
13	Elviras (Collective of Women Film Critics)	Mulheres na Direção—O Cinema Sergipano sob a ótica feminina (Women in the Director's chair—The cinema of Sergipe under the female perspective)	Filme de Mulher—Cineclube da Fundação Cultural Bradesc (Women's Cinema—Bradesc Foundation's Cinema Club)	Coletivo de Mulheres de Cinema e Audiovisual da Baixada Santista (Collective of Women in Film and in the Audiovisual Industry in Baixada Santista)
14		Mostra Cineastas Mineiras (Women Filmmakers from Minas Gerais' Film Exhibition)	Debate about Violence Against Women—Cineclube de Tauá	Mulher na área de Fotografia e Audiovisual (Women in the fields of photography and audiovisual productions)

continued on next page

Table 3.1 (Continued)

	Film Collectives	Cinema Clubs	Women's film festivals and smaller screenings	Events	Awards	Facebook Groups
15			Mostra de Cinema Feminista: Corpo, Interseccionalidade e Democracia (Feminist Film Exhibition: Body, Intersectionality and Democracy)	Cine Mulher—Forum de Mulheres ES (Women's Cinema—Women's Forum in Espírito Santo)		Mulheres no Audiovisual MT (Women in the Audiovisual Industry in the State of Mato Grosso)
16			Artemis Cine (Artemis' Cinema)	Debate: Onde estão as Mulheres no Cinema?—Festi France—Mostra Francesa de Cinema (Debate: Where are the women in film?—Festi France—Exhibition of French Cinema)		Coletivo "A Mulher no Audiovisual" (Collective "Women in the Audiovisual Industry)
17			Mostra Olhares Femininos no Cinema Negro (Female Perspectives on Black Filmmaking)	Quem tem medo das Mulheres no Audiovisual—Ciclo de Debates—Coletivo Vermelha (Who's afraid of women in the audiovisual industry—Cicle of Debates—Red Collective)s		Coletivo de Diretoras de Fotografia do Brasil (Collective of Women Cinematographers)

18	Mostra A Magia da Mulher Negra (The Magic of Black Women Film Exhibition)	I Encontro de Mulheres Críticas—49º Festival de Brasília de Cinema Brasileiro (First Meet-up of Women Film Critics—49th Brasilia Film Festival)	Minas da Pós-Produção (Women in Post-Production)
19	1ª Mostra de Cinema Feministas de Quinta (Quinta Feminist's First Film Exhibition)	Reunião Mulheres Críticas de Cinema—Festival do Rio (Meet Up of Women Film Critics—Rio de Janeiro Int'l Film Festival)	Minas do Audiovisual—ECO (Women in the Audiovisual Industry at the School of Communications of the Federal University of Rio de Janeiro)
20	I Mostra Competitiva de Cinema Negro Adélia Sampaio (First Competitive Exhibition of Adelia Sampaio's Black Cinema)	Quebrando Vidraças; desconstruindo o machismo no audiovisual pernambucano (Breaking Panes: deconstructing sexism in Pernambuco's audiovisual industry	Minas do Audiovisual UnB (Women in the Audiovisual Industry at the University of Brasilia)

continued on next page

Table 3.1 (Continued)

	Film Collectives	Cinema Clubs	Women's film festivals and smaller screenings	Events	Awards	Facebook Groups
21			Terceira Mostra de Cinema Feminista—Coletivo Malva (Malva Collective's third feminist film exhibition)	Mulher no Cinema Brasileiro—Cine Guarani (Women in Brazilian Film—Cine Guarani)		Fotógrafas Brasileiras (Brazilian Female Photographers)
22			Mostra Mulheres no Cinema (Women in Cinema Film Exhibition)	Mostra Especial MAPE—Cineclube Amoeda Digital (MAPE's Special Exhibition—Amoeda Digital's Cinema Club)		Minas do Audiovisual DF (Women in the Audiovisual Industry in Brasilia)
23			Mostra Diretoras Negras no Cinema (Black Filmmakers' Film Exhibition)	Cine-Debate Mulheres no Cinema—Outras Palavras & Mulher do Pai (Film Debate Women in Fil hosted by Outras Palavras and Mulher do Pai)		Minas do Audiovisual MG (Women in the Audiovisual Industry in the State of Minas Gerais)
24			Mostra Edital Carmem Santos—Cinema de Mulheres e Filmes Convidados (Carmem Santos' Film Exhibition—Women's Cinema and Guest Films)	Criativas—Oficina de Roteiro Audiovisual para Mulheres Jovens (Criatives—Screenwriting Workshop for Young Women)		Minas do Audiovisual (Women in the Audiovisual Industry)

25	(a)mostra de mulheres no cinema (Women in Film Exhibition)	Encontro Internacional de Cineastas e Produtoras Negras (International Meet-Up of Black Filmmakers and Producers)
26		Empoderamento Feminino e a Condição Democrática—Cineclube de Março (Female Empowerment and the Democratic Condition—March's Cinema Club)

Tocantins. Some initiatives were excluded from the map due to their exclusive virtual presence (Facebook groups) or their decentralized formation with members and actions located in multiple states. The latter are the Coletivo DAFB (Coletivo das Diretoras de Fotografia do Brasil [Collective of Women Cinematographers]), Elviras—Coletivo de Mulheres Críticas de Cinema (Elvira's Women Film Critics Collective), Somos Mais que 30 (We Are More Than 30), and the Cabíria Prêmio de Roteiro (Cabíria Screenwriting Award). Furthermore, it was not possible to identify the location of the Coletivo Mangaba (Mangaba Collective). Table 3.2 shows their numbers by region in more detail.

The distribution of initiatives across the country reveals a disparity between regions. It is clear that there is a higher concentration of these groups in the southeastern states of Rio de Janeiro and São Paulo. According to IBGE (2011), Brazil's Institute of Geography and Statistics, this is the most populous region in Brazil. However, population is not a factor for the emergence of these groups. The northeast, a region that ranks second in the country's population (IBGE 2011), has the lowest number of initiatives developed in this period. Aristides Monteiro Neto (2014) demonstrates that the economy of the northeast is least favorable when compared with the rest of the country. He also highlights a process of reconcentration of economic activities in the southeast and south of Brazil. However, it is important to highlight that the northeast has one of the most diverse and prolific independent film scenes in the country.

Considering the year of foundation, table 3.3 reveals that five initiatives were created in 2014, fifteen in 2015, fifty-two in 2016, and sixteen in 2017.[2]

Table 3.2. Regional Distribution of Initiatives by Category

	North	South	Southeast	Central-West	Northeast
Film collectives		1	6		2
Cinema clubs		1	10		
Film Festivals		5	13	4	4
Events		4	12	7	4
Awards			1		
Total		11	42	11	10

Table 3.3. Initiative's Year of Foundation

	2014	2015	2016	2017
Film collectives	1	3	6	1
Cinema clubs	1	—	5	3
Film Festivals	—	4	13	7
Events	2	5	16	3
Awards	—	—	2	—
Facebook Groups	1	3	10	2
Total	5	15	52	16

It is interesting to note a peak in 2016 when the numbers tripled. The political context described in the beginning of this section is highly relevant here to understand this growth. However, an in-depth analysis of this topic will not be addressed in this chapter.

A pioneering initiative developed in this context is the Coletivo Vermelha (Red Collective). It started off as a study group of gender inequality and sexism in the film industry. The idea of forming the collective was inspired by the Film Fatales collective, an advocacy platform for equality in film in the United States (Iana Paro, Skype interview with author, February 14, 2017). Since its creation, the Red Collective has organized groundbreaking actions and events, such as the Prêmio Vermelha (Red Award), a prize created in partnership with Spcine, São Paulo's state film agency, to award short films directed by women. Another example is the workshop "Quem Tem Medo das Mulheres no Audiovisual?" ("Who Is Afraid of Women in the Audiovisual Industry?") that gathered Brazilian scholars, film professionals, and international campaigners for gender equality, such as Ellen Tejle. The Red Collective has inspired many women across the country, including Isabel Cardoso (2017), one of the organizers of the film festival Ela Na Tela (Her on Screen), who states that she regularly follows its activities. According to Cardoso, the Red Collective's Facebook posts have been highly important for her understanding of the condition of women in the market. Together with some colleagues she created the festival Her on Screen with the goal of making women in the film industry more visible:

> Many times, we don't identify with female characters and the way they are represented. [We decided to discuss] the pivotal role of women as directors, of women occupying pivotal roles in a crew, where they direct and also develop a concept for a film. How would it be to talk about ourselves? (Isabel Cardoso, Skype interview with author, January 30, 2017)

Similarly, FINCAR was created as a space of debate around women's cinema and its multiple perspectives. The main theme of its first edition was resistance to invisibility and autonomy of representation. For Maria Cardozo (2017) the turning point was a case of gender-based discrimination in the state of Pernambuco. She recalls:

> There was a specific case of sexism here in Recife against a woman filmmaker. As a reaction, many female peers addressed this topic in a public statement. From this action, the movement "Breaking Panes: Deconstructing Sexism in Pernambuco's Cinema" emerged. This for sure influenced the creation of FINCAR. (Maria Cardozo, Skype interview with author, January 9, 2017)

Invisibility and autonomy of representation were also important topics for Malu Andrade when she created the group Mulheres do Audiovisual Brasil (Women in the Audiovisual Industry in Brazil). Andrade (2017) notes that the catalyst for her engagement with gender equality in film was the various campaigns and statements from film professionals around the world:

> My awakening happened during an Oscar[s]. It was . . . when Cate Blanchett won and she made that feminist speech. Before that there was the #AskHerMore campaign to urge [the media] to ask more [of actresses] than what they were wearing. It was then that I thought: Wow. It's true. They only ask about their clothes and not about their work. It never occurred to me before. It was then that I started to observe the audiovisual industry. (Malu Andrade, Skype interview with author, February 22, 2017)

The group's foundation is a result of her engagement at Spcine, where she worked as coordinator of innovation. Initially composed of twenty women, in two years it reached 14,000 members. In January 2020, the group had

20,000 members. The size of this group reveals the importance of those topics for women in Brazil's audiovisual industry today. According to Érica Ramos Sarmet dos Santos and Marina Cavalcanti Tedesco (2017), from a poll of 1,130 members in 2016, only 52.2 percent of the women reported earning a living in the audiovisual industry and only 44.7 percent reported having a regular monthly income. It is therefore clear that precarious work, financial instability, and unemployment are daily realities of Brazilian women filmmakers.

Apart from the high levels of inequality in the audiovisual industry, another important field to address is inequality in academia. Many mechanisms of exclusion led to the invisibility and/or marginalization of women in spaces of knowledge production. Franciele Campos (2017) says that while studying at a film school in Rio de Janeiro:

> One of my friends asked a professor why he did not mention any woman filmmaker in his classes. His response was "Because there are no women filmmakers worth mentioning in the history of filmmaking." This was the time when we decided to create the collective. (Franciele Campos, WhatsApp interview with author, October 1, 2017)

Adélia's Cartel addresses multiple perspectives of poor and Black young women filmmakers in the state of Rio de Janeiro. The collective is named after the Brazilian filmmaker Adélia Sampaio. After decades on the margins of historiography, Sampaio was recently identified by Professor Edileuza Penha de Souza from the University of Brasília as the first Black woman to direct a feature film in Brazil in 1984 (Marques 2017). The invisibility of women filmmakers in academia reveals the structural nature of this problem. Another case that further sheds light on this issue is the application guidelines for the graduate program at the School of Arts and Communications of the University of São Paulo, a reference for audiovisual studies in Latin America. In 2018 the list of works required for entrance in the program included just one film and one book solely written/directed by a female author/filmmaker in a total of forty six books and thirty one films (Universidade de São Paulo 2018). This information was shared at the time by a member of the Facebook group Women in the Audiovisual Industry in Brazil.

The exclusion and/or marginalization of women as references in the field of knowledge production also affects the profession of film criticism.

Samantha Brasil (2017), cofounder, member, and cocurator of the Women's Cinema Club and the film critics collective Elvira's, explains:

> We are not in the places where people [film critics] usually read. And what is that? Newspapers *O Globo, Folha de São Paulo, Estadão*, which are the vehicles where film critics' references are articulated in Brazil today. There are also online media, which are currently growing . . . [but] there are also no women there. Accordingly, we can't see/read each other [in these channels]. (Samantha Brasil, Skype interview with author, March 10, 2017)

The case of Elvira's calls attention to the connection between gender inequalities in filmmaking and in media practices. It is highly important that women filmmakers and their work circulate in the public sphere. A public sphere that allows multiple perspectives to flourish is a public sphere committed to democratic principles. In face of unequal practices both in filmmaking and in the media, social networks have become important platforms of resistance, where women filmmakers expose processes of exclusion and build affirmative actions. To investigate this process is therefore essential to comprehend this movement.

Strength through Circulation: Brazilian Women Filmmakers on Facebook

It is not possible to understand the contemporary movement of Brazilian women filmmakers without an analysis of their online activism. Facebook is more than just a platform for them to communicate and to be visible in the public sphere. It is an integral part of the movement. It is where they get informed, where they share their experiences, where they learn about the diverse conditions of women in the industry, and where they produce knowledge. This set of practices is reshaping social relations between women filmmakers while creating new forms of literacy that have the potential to challenge institutions and the film market. In order to understand this online activism, it is important to take a look at the specificities of social media practices.

Brazil has one of the largest number of Facebook users. According to recent studies, eight out of ten Brazilians have Facebook accounts (Diário de Pernambuco 2016) and 55 percent of them conflate Internet access with Facebook access (Valente 2017). This means that its 93.2 million users are accessing most of the information and content they consume online through the platform (Redação 2016). Brazil is therefore a powerhouse for online content production and consumption.

Many theorists have discussed whether the Internet and social media represent the materialization of the Habermasian public sphere, due to its promise of democratizing access and production of content. According to Elisabeth J. Friedman (2017, 13), "Internet-based technology has (re)produced and (re)configured offline inequalities," therefore not guaranteeing equal visibility and access. Not only has the Internet been a territory for discriminatory practices with the circulation of hate speech and fake news, but it has also enabled individual data collection practices by companies like Facebook. Furthermore, José van Dijck (2012, 168) notes that Facebook "heavily invests in tracking, interpreting, repurposing, and selling information generated by its users. . . . Access and exploitation of these data are mostly unregulated territory." Even though the platform is a business that profits through data collection from personal accounts, Facebook users have been able to resignify and reshape the network according to their needs. Manuel Castells (2007, 249) notes that "the emergence of mass self-communication offers an extraordinary medium for social movements . . . to build their autonomy and confront institutions of society in their own terms and around their own projects." The interaction between individuals and technology has resulted in new "imagined collective(s)" where social, cultural, and civic gatherings take place (Boyd 2010) and where digital networks have become a space for civil society to act on pressing matters (Fotopoulou 2016). Furthermore, "public concerns can be framed in unique ways, as actors come together in real time to 'make things public' . . . and to claim voice and recognition" (Fotopoulou 2016, 991). Courtney Martin and Vanessa Valenti (2012, 6) also note that "no other form of activism in history has empowered one individual to prompt tens of thousands to take action on a singular issue—within minutes." In this context, social media can be considered powerful channels for social justice movements.

Facebook has been employed by women filmmakers to address five main goals: First, fighting against gender-based discrimination by exposing acts of sexism and racism; second, fighting against exclusion in institutions, film industries, and the media; third, promoting the work of women filmmakers; fourth, creating a network of support and exchange among women filmmakers; and fifth, improving working conditions for women in the industry. Isabel Cardoso (2017) notes the importance of this platform:

> Of course we have theoretical references through the university and through other filmmakers, whose works we learn in the university. But, basically, information [about women filmmakers] we find on Facebook. We learn about the percentage of women's participation [in the film industry], about Hollywood's relation with gender, and the possibility that women have in the international market. All of this we access basically through Facebook links. (Isabel Cardoso, Skype interview with author, January 30, 2017)

Malu Andrade (2017) adds that "social media in combination with filmmaking has the power to share unique content with other publics, who would never have access otherwise" (Malu Andrade, Skype interview with author, February 22, 2017). This means that films that were excluded from mainstream circuits of exhibition are now available through the platform. In addition to discussing the role of social media in democratizing knowledge, Samantha Brasil (2017) points to an impossibility of the existence of Elvira's Collective without social media. She explains: "We can only see ourselves today writing film criticism in Brazil because of Facebook and because of the internet. . . . The popularization of the internet and of social media made visibility possible to those who were previously marginalized or invisible" (Samantha Brasil, Skype interview with author, March 10, 2017).

Brazilian women filmmakers have used several mechanisms to perform their online activism on Facebook. The two most important tools are Facebook pages and Facebook groups. According to Facebook (n.p.), pages are channels of visibility for businesses, companies, institutions, brands, artists, public figures, and/or causes or communities. The content published on this platform is public and visible to all users. Through Netvizz (Rieder 2013) it was possible to build an overview of the initiative's Facebook page presence.

Figure 3.1 reveals that Facebook pages are heavily used by Brazilian women filmmakers. All film collectives, 80 percent of cinema clubs, 28 percent of film festivals, 11 percent of events, and 50 percent of awards have Facebook pages. However, 42 percent of festivals are online as Facebook events and 32 percent have no Facebook presence. Additionally, Netvizz

Resistance and Online Activism | 91

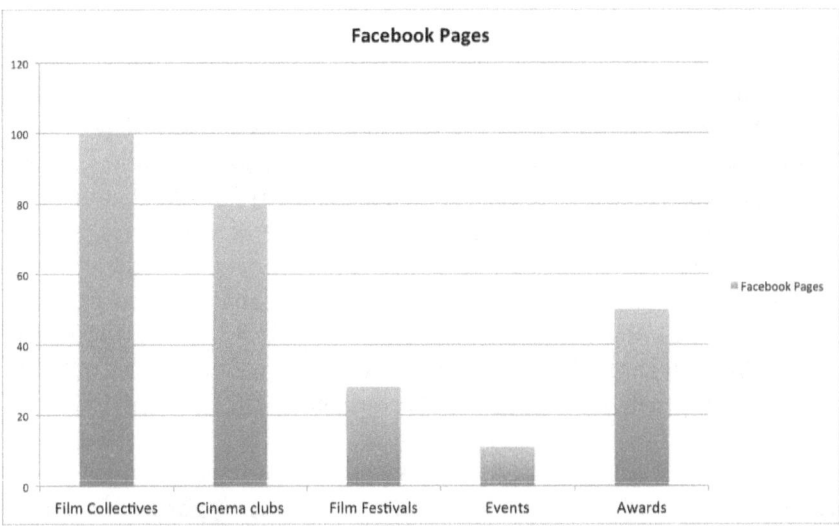

Figure 3.1. Percentage of Facebook pages by initiative.

(Rieder 2013) revealed that the initiatives produced and published online content through the platform in 2016.

As can be seen in figure 3.2, in that year, Brazilian women filmmakers circulated 2,594 posts, 7.08 posts per day, through their Facebook

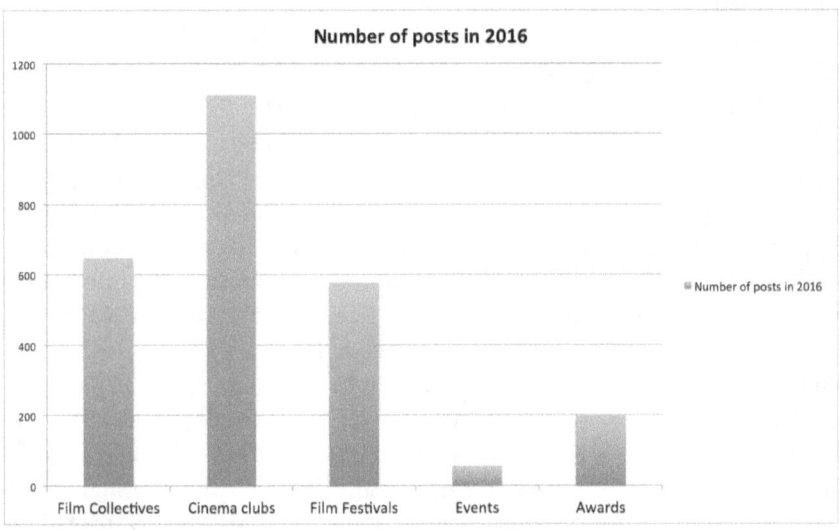

Figure 3.2. Total of posts by category in 2016.

pages. The film collective that most circulated content on Facebook was the Red Collective with a total of 168 posts. Among cinema clubs, the Cine Clube Mulheres do Brasil (Women's Cinema Club) circulated 446 posts. The women's film festival Her on Screen circulated 322 posts, the event Criativas: Oficina de Roteiro Audiovisual para Jovens Mulheres (Creatives: Screenwriting Workshop for Young Women) published content 28 times, and the Cabíria Prêmio de Roteiro (Cabíria Screenwriting Award) published 202 posts. An analysis of the Facebook pages of the Women's Cinema Club, Adélia's Cartel, and Her on Screen showed that a total of 149 posts were published in September 2017 alone. The main topics were (1) information about films directed by women (forty-one posts); (2) content featuring their own work (twenty-two posts); (3) content featuring the work of other initiatives (twenty-one posts); (4) information about film festivals (sixteen posts); (5) interviews with women filmmakers and scholars (six posts); (6) information about training opportunities (three posts); (7) information about crowdfunding opportunities (five posts); (8) content shared from individual Facebook profiles and women filmmakers (two posts); (9) livestreaming events (six posts); (10) content from the site Mulher no Cinema (Woman in Film) created by the journalist Luisa Pécora (thirteen posts); and (11) other content (twelve posts).

Through the circulation of content, both festivals and cinema clubs have been able to receive more films made by women, as explained by Samantha Brasil (2017): "The Women's Cinema Club received forty-two films [exclusively directed and photographed by women] through Facebook without any funding involved" (Samantha Brasil, Skype interview with author, March 10, 2017).

Content production through Facebook is therefore a fundamental advocacy tool for women filmmakers. Making these topics public is not only generating traffic to their pages but also challenging mainstream narratives and having a real impact on the circulation of films made by women. Furthermore, initiatives are circulating content produced by each other, which reveals the high levels of connectivity and interaction between them. Henry Jenkins, Sam Ford, and Joshua Green (2013) note that circulation is never an isolated process. It requires individuals to be connected through networks or communities, where they can "spread" content. Furthermore, Ulf Hannerz (Brosius and Wenzlhuemer 2011, 14) highlights that "only by being constantly in motion, forever being recreated, can meanings and meaningful forms become durable." Therefore, practices of "spreading content" across platforms not only are deeply rooted in collective forms of collaboration but also provide strength and visibility to the movement of Brazilian women filmmakers.

Apart from the importance of sharing content publicly, Facebook groups allow women filmmakers to communicate with each other in a private manner. This is highly important to (1) boost women's employment by posting job opportunities nationwide; (2) give visibility to women filmmakers, their projects, and initiatives; (3) accelerate processes of exchange among women, which can range from forming a film crew to coproducing knowledge; and (4) offer women safe spaces to share their experiences of harassment and their struggles in the film industry. Between 2014 and 2017, twenty-five Facebook groups were created by Brazilian women filmmakers. They can be distributed into four categories: (1) national groups, such as Women in the Audiovisual Industry in Brazil and Black Women in the Audiovisual Industry; (2) regional groups, such as Women in Film in the State of Rio de Janeiro and Women in the Audiovisual Industry in the State of Bahia; (3) student groups, such as Women in the Audiovisual Industry at the School of Communication of the Federal University of Rio de Janeiro and Women in the Audiovisual Industry at the University of Brasília; and (4) occupational groups, such as Women in Post-Production.

It was not possible to assess the content shared in these groups or the number of posts due to Facebook's privacy policies. However, Brazilian women filmmakers have stated that these groups have been very helpful for their initiatives and their positioning in the audiovisual market. Isabel Cardoso (2017) explains that the outreach of the festival Her on Screen was positively influenced by the platform: "We mainly did our publicity through Facebook. We went to women filmmakers groups online. Through these groups we knew that we would address our public. . . . And it worked" (Isabel Cardoso, Skype interview with author, January 30, 2017). Iana Paro, member of the Red Collective, further states that

> I think these groups are very important. In fact, when we [the collective] need to publish something or when we are looking for someone [to work] or for specific films [they can be very useful]. It is also great for us to understand what other women are discussing. (Iana Paro, Skype interview with author, February 14, 2017)

Women in the Audiovisual Industry in Brazil is the biggest group of its kind. Its social profile is very diverse and it includes more than just

Brazilian women filmmakers. For example, group members include Ellen Tejle, the Swedish campaigner for gender equality in film, and Marina Costin Fuser, activist and PhD in gender studies and film. Fuser explains her activities as follows:

> I think my activities are a bit different. I go there to do feminist activism. I pose questions. I see a lot of people mostly looking for work or publishing opportunities ... [people aiming] to form crews, which employ mostly women to make movies. ... A lot of events we also know because of the group. ... The part which interests me the most are the articles being published, film criticism written by women, reflexive posts, and their comments. (Marina Costin Fuser, Facebook interview with author, April 7, 2017)

Fuser calls attention to the importance of social media to women's rights movements and highlights that the popularity of feminism today is not necessarily a result of readership practices of feminist authors but an outcome of an intense engagement with social media. Facebook groups, specifically, can be formative for Brazilian women filmmakers since these are spaces of information, reflection, and debate. Additionally, participation in these networks offer women the possibility of empowerment through the organization of affirmative actions. An example of the latter was a petition in support of Débora Ivanov signed by six hundred members, including filmmakers Anna Muylaert, Laís Bodanzky, Tata Amaral, and Lúcia Murat (Pontes 2017). As president of Ancine, Ivanov was responsible for several policies that made a targeted effort at greater inclusion of women in the audiovisual industry. This petition circulated in the Brazilian public sphere and was articulated to specifically address the interim president Michel Temer. This example reveals the potential of this group to assemble activists and make their concerns publicly known.

Aristea Fotopoulou (2016, 1000) notes that "what makes the digital potentially political is the determination of people to connect, and to embody, in their communication practices, new forms of solidarity." On Facebook groups, it is possible to observe the intense exchange among women and the creation of networks of support, especially for those who experienced abuse. Malu Andrade has reported receiving daily messages from group members concerning harassment experiences in the workplace (Mori 2017). She highlights, however, that it is not easy to address these topics in the public sphere as many women fear retaliation in the film market. Tarana Burke (UN Women 2018) also highlights that "there are many women on jobs right now who are being sexually harassed . . . [and] who have complicity in their abuse for their own livelihoods." This clearly reveals the structural nature of gender-based violence and discrimination.

Ariella Azoulay (2008, 224) explains that the emergence of the definition of rape and its inclusion in dictionaries and in public policies were influenced by "the fact that women began to talk about rape themselves, in the first person, to attest to the experience of rape from the primary source, and they began to do so both among themselves and generally in the public sphere." Even though not all cases of abuse have reached the public, the fact that Brazilian women filmmakers are addressing these topics in private forums such as Facebook groups means that women are seeking support and reflecting on the structural nature of this issue together. Speaking out about harrassment and violence against women in these forums can lead not only to future affirmative actions but also to positive outcomes related to cultural and institutional changes in Brazil.

In this context, speaking out both publicly and in closed forums is highly important for the movement of Brazilian women filmmakers. As demonstrated in this section, Facebook is a platform by which to address concerns, voice perspectives, and build significant connections with each other. Being part of these networks also means building communities, which allows the movement to gain strength and to develop further. Their activism on Facebook therefore has given them greater agency while amplifying their voices.

Concluding Remarks

Between 2014 and 2017, Brazil underwent a period of democratic and political turbulence, when political figures and women's rights policies were under attack. As a counterpoint to this process, many social justice and feminist movements flourished across the country. In the face of systemic gender-based discrimination and exclusion, Brazilian women filmmakers developed several initiatives with the purpose of building new possibilities and spaces for women in the industry. In a context of democratic instability, which threatened further restrictions to their rights, these filmmakers have become important voices for social justice and equality on a national level.

As demonstrated in this chapter, Brazilian women filmmakers developed actions and articulated their perspectives both online and offline. We argue that their movement cannot be dissociated from their online activism. The platform of Facebook has had major significance for them to speak out against injustices and to build positive propositions to address imbalances and struggles in the film industry. In this context, circulation of content has a special impact on the movement, granting it durability and strength. Since Brazil has one of the hightest number of Facebook users in the world, the outreach women can achieve from their activism is immense. Although not a focus of this chapter, it is important to recognize this potential and note that social media has been a major channel for movements to challenge dominant narratives. It is, however, also essential to remember that online mobilizations are temporary forms of protests. This research covers only the period of 2014 to 2017. Future research on this topic is therefore called for to identify new practices among women filmmakers as well as the continuity of the movement itself.

The activism of Brazilian women filmmakers has an imperative to challenge women's roles in society. By building new narratives and imaginings of womanhood, filmmakers can challenge traditional representations, which place women in oppressive and/or marginal positions. A transformation in society comes together with a change in how women are seen and represented. Brazilian women filmmakers are, therefore, developing groundbreaking efforts in this direction. With the plurality of their voices, the whole structure of society moves with them.

Notes

1. See Cacilda M. Rêgo's chapter in this volume for further discussion.

2. It was not possible to identify the year of creation of We are Magnolias Film Collective, Mulheres no Audiovisual Pernambuco (Women in the Audiovisual Industry in Pernambuco), Cineclube Academia das Musas (Academy of Muses Cinema Club), Coletivo de Mulheres de Cinema e Audiovisual da Baixada Santista (Collective of Women in Film and in the Audiovisual Industry in Baixada Santista), Mulheres da Produção Audiovisual e da Fotografia (Women in the Fields of Photography and Audiovisual Productions), Mulheres no Audiovisual no Estado de Mato Grosso (Women in the Audiovisual Industry in the State of Mato Grosso), Coletivo de Mulheres no Audiovisual (Collective Women in the Audiovisual Industry), Coletivo de Mulheres Diretoras (Collective of Women

Cinematographers), Mulheres na Pós-produção Audiovisual (Women in Post-Production), Mulheres na Direção de Fotografia (Brazilian Female Photographers), Mulheres no Audiovisual Brasília (Women in the Audiovisual Industry in Brasilia), and Mulheres no Audiovisual (Women in the Audiovisual Industry).

Works Cited

Ancine. 2018. "Ancine apresenta estudo sobre diversidade de gênero e raça no mercado audiovisual." *Ancine*, January 25, 2018. https://www.ancine.gov.br/pt-br/sala-imprensa/noticias/ancine-apresenta-estudo-sobre-diversidade-de-g-nero-e-ra-no-mercado.

Azoulay, Ariella. 2008. *The Civil Contract of Photography*. New York: Zone Books.

Brosius, Christiane, and Roland Wenzlhuemer. 2011. *Transcultural Turbulences Towards a Multi-Sited Reading of Image Flows*. Berlin, Heidelberg: Springer.

Biblioteca. 2016. "Ministério das Mulheres, da Igualdade Racial e dos Direitos Humanos." Presidência da República. September 29, 2016. http://www.biblioteca.presidencia.gov.br/base-legal-de-governo/orgaos-extintos/das-mulheres-da-igualdade-racial-e-dos-direitos-humanos.

Boyd, Dannah. 2010. "Social Network Sites as Networked Publics: Affordances, Dynamics, and Implications." In *Networked Self: Identity, Community, and Culture on Social Network Sites*, edited by Zizi Papacharissi. New York: Routledge.

Bowerbank, Joel. 2013. "Facebook and Communicative Action: The Power of Social Media during the 2011 Egyptian Revolution." Master's thesis, University of Ottawa.

Candido, Márcia Rangel, Cleissa Regina Martins, Raissa Rodrigues, and João Feres Júnior. 2017. "Raça e gênero no cinema brasileiro: 1970–2016." Rio de Janeiro: Boletim GEMAA 2, 1–5. http://gemaa.iesp.uerj.br/wp-content/uploads/2017/06/Boletim_Final7.pdf.

Castells, Manuel. 2007. "Communication, Power and Counter-Power in the Networked Society." *International Journal of Communication* 1, 238–66.

———. 2015. *Networks of Outrage and Hope Social Movements in the Internet Age*. 2nd ed. Cambridge: Polity Press.

Crenshaw, Kimberlé. 1989. "Demarginalizing the intersection of Race and Sex: A Black Feminist Critique of Antidiscrimination Doctrine, Feminist Theory and Antiracist Policies." *University of Chicago Legal Forum* 1: 139–67.

Diário de Pernambuco. 2016. "A cada dez brasileiros, oito estão no Facebook." *Diário de Pernambuco*, January 28, 2016. http://www.pernambuco.com/noticia/tecnologia/2016/01/a-cada-dez-brasileiros-oito-estao-no-facebook.html.

Dijck, José van. 2012. "Facebook as a Tool for Producing Sociality and Connectivity." *Television & New Media* 13(2), 160–76.
Ernesto, Marcelo. 2017. "Vereadores denunciam decreto de Kalil que retira a palavra 'gênero' de políticas de educação." *Estado de Minas*, October 2, 2017. https://www.em.com.br/app/noticia/politica/2017/10/02/interna_politica,905 333/vereadores-denunciam-decreto-de-kalil-que-retira-a-palavra-genero-de.shtml.
Facebook. n.d. "Facebook Pages Terms." https://www.facebook.com/page_guidelines.php.
Finco, Nina. 2017. "Filósofa Judith Butler é agredida em Congonhas antes de deixar São Paulo." *Época*, November 10, 2017. https://epoca.globo.com/cultura/noticia/2017/11/filosofa-judith-butler-e-agredida-em-congonhas-antes-de-deixar-sao-paulo.html.
Förster, Annette. 1997. "Alice Guy in der Filmgeschichtsschreibung." *Frauen und Film* 60, 185–94.
Fotopoulou, Aristea. 2016. "Digital and Networked by Default? Women's Organisations and the Social Imaginary of Networked Feminism." *New Media and Society* 18 (6): 989–1005.
Francheschini, Marina. 2015. "Brasil é o quinto país do mundo em ranking de violência contra a mulher." *G1*, November 10, 2015. http://g1.globo.com/hora1/noticia/2015/11/brasil-e-o-quinto-pais-do-mundo-em-ranking-de-violencia-contra-mulher.html.
Friedman, Elisabeth J. 2017. *Interpreting the Internet: Feminist and Queer Counterpublics in Latin America*. Oakland: University of California Press.
IBGE. 2011. "Sinopse do censo demográfico 2010." *Instituto Brasileiro de Geografia e Estatística*, July 27, 2020. https://biblioteca.ibge.gov.br/visualizacao/livros/liv49230.pdf.
Jenkins, Henry, Sam Ford, and Joshua Green. 2013. *Spreadable Media. Creating Value and Meaning in a Networked Culture*. New York: New York University.
Kilomba, Grada. 2010. *Plantation Memories: Episodes of Everyday Racism*. 2nd ed. Münster: UNRAST-Verlag.
Marsh, Leslie L. 2012. *Brazilian Women's Filmmaking: From Dictatorship to Democracy*. Urbana: University of Illinois Press.
Martin, Courtney, and Vanessa Valenti. 2012. "#FemFuture: Online Revolution." *New Feminist Solutions* 8, 1–34. http://bcrw.barnard.edu/wp-content/nfs/reports/NFS8-FemFuture-Online-Revolution-Report.pdf.
Marques, Marilia. 2017. "Primeira cineasta negra do Brasil, Adélia Sampaio exibe filme em Brasília." *G1 DF*. April 11, 2017. https://g1.globo.com/distrito-federal/noticia/primeira-cineasta-negra-do-brasil-adelia-sampaio-exibe-filme-em-brasilia.ghtml.
Matos, Carolina. 2017. "New Brazilian Feminisms and Online Networks: Cyberfeminism, Protest and the Female 'Arab Spring.'" *International Sociology* 32 (3), 417–34.

Mori, Letícia. 2017. " 'Caso Weinstein não me choca': mulheres falam sobre assédio na indústria brasileira do entretenimento." *BBC Brasil*. October 12, 2017. http://www.bbc.com/portuguese/brasil-41602756?ocid=socialflow_facebook.

Neto, Aristides Monteiro. 2014. "Desigualdades regionais no Brasil: características e tendências recentes." *Ipea: Boletim Regional, Urbano e Ambiental*, January 9, 2014. http://repositorio.ipea.gov.br/bitstream/11058/5582/1/BRU_n09_desigualdades.pdf.

Observatório Brasileiro do Cinema e do Audiovisual (OCA). 2016. "Informe de acompanhamento do mercado. Produção de longas-metragens." *Observatório Brasileiro do Cinema e do Audiovisual*, October 13, 2016. http://oca.ancine.gov.br/sites/default/files/cinema/pdf/informe_producao_2014.pdf.

Pereira, Leonardo. 2016. "Michel Temer extingue o Ministério das Comunicações." *Olhar Digital*, May 13, 2016. https://olhardigital.com.br/noticia/michel-temer-extingue-o-ministerio-das-comunicacoes/58301.

Pontes, Fernanda. 2017. "Mulheres do audiovisual pedem a Michel Temer a permanência de Debora Ivanov na presidência da Ancine." *O Globo*, June 17, 2017. https://blogs.oglobo.globo.com/gente-boa/post/mulheres-do-audiovisual-pedem-michel-temer-permanencia-de-debora-ivanov-na-presidencia-da-ancine.html.

Redação Pragmatismo. 2015. "Vereadores de Campinas aprovam 'moção de repúdio' a Simone de Beauvoir." *Pragmatismo Político*, October 30, 2015. https://www.pragmatismopolitico.com.br/2015/10/vereadores-de-campinas-aprovam-mocao-de-repudio-a-simone-de-beauvoir.html.

Redação. 2016. "Brasil é o país que mais usa redes sociais na América Latina." *CanalTech*, June 20, 2016. https://canaltech.com.br/redes-sociais/brasil-e-o-pais-que-mais-usa-redes-sociais-na-america-latina-70313/.

Rieder, Bernard. 2013. "Studying Facebook via Data Extraction: The Netvizz Application," *University of Amsterdam*. https://apps.facebook.com/netvizz/?fb_source=search&ref=br_rs.

Santos, Érica Ramos Sarmet dos, and Marina Cavalcanti Tedesco. 2017. "Iniciativas e ações feministas no audiovisual brasileiro contemporâneo." *Estudos Feministas* 25 (3), 1373–91.

Smith, Stacy. L., Mark Mac Choueiti, and Katherine Pieper. 2014. "Gender Bias without Borders: An Investigation of Female Characters in Popular Films Across 11 Countries," 1–41. *Geena Davis Institute on Gender in Media*. Los Angeles: University of Southern California.

Universidade de São Paulo. 2018. "Processo de seleção para ingresso no mestrado e doutorado no programa de pós-graduação em meios e processos audiovisuais em 2018." *Universidade de São Paulo*. http://www3.eca.usp.br/sites/default/files/form/ata/pos/Edital.PPGMPA.2018.Retificado.pdf.

UN Women. 2018. "Six Activists Who Are Using Social Media for Change Offline." *UN Women*, June 29, 2018. https://www.unwomen.org/en/news/stories/2018/6/compilation-social-media-day.

Valente, Jonas. 2017. "Internautas brasileiros acham que a internet se resume ao Facebook." *Carta Capital*, January 24, 2017. https://www.cartacapital.com.br/blogs/intervozes/internautas-brasileiros-acham-que-a-internet-se-resume-ao-facebook.

Verztman Bagdadi, Daniela. 2017. "Inclusive Futures and Diversity on Screen: Contemporary Online Activism of Brazilian Women Filmmakers." Master's thesis. Ruprecht-Karls-Universität Heidelberg.

Verztman Bagdadi, Daniela. 2016. "Politics, Women's Rights and the Evangelical Parliamentary Front in Brazil." *HERA Single*. http://www.hera-single.de/women-brazil/.

Chapter 4

Interview with Maria Augusta Ramos

Maria Augusta Ramos (MAR), Jack A. Draper III (JD), Cacilda Rêgo (CR), and Gustavo Procopio Furtado (GF)[1]

Figure 4.1. Maria Augusta Ramos. (Photo credit: Ana Paula Amorim)

Maria Augusta Ramos began her career as a documentary director in the Netherlands in 2000 with *Desi*, a film about the life of an adolescent Dutch girl growing up poor, without her mother, who died when Desi was still a toddler. An interest in subaltern perspectives would continue in her later films, along with a consideration of the complex operations of institutional power in Brazil on subaltern populations. Her later films include a trilogy about the justice system (*Justiça / Justice*, 2004; *Juízo / Judgment*, 2007; and *Morro dos prazeres / Hill of Pleasures*, 2013), focusing on judges, prosecutors, public defenders, and police as well as the citizens, often working-class and/or Black, who get caught up, tried, and/or imprisoned by this system. As discussed in this interview, in her *O processo / The Trial* (2018), the theme of the trial was taken up again in a legislative context, the 2015–2016 congressional impeachment proceedings and trial of President Dilma Rousseff. This interview took place on the Pontifical Catholic University campus in Rio de Janeiro, after the three interviewers and the director had participated in a roundtable discussion of Brazilian women filmmakers and protagonists and the cinematic oeuvre of Maria Augusta Ramos, particularly *The Trial*. Ramos was one of several women directors, including Petra Costa (also interviewed in this volume), to focus one of her films on the struggles of Brazil's first woman president with a largely *machista* political culture, major corruption investigations, and the economic crisis that interrupted the prior period of economic growth and low unemployment during the first decade of the Workers' Party's occupation of the presidency. Ramos explains here how *The Trial* was a return of the director to her native city of Brasília. She says Brasília shaped her understanding of what a city should look like, and even suggests that, by extension, perhaps the modernist style of its urban plan and architecture contributed to the formalism of her filmmaking style.[2]

CR: Some years ago, I heard an interview with [Brazilian director] Tata Amaral against Globo Films. There is a criticism of some women directors because it is a system unfortunately extremely dominated by male directors.
How can you get past these barriers as a woman?

MAR: I think that one has to think about how there was a considerable change during the era we are talking about. Nowadays, in the last ten years, and during the years of the Workers' Party [since 2003], of Ancine,[3] some cinema policies have been adopted that allowed for many—that is, a minority principally of women—to be able to make films. And not just women—alternative, reflective cinema, which was not necessarily harnessed to the interests of the big media or Globo Films or which does not need television and does not necessarily depend on the big corporations in the audiovisual sector, which can finance itself through public incentive. In truth, it is the tax revenue from the cinematic industry. I think it is interesting, how it is that a woman, how this happened, this change, because in the beginning it did not happen that way; it took a good twelve years before this policy really reached films that are not commercial. The money arrived for the commercial films, [but] that advance which happened six years ago occurred after the policies. For example, the Sectorial [Fund of the Audiovisual Sector] was extremely important.

Débora Ivanov, one of the directors of Ancine, has been there for quite some time already, she has cinema experience, was an executive at Gullane Films, is an important producer in São Paulo, and then became the director of Ancine. [Ivanov also produced *Que horas ela volta? / The Second Mother* (2015), analyzed in Jack Draper's chapter in this volume.] She is a cool person . . . she was placed in that position by Sérgio Sá Leitão, and then produced some films, and pursued a policy different than that of Temer. She is a woman, and to tell you the truth, two or three years ago, they did a laboratory for women in the field of cinema. It is a kind of workshop, with her, with women in cinema, with people, women, also from Ancine. [She could tell some stories] about the situation, the difficulties, the issue of the funding cycles [*editais*], of all the bureaucracy of Ancine, about what we achieved. Only in the past five years, great films were made; all this richness of current Brazilian cinema was created through the funding cycles of Ancine, with this change in policies. Also, obviously in Pernambuco, the state also adopted a very cool policy of stimulating cinema; in São Paulo with Haddad and Spcine.[4] So all of this is going down the drain.

It's interesting that it's by women, there are a lot of women making films.

GF: And they are very important films, very notable. We see various films with an impact beyond yours. Women directors, cinematographers, editors.

CR: And producers, right?

MAR: There are a lot of women producers. A lot of editors. I think there are more women editors.

GF: Than men, you think?

MAR: Than men, yes, or if there are more men, there are still a lot of women. I myself have already worked with three.

JD: [In terms of screenwriters] there are various women, for example Antônia Pellegrino who wrote the screenplay of the film *Tim Maia* [2014] [and also of *Primavera das mulheres / Women's Spring* (2017)].

MAR: Look, just in terms of editors, in the Netherlands I worked with men, but in Brazil they are all women.

CR: You work here in Brazil, but live there?

MAR: I live in both places. I spend some time here making films, I edit here, I do everything here with my Brazilian films. The crews . . . unless they are coproductions with the Netherlands, they are all made, filmed here, edited here, *Justice* as well. Then I go and do the finishing touches in the Netherlands, and I come back and show it here all over, on public television, I discuss it with the public because there should be a participation with the film.

But there are a lot of women producers; there is Vânia Catani, who produces national films, who produced Lucrécia Martel's *Zama* [2017]. Anita Rocha [da Silveira], a young girl who made her first fictional film, *Mata-me* [*por favor / Kill Me Please* (2015)], who is making her second, that one Vânia Catani produced as well, and she produced several films [directed] by Selton Mello. She has produced a lot.

JD: I wanted to ask about the international context, in terms of stylistic influences, if you see your films as part of an international dialogue of cinema, of documentary, of women's cinema? Or simply of international cinema, of arthouse or independent cinema? And you want to show this film *O processo / The Trial* [2018] in the United States—how do you think it should be received, as a Brazilian film, or is it a more universal story that you are interpreting?

MAR: I don't think in that way, you know? If I am making a Brazilian or a Dutch film, one for a specific audience . . . short, fat [laughter]. I just believe that I have a narrative with which I manage to identify completely, the product of a cinematographic discovery, and through that discovery one goes in accordance with the language developed . . . so I have a process of discovery of a language, a narrative that I keep refining. And I hope that the film, certainly, reaches every kind of audience including the international audience. It might seem that *The Trial* is a very specifically Brazilian film because it deals with the issue of an event, a historic moment like the impeachment. But I think it does indeed have universal elements. I think that we see in the world a polarization, a tendency toward neoliberalism, a theatricalization [*teatralização*] of the justice system, of politics. But I agree, and I cannot manage to say what an aesthetically Brazilian film is; I would not say that it is a Brazilian film. There are so many Brazils within Brazil! It is complicated for us to reduce it: a women's film, a Brazilian film. Pernambuco comes to mind; you have Pernambucan directors who make very different films, who make all kinds of cinema. And then, for example, I was influenced much more by Dutch, European documentary, and fiction cinema than Brazilian in my development [*formação*]. But when I was a university student, I went to the movies and watched the Brazilian classics. I identify with cinema, independently of whether I am here or in the Netherlands. I think that I had access to an education that is universal, and I think that today, more than ever, every film that is produced, everyone has access to it. So all this new generation, all these directors, they are drinking from this . . . from every mediatic place, from Russian cinema, etc. In the end, it is difficult in this moment, in this era of globalization, to say what is Brazilian cinema. For example, today in Brazil, the documentarian Eduardo Coutinho is considered an important filmmaker, perhaps one of the greatest. I also find him a great documentary filmmaker, but I don't identify myself with his work. I never identified with it. I never identified with a work of conversations, of interviews—I watch it, I find it all interesting, but sometimes it is not just what we are familiar with; it is a question of identification. What makes me feel, what moves me, what interests me in reality. So why a more formal cinema, and who makes more formal cinema? The Japanese, the French, the Italians, the Belgians. So that is, at least in its form, the cinema which touches me, the cinema I want to make. So it is difficult to say if I find the film Brazilian; if you watch my films, in a certain way, you will see that it is a Maria Ramos film.

GF: Of course!

MAR: *Desi* [2000] is a Dutch film made in Dutch. It has English subtitles, but it is not a film that takes place in Brazil.

CR: But *The Trial*, that is a Brazilian film, or is it not? Because it is a question of content. But for example, I was reading just recently a news article about [Fernando] Meirelles, because he has several films made in English, financed and made with actors from Hollywood—are those Brazilian or not? Today in this age of the transnational.

MAR: In the case of *Desi*, it is not. It's a Dutch film. Well, it has a Brazilian director and is Dutch.

CR: And *The Trial*, Brazilian or not?

MAR: I don't know.

CR: We in the academic arena attempt to apply theory. You have your practice and can apply it within theory, or not. And we come along full of theory [laughter]! Let's talk about your gaze. You can make something that could be screened internationally with characters and stories that are not Brazilian, but your gaze can be, or not be, a Brazilian gaze. That is the question.

GF: We can also add that there is a specific perspective, indeed—every perspective is a specific one—beyond that, your filmmaking has a very strong vision to determine what type of gaze you will adopt, and which is a very disciplined adherence to a perspective. So up to what point do you enter into the historical situation? That is, is there something that you bring when looking at *Desi*, which a Dutch director would not see? Or to extend this to the theme of that roundtable[5] itself, you do not make your films as women's films, as feminist films, but up to what point does the fact of you being a woman determine that you choose this element as something which merits attention, or this gaze, or this closeness?

MAR: I think that certainly I have a role, but to what extent? There is a complexity there. I was born in '64 in Brasília. I'm from the generation of the revolution. I experienced the return [of democracy]. I would say that I am not just Brazilian—I am a Brazilian woman, middle-class, white, who had access. How can you define as "Brazilian" all of this myriad of experiences?

GF: Too broad.

MAR: Too broad! I am not one city since I am several states. At the same time, indeed, I am a person who lived twenty-four/twenty-five years in Europe. Now, my formalism, it does not necessarily have to do with the Netherlands. That is to say, my first film is already extremely formal. The Dutch themselves called it "so formal," which maybe has something to do with my experience of music, which maybe has to do with having been born in Brasília. I don't know! My mental representation of a city was Brasília. I would leave Brasília to visit my grandparents in Rio and I found that all chaos! I have an identification with that type of cinema. Feminine, certainly! There are elements to which I am able to relate, having to do with the family—all my films have these people eating dinner [together], the family. The familial relationship, the father, the mother; there are children. So there are elements that I would say come from being a woman. Which is also to say that a Brazilian gaze is possible. I am considered in Brazil to be a Brazilian director.

GF: I recommend *Desi* very highly as well, I think it is extremely—especially on the feminine question—it is a very, very strong film. It is an older film, it is a Dutch film, but it is a film which indeed pays attention to domestic, private life and the like. And there is a fragile female figure who is at the same time very potent. Vulnerable. I see a relation between *Desi* and the film *The Trial*, as well as the justice system films, which are films about the relation between institutions of power and their operation, the minutiae of their operation. And *The Trial*, which takes place in Congress, is not so much about the justice system, it is a little bit theater, a farce, but it is a denunciation, and what is in play are human beings whose destinies lie in the hands of the institutions. So there is a very strong relationship; I even see it as a continuation of the trilogy of the justice system, moving to the area of legislative power but acting in judgment.

MAR: Yes, the impeachment is a juridical-legislative process. It is a juridical process, too.

CR: It would be interesting also to know how you see yourself. What would you like us to know about you as a person or an artist, and as a director?

MAR: We are all various, that is the issue. I am a filmmaker, a documentarian, and also other people. I am the daughter of my mother, I am a friend, I am Brazilian, I am also Dutch, I am middle class. Not even I know how to define myself. I also think that we don't know how to define ourselves, right? Who am I? We do therapy for years to define ourselves, too.

GF: It is a task that relates to your films, right? That is, for example, in the case of the justice system, it is "Who are you?" that is in question. You are so-and-so from such-and-such place, you did such-and-such crime—who is the subject defined as a subject of law? All these films have some subject looking for a space of resistance, and sometimes without finding it.

MAR: Yes, that is the question of truth. I don't want the truth. The truth has various versions, doesn't it? That search for truth, the only truth.

GF: And the discourses do not match up sometimes. "When were you born?" "I don't know." That is, there is a mismatch of language itself which seeks to define the subject. So there is a fragility, an instability of the place of the subject.

CR: Well then, that answer could be her answer. My gaze is that of a woman, simply a woman director, or a Brazilian woman or a woman of two cultures, or simply nothing.

MAR: A woman in search of understanding, right?

CR: Yes, because in truth, you are saying who you are in your films. By the very fact of you seeking out a subject, the theme which is proposed or which you identify, you are saying who you are.

JD: Do you think that this is a question that you are posing to the subjects of your films, "Who are you?"

MAR: No.

JD: Or who are the different sides of you? Because I am thinking of *Justice*, in which you want to show the workplace of the lawyer, of the defense, and also show her at the dinner table with her family, as well as the family of the accused, like the mother, and the mother also enters the courthouse. So, certainly you are showing different sides of these people. Is it also about creating a space for this to be revealed? How do you see it?

MAR: I think it is a search to understand Brazilian society, in a certain way. I think that *Justice* is a fruit of that. It is a return to the country after many years to understand the power relations, social relations, human relations, how these operate. Truthfully it is about those various Brazils I was talking about, or at least about those two Brazils.

CR: And about those various Marias, too? For example, I have been living more than thirty years in the United States. I do not see Brazil like my family sees it. And certainly you do not see Brazil like many people who have not left Brazil. That gaze that you have, it has to be different, it has to be you in some way. What your experience is, not my experience, not anyone else's experience.

MAR: Yes, it is a unique vision, surely.

CR: So that gives you a distance, an objectivity?

MAR: No doubt. It gives me an objectivity, certainly. But it is not one of searching for the truth of the characters, for example. It is trying to reveal or discover various elements, various characteristics of that complexity in each one of the characters who make up the film. For example, the judge, the accused, the mother of the accused, they are social, cultural, political, products of a society—of a culture, of a social class, of Brazilian culture. But they are also unique beings. This is very important—how I believe, how I work, how I film, and how I edit the characters, these people in my films. So Brulaine [dos Santos, of *Morro dos prazeres / Hill of Pleasures* (2013)], she is not just a drug trafficker, a product of an unequal society—she is Brulaine. She is all of this, and also something individual. That individual, or other various individuals, they reveal those institutions. In the case of the justice system, in the case of the favela. Through them I can speak about all of that . . . I believe in that unique mystery of each unique being. For that reason it is difficult for me to say who I am. I am a series of elements which are effervescent because I am not the person who I was twenty years ago. The complexity . . . it is absolutely contradictory as well, we are contradictory beings. We have to understand what it is that moves us, at least my desire is [to achieve] an understanding for myself. If other people who watch the film manage to see what I see or discover other things, identify with other things, or indeed, discover that cinema is a reflection of themselves, of a society, great! But my films are a quest, a quest for understanding, to see the world in some manner.

CR: In this context, you have the criticism of newspapers, the reaction of the people. How does this work currently?

MAR: Currently it works in every way: through movie critics; through spectators who go to see the films and write to me—leave reactions or thoughts on the Facebook page or send them to the distributor; people who view the film when I am present and come afterwards and speak with me. So I have contact with every kind of direct reaction or intellectual [reaction] through movie critics, intellectuals, jurists, or people directly . . . as much via the internet as physically. We did advance screenings in practically all the capitals of Brazil. I went to all the capitals. So it was a film, in the case of *The Trial*, a film which has a great impact on the audience. They cry. They have a relationship. It's a film in which you can see again, as someone said, a regression without a cure, you will review a moment.

CR: I am asking because I continue to be very surprised to see, for example on the Internet, the hate which the PT [Workers' Party] receives. The aggressions, the people are so aggressive. Family members, friends, but you are PT or you're anti-PT.

JD: That political-social division in the country, in the film [*The Trial*] I think that you showed that very well, on the individual level. Janaína Paschoal is a very good antagonist. As a character, for these senators like Gleisi Hoffman and Lindbergh [Farias]. I know Paschoal principally through criticisms that I read of her and her analysis in newspapers and magazines with a more left point of view. But it is possible to see that individual side to her, a passion that could be considered a little bit crazy from a certain point of view, but as an antagonist or protagonist it is very interesting to see this conflict in the Senate between her and Lindbergh. It is somewhat dramatic, isn't it?

MAR: Yes, I think that in the trial there are always two sides, right? The prosecution and the defense, and she represents the prosecution.

JD: But Gleisi [Hoffman], I learned more about her in your film. How it is so important for her to continue with this struggle, with Lula's cause? How he represents something bigger.

MAR: For the whole left.

JD: For democracy. But she has a personal interest; she could have put herself forward as a candidate instead of [former mayor of São Paulo, Fernando] Haddad, for example.

MAR: Ah, yes. But it's an issue for the party, complicated. But just to let you know, three weeks ago, the STF [Federal Supreme Court] finally adjudicated her case and the trial was suspended. The STF found her innocent.

JD: That was along with her husband?

MAR: Yes, that trial was connected to her husband.

JD: Ah. That was another mediatic game of the—

MAR: Of [the] Car Wash [federal corruption investigation], yes. There was no proof and beyond that, it seems that the State witnesses contradicted themselves. They said one thing, then they said another.

Notes

1. Translation to English and preface by Jack A. Draper III.
2. This interview has been edited for reasons of length and clarity and to conform with the format of the other interviews in this book.
3. Brazil's national film agency, which provides funding and other incentives for domestic filmmaking.
4. The cinema and audiovisual company of the city government of São Paulo.

5. A roundtable conversation organized by JD and CR, on the same day as this interview, on the theme of woman-centered Brazilian cinema. The roundtable discussion was a panel event during the Congress of the Brazilian Studies Association.

PART 2

POLITICS OF PUBLIC/PRIVATE SPACES

Chapter 5

From Tweets to the Streets

Women's Documentary Filmmaking and Brazil's Feminist Spring

REBECCA J. ATENCIO

On October 20, 2015, the name of a twelve-year-old female contestant on the Brazilian edition of *Master Chef Junior* became a trending topic on Twitter when male viewers posted disturbing, sexual tweets about the girl during the show's premiere. The next day, Juliana Farias, the founder of the São Paulo–based feminist nongovernmental organization Think Olga, encouraged women to channel their outrage over the incident by tweeting personal stories of childhood sexual harassment under the hashtag #PrimeiroAssédio (First Harassment/Assault). The hashtag quickly went viral on Twitter and Facebook, catapulting the issue of sexual violence into the national spotlight to an extent never before seen in Brazil.[1] As Farias's Twitter campaign was unfolding on social media, conservative Brazilian congressman Eduardo Cunha proposed a bill seeking to deny abortion access to rape survivors (federal law currently prohibits abortion except in cases of rape, endangerment to the pregnant person's life, and fetal microencephaly) and to change the legal definition of sexual violence in the Penal Code from a consent-based model to a much more restrictive one hinging on the presence of both physical and psychological threat. The bill unleashed a wave of protest by Brazilian women, who tweeted their infuriation under the hashtag #MulheresContraCunha (Women Against Cunha) and participated in over fifty demonstrations in cities across the country from October 27 to December 13, including the historic Marcha das Negras (Black Women's March) in Brasília on November 18. Consequently, Cunha's bill stalled. That same period saw the introduction and viral circulation of a number of other hashtags denouncing misogyny and demanding gender equality, such as #MeuAmigoSecreto (My Secret Friend, an invitation for women to post ironic commentaries about everyday instances of misogyny), #AgoraÉQueSãoElas (Now It's the Women's Turn, a campaign demanding that male journalists create space for women's voices in the media), and #NãoPoetizeOMachismo (Don't Romanticize Machismo, an effort to denounce male chauvinism in the realm of culture and the arts). The confluence of so many gender-related protest initiatives online and in the streets invited comparisons to the Arab Spring of 2010, prompting some participants and observers to propose that Brazil was witnessing a Primavera Feminista (Feminist Spring, a designation popularized by the national media).²

Brazil's Feminist Spring is largely associated with social media and city streets, but it was also amplified by the documentary filmmaking of emerging women directors, some of whom played an instrumental role in helping bridge the divide between the two spaces, virtual and physical. Not long after Farias launched her hashtag campaign, director Paula Sacchetta began production on her documentary *Precisamos falar do assédio* (*We need to talk about harassment*, distributed in English as *Faces of Harassment*), which was released in September 2016, less than year after the fateful *Master Chef Junior* premiere. Farias, for her part, partnered with directors Amanda Kamanchek Lemos and Fernanda Frazão, leveraging the momentum generated by #PrimeiroAssédio to parlay an earlier Think Olga project involving an online platform for denouncing sexual violence into the production of a crowd-funded documentary film on street harassment in Brazil titled *Chega de fiu fiu*, released in 2018 (and distributed in English as *Enough with Catcalling*).³ Sacchetta and the duo of Kamanchek and Frazão, all in their early thirties when their films were launched, continue a long tradition of Brazilian women directors for whom filmmaking is a vehicle for feminist praxis.⁴ What sets *Faces of Harassment* and *Enough with Catcalling* apart is, above all, their intersectional feminist sensibilities and synergistic relationship with social media.

#PrimeiroAssédio Hits the Streets

In the tweet that officially launched what was to become a viral hashtag campaign, Juliana Farias wrote: "#FirstHarassment happened at age 11.

It didn't end there. I was harassed in the street, on the subway, at school, by strangers and by the men who were supposed to be there to protect me."[5] Many followers of Think Olga's Twitter account were likely already familiar with the incident alluded to in that tweet, since Farias had related the story in a TED Talk that she gave on the subject of street harassment just a few months earlier. In the talk, the journalist mentions an unspecified form of harassment she experienced, drawing attention not to the man who enacted the aggression but rather to an older female bystander:

> I was an eleven-year-old girl . . . but men on the street . . . thought it was already time to start talking to me about sex. The first time I was harassed happened on the way home from the bakery and I cried. An older lady saw me walking and crying, and tried to console me. When I told her what happened she replied that I was being silly—that there was no reason to cry, that I should feel flattered because it was a good thing, a compliment. And that when I got to be her age I would miss it.[6]

As Farias noted in another tweet, many viewers who posted comments on the video sought to undermine this testimony either by questioning its veracity or by insisting that her experience was an exception rather than the rule. Her point was that the disturbing tweets about the preadolescent *Master Chef Junior* contestant proved how wrong such viewers were. Farias's tweets and the account of harassment she shared in her TED Talk encapsulate what were to become central themes in the #PrimeiroAssédio Twitter campaign, namely (1) the early age at which girls are first exposed to sexual behavior by adult men in Brazil; (2) the doubt and disbelief that greet women's and girls' testimonies of such experiences; (3) the frequency of abuse by men occupying positions of trust, such as male family members, teachers, religious leaders, and policemen; (4) and the complicity of older women in normalizing and minimizing this harmful sexual culture.[7]

It is no coincidence that these same themes run through *Faces of Harassment*. Sacchetta explicitly conceived her documentary as a continuation of the viral #PrimeiroAssédio hashtag campaign, as reflected in the project's title, which transforms the buzzword *assédio* into a slogan or call to action. This conceptualization shaped the film in important ways, including both its production and its distribution. In terms of the production process, the director converted a large van into a studio on wheels and parked it in nine locations throughout Brazil's two largest cities, São Paulo and Rio de Janeiro; any woman was invited to step into the privacy of the empty vehicle and record her story. Sacchetta and her crew outfitted the van for this purpose by installing a camera, stool, and lighting in the back. As the director explains in a piece posted on the blog of the *Folha de São Paulo* newspaper and reprinted in the press kit for the documentary, "We could have invited women to come to our production company headquarters to record their testimonies, but we decided to deploy a mobile studio that would circulate in different parts of the city, without vetting the participants in advance [*sem pesquisa prévia*], so that the production process would itself be a campaign" ("Press Kit" 2016). From the outset, then, she framed the documentary as an extension of the #PrimeiroAssédio movement but taking place out in the streets, the idea being to gather as many different stories from as many different women as possible in a single week. To help conjure the atmosphere of a campaign, the van's exterior became a kind of mobile billboard for the project, with the slogan "Faces of Harassment" emblazoned in large letters on all sides, alongside huge, attention-grabbing images—reminiscent of graffiti—of women with their mouths open as if telling or shouting their stories.

In the same spirit, Sacchetta issued an open call for any *paulistana* or *carioca* (São Paulo or Rio de Janeiro) women to participate via announcements posted on social media, as well as through local newspapers, television, and radio, and made a point of stationing the van in a variety of

Figure 5.1. Sacchetta's studio van parked at the Cidade Tiradentes bus terminal in São Paulo.

Figure 5.2. Image of a woman speaking out on the side of the studio van. (Photo credit: André Bonfim)

Figure 5.3. The studio van parked at São Paulo's City Hall (Photo credit: André Bonfim)

different public spaces and neighborhoods, from downtown to the urban periphery. Timed to coincide with International Women's Week (March 7–14, 2016), production of the documentary capitalized on the heightened public attention on gender-based violence and other women's issues that typically accompany such commemorative dates. By all accounts, the production process/campaign was a success, generating over twelve hours of footage containing the recorded testimonies of 140 different women from all over São Paulo and Rio, twenty-six of which appear in the film.

Sexual harassment and assault are by definition highly traumatizing experiences, and any documentary filmmaker working with this subject matter is ethically obligated to adopt an interview protocol that minimizes the risk of retraumatization or other harm to the person sharing their testimony, as Lisa M. Cuklanz and Heather McIntosh stress in the introduction to their edited volume *Documenting Gendered Violence* (2015, 8–12). To this end, Sacchetta took a number of measures to preserve the safety, comfort, and agency of the women who taped their testimonies for the project. Most significantly, she did away with interviews altogether. Participants who recorded their accounts did so in complete privacy, directly addressing the camera without the presence or mediation of an interviewer. In addition, safeguarding the anonymity of women who didn't feel comfortable going completely public with their stories was a concern of utmost importance, as Sacchetta explains: "We know that women tend to be blamed for the violence inflicted upon them. [In the case of the participants who wished to keep their identities private] we didn't want to blur their faces the way it's done with criminals who appear on television. And we needed to make clear the reasons why women wanted to speak out without identifying themselves" ("Press Kit" 2016). The solution the director devised was to offer the participants the option of partially concealing their faces inside the van with special masks that she commissioned from artist Juliana Souza, who created expressive pieces in four different colors representing the emotions most commonly verbalized by survivors of sexual assault: anger (red), sadness (blue), shame (purple), and fear (yellow). Each mask was designed to cover all but the bottom third of the wearer's face so that only the mouth and chin remained visible, revealing some body language (a trembling chin, the chewing of a lip) without compromising anonymity in addition to ensuring a clear, unmuffled recording of the subject's voice.[8] Women who donned a mask in front of the camera—one-third of all those who participated in the campaign and in the documentary—also had the option of having their voices electronically distorted in postproduction (they also had the opportunity to change their minds about the voice distortion after viewing a rough cut of the film). The number of women who opted for the masks speaks to the continued power of cultural taboo around denouncing gender-based violence. Yet the fact that twice as many participants turned down the masks is just as telling insofar as it suggests that this power is waning in the wake of #PrimeiroAssédio, as Sacchetta points out in the press kit: "One-third of 140 . . . is a big number, yes, but the majority spoke out with their faces showing. Without fear or shame."

The production process of *Faces of Harassment* was relatively participatory and reflected a feminist sensibility in the sense that the survivors were empowered to decide what kind of personal story they wanted to tell and when to start and stop recording. The general protocol is demonstrated in the few instances in the documentary in which Sacchetta includes footage of her interactions with the women right before closing the van door:

Figure 5.4. Masks designed by Juliana Souza representing (from top left to bottom right) sadness, shame, anger, and fear. (Photo credit: Bruno Horowicz)

SACCHETTA: Are you going to cover your face?

WOMAN 17: Yes. Is there a way I should begin, or . . . ?

SACCHETTA: No. Just look into the camera and tell your story. There won't be anyone asking you questions.

WOMAN 17: Ok.

SACCHETTA: Just say whatever you like. I'll know when you're finished. You don't need to speak for five minutes. Take as long as you like.

WOMAN 17: Ok. [Sound of the van door closing.]⁹

This scene and a few others like it represent one of the few times that Sacchetta is visibly or audibly present in the documentary.

For the most part *Faces of Harassment* consists of one testimony after another. There is no music or other cinematic effects, resulting in a minimalist aesthetic that focuses all attention on the faces and voices of the twenty-six women whose testimonies were included in the final cut. It is as if Sacchetta transposed the viral #PrimeiroAssédio hashtag into cinematic form, and indeed the documentary addresses what the director viewed as a major drawback of the Twitter campaign, as she explains in the interview contained in this volume: "What most struck me when women began posting under the hashtag #PrimeiroAssédio was that there were no faces, no voices to go with the many, many testimonies I was reading. . . . I wanted to give voices and faces to all the stories that up until that point were just a bunch of words typed in an impersonal tweet or Facebook post." If the production process (with the attention-grabbing studio van) was an effort to intervene in or occupy public space with women's stories of harassment and assault, so too was the subsequent initiative to hold outdoor screenings of the finished documentary in urban environments. As Sacchetta is quoted in an article publicizing the open call for women to record their testimonies in March 2016: "We want to occupy the spaces of the city with the project. It's like, 'dude, you don't feel like reading the testimonies posted on the internet? Well, when you're walking on the street you're going to watch that account being projected on the side of a building'" (Quoted in Eiroa 2016).

Faces of Harassment consists of eighty minutes of back-to-back testimonies, all identical in format (direct address, with the subject sitting in front of a black background), prompting some critics to complain that the full-length documentary "would have been better as a short because some of the participants' accounts come off as repetitive" ("Press Kit" 2016). This perceived repetitiveness is indeed a defining feature of the film, but far from being a weakness, it arguably constitutes the work's most powerful rhetorical device from the perspective of feminist praxis. Repetition serves to underscore the same four key points that Juliana Farias and Think Olga underscored at the outset of #PrimeiroAssédio: girls start experiencing male sexual aggression when they are shockingly young (the average age being 9.7 years), accounts of such experiences are widely met with disbelief (often in the form of victim-blaming), the vast majority of aggressors are their supposed male protectors, and older generations of women tend toward complicity with this state of affairs.

The selection of the twenty-six testimonies that appear in the film and the thoughtfulness with which they are strung together creates complex meanings out of abundant repetition, constituting the most significant manifestation of the director's creative vision given the documentary's austere aesthetic. As far as selection is concerned, the various experiences featured in *Faces of Harassment* reflect the diversity of experiences recounted by the 140 women who participated in the project, with ages ranging from fourteen to eighty-five and representing a variety of racial, sexual, class, and religious backgrounds. The campaign to collect testimonies yielded a random sample that, as Sacchetta points out in the interview included in this volume, ended up hewing closely to official Brazilian statistics for sexual violence against women. The forms of male sexual aggression they denounce run the gamut and include ogling and voyeurism, stalking, street harassment, and everything from stranger and group rapes to father-daughter incest. Sacchetta notes that she deliberately chose to center her project around the word *assédio*, which can be translated into English as harassment or assault, as an allusion to #PrimeiroAssédio and to make the testimony-gathering campaign as inclusive as possible. Moreover, the lack of cultural consensus regarding the meaning of words like *assédio*, sexual violence, and rape becomes a recurring motif in the documentary. One survivor, Woman 20, wonders aloud about the meaning of *assédio* during a brief exchange with the director as she waits to record her testimony: "I'm actually a rape victim. It was a stranger. Anyway, does that count as harassment? Because I think it's the utmost form of it." Another,

Woman 9, concludes her account of catching a Peeping Tom while in the shower by affirming that, despite her friends' opinion that it was nothing because the man never touched or spoke to her, the experience merits denunciation as harassment: "This story goes to show how a look can be just as aggressive as a touch or a word, you know? The issue isn't so much the act itself as the violence it represents." A rape survivor, Woman 26, expresses her frustration at her friends' unwillingness to admit that what happened to her was rape: "Telling [people] . . . that I was drunk when it happened was pointless. . . . When someone doesn't consent, it's called rape." The inclusion of this observation and its placement at the very end of the film highlight the political struggle over the meaning of rape encapsulated in Cunha's failed bill and its attempt to remove the question of consent from the legal definition.

The ordering of the testimonies is particularly important in developing the film's argument. During her interview in chapter 12, Sacchetta explains that one of her main preoccupations during the editing process was to pace the testimonies in such a way as to avoid overwhelming viewers. The participants embody a range of emotions beyond the four represented by the masks. Some are empowered, sardonic, or hopeful, others are anguished, ashamed, or angry. The testimonies are ordered to alternate between these reactions, or, to paraphrase the filmmaker, going heavy and then taking a breather (*pegar pesado, dar uma respirada*). The first and last testimonies play a crucial role in transmitting the message of the documentary. Although a significant portion of the women either chose to wear masks or declared themselves to be "broken" by their harassment experience, none of these were suitable to open or close the documentary. The opening testimony is fitting because Woman 1 concludes her story by not only denouncing her experience but also unequivocally making clear that sexual violence is above all about power and stems from a toxic patriarchal culture: "He [the abuser] thought the fact that I'm a woman and he's a man gave him more power, more rights, and that's absurd." As Woman 12 observes, "These things usually happen with people who . . . abuse the power they have over us." A Black participant, Woman 16, calls attention to the intersection of sexism and racism in recounting how a man hurled a racist epithet at her when she rejected his advances after reluctantly accepting a drink he insisted on paying for despite her protestations: "It's important that we observe this kind of oppression, which starts off looking like chivalry, but is really about humiliating you and placing you in a position of servitude. As soon as I rejected him, he came at me with that bit of racism." Of all the testimonies, it is the one that closes the film, by Woman 26, that most emphatically reinforces the film's titular declaration regarding the necessity of speaking out about harassment:

> Two days ago, I told my mother [that I had been raped by a friend] over dinner. . . . And she looks at me and says: "But you were drunk. Who's to say you weren't leading him on?" Although I know what victim blaming is, when you hear that from your family it's devastating. . . . I had to point a finger at her and say: "Even if I were completely naked, said I wanted to, and then changed my mind a second later—'No, I don't want to'—he didn't have the right to do what he did." She looked at me silently for a while and said, "You're right, daughter. All this time I've blamed myself [for similar things I've been through]. I'm going to rethink my own experiences in light of what you've just said."

These are the final words spoken in the documentary, underscoring the generation gap in how women perceive Brazil's sexual culture and suggesting the power of speaking out to change hearts and minds. The mother's statement, as recounted by Woman 26, serves as an invitation for female spectators to reflect on their own lives and rethink similar experiences as well.

The imperative and empowering potential of denunciation that *Faces of Harassment* endorses has long been the cornerstone of feminist anti-rape activism. As admirable as this position might be, it is worth questioning whether it constitutes a sufficient basis for an effective movement aimed at eliminating sexual violence, as Tanya Serisier (2018, 12) argues in her book *Speaking Out*. As she bluntly puts it, "Breaking the silence, despite its significant cultural impact, has not ended sexual violence, nor does it seem to have significantly reduced it, or to have eradicated the stigma associated with being a rape victim." Serisier is particularly critical of hashtag campaigns in the United States that hinge on calls to speak out, noting, "The question . . . of what kind of a politics speaking out might produce that goes beyond more speech seems difficult or even impossible to answer within a political frame in which the act of speech is so dominant" (115). Sacchetta's film, conceived as the outgrowth of such a campaign, is precisely the kind of project that Serisier critiques. After all, the political project of the documentary is encapsulated in its titular call for women to speak out. The film's entire logic is predicated on the importance of survivor testimonies, and *Faces of Harassment* ends with an invitation for women to visit the project's companion website, where visitors can listen to the uncut version of all 140 testimonies (including those not featured in the film) and even record and submit their own testimonies for possible inclusion on the site. These points notwithstanding, the very fact that one-third of the women who participated in Sacchetta's projects chose to wear masks while recording their testimonies suggests that there was, at the time of the film's production, a social need to validate speaking out. Several participants attest to this need, such as Woman 3, who recounts being molested by a school aide: "I'd like to share this not only because they are terrible things but because I want to send a message to all the women and girls who have suffered any kind of abuse or harassment: don't remain silent, and don't wait as long as I did—fifteen years—to open up and speak the truth." Reflecting on relatives' advice that she not disturb the family peace by denouncing recurrent sexual abuse by her step-grandfather to her grandmother, Woman 8 declares, "I wish I'd done something about it at the time. If this feminist surge had happened three years ago, I might have brought it up with my family." Upon describing inappropriate comments by a radiologist during her cancer treatments, Woman 12 concludes, "I didn't tell anyone about it. I didn't confront him. But I should have, so I think this is a great opportunity to speak out now." Woman 14 echoes these sentiments, opining, "It's good to expose these stories. . . . Yes, I think harassment has to be reported—if someone makes a pass at you or whatever—so that other women won't have to go through what I did." Moreover, speaking out means different things to the different women who participate in *Faces of Harassment* and Sacchetta refrains from imposing a unifying message in this regard.

Another critique Serisier makes of mainstream feminist anti-rape politics is that its message championing speaking out has historically centered white, cisgender, heterosexual, middle-class, highly educated women whose privileges afford them platforms unavailable to women who are marginalized on the basis of race, gender identity, sexual orientation, class, and/or educational status, among other axes of difference. In *Faces of Harassment*, however, women who represent the normative intersection of whiteness, heterosexuality, middle-class or elite economic status women, and youth appear to constitute less than half of the participants featured.

One-third of the women wear masks and relatively few specify their sexual orientation or class (although some do), complicating attempts to ascertain the racial, sexual, class, and other identities of all twenty-six participants. Nevertheless, it is safe to say that over half of the women occupy some intersection of racial, sexual, class, age, and/or religious difference, suggesting that Sacchetta's documentary goes beyond mere inclusiveness to actively center marginalized perspectives and decenter privileged ones.

This prioritizing of less privileged voices is most readily apparent in the film's treatment of the issue of whether to report sexual abuse to the police. Sacchetta selects and orders the testimonies in a way that avoids presenting the police as women's saviors and that suggests an intersectional sensibility. Of the handful of participants who explicitly mention police involvement in their cases, only one—Woman 17—explicitly advocates it as a solution for other women. This participant, who wears a mask and appears to be white, relates how she filed a police report after learning that she had been gang raped while passed out at a party and that members of her social circle were circulating a video of what happened:

> Woman 17: The right thing to do is to report it to the police. That's what I did and it made me feel much better, even though I know it [the ensuing investigation and court case] is going to be hard and may take years to get resolved. You have to confront people [the abusers] and stand up for your rights. And that's exactly what I did.

On its own, this statement paints the police as a one-size-fits-all solution. Yet within the context of the documentary, it is disputed and qualified by multiple statements by Black women, the most forceful example being Woman 18, whose testimony is placed immediately after the one quoted above. In one of the longest and most anguished parts in the documentary, this participant, a light-skinned Afro-Brazilian woman, recounts how police officers who are supposedly specialists in assisting women survivors egregiously mishandled her report of being assaulted during a consultation with a ninety-six-year-old pai-de-santo. Recounting how a detective, skeptical of her account, ordered her to subject herself to the same abuse a second time and record it (which she did), she states, "When the police—the very people who should protect us and care for us—make us go through this violence twice, they are only multiplying the number of violence cases against women." The case is poignant for its revelation of the intersection of gender, race, and religion. In a similar vein, another Black participant, Woman 4, relates how the police dismissed her desperate pleading for them to protect her mother from her abusive father, calling viewers' attention to the intersections of sexism, racism, and classism, declaring, "This is one of my best examples of how the police don't protect us, especially in the poorer parts of town." Woman 11, an Afro-Brazilian lesbian who was dating a trans man at the time of her assault, describes the indifference of the police, who watched impassively and left her to fend for herself as two men attempted to rape her while spewing homophobic and transphobic slurs: "I started screaming and the policemen in the bar only looked at me as if nothing was happening. And they [the assailants] said, 'You like dating a woman who looks like a man, so I'm going to show you what a real man is. Because you don't know what that is. That's why you date women.'" The strategic placement of these four testimonies center the experiences of Black women and make clear that Woman 17's recommendation that survivors seek out the assistance of the police is grounded in her own racial, sexual, class, and other privileges. In this way, *Faces of Harassment* underscores how women's recourse in the wake of sexual violence drastically varies according to their social location.

Sacchetta's campaign to collect women's stories in March 2016 yielded a total of 140 testimonies, of which she was only able to use twenty-six in her film. The time constraints of the project posed an ethical quandary, as she explains in her interview:

> In making the film we took thirteen hours of footage and edited it down to eighty minutes. And I said to myself, I can't collect 140 testimonies only to use pieces of twenty-six of them and leave the rest on the cutting room floor. We wanted all of the voices to be heard, but we weren't about to turn all of the footage into a thirteen-hour film! So, we needed another container for the material that we couldn't use in the documentary.

The filmmaker resolved the dilemma by creating a companion website where visitors could also view all 140 testimonies uncut and even record and upload their own testimonies for potential inclusion on the platform. Although it was unplanned, *Faces of Harassment* became, in this way, billed as a transmedia project. This transmedia component has multiplied the documentary's dialogue with social media, enabling viewers to share clips with the individual testimonies on their Twitter and Facebook accounts in the same way people shared women's #PrimeiroAssédio posts on social media during the Feminist Spring.

Street Harassment in *Enough with Catcalling*

Similar to *Faces of Harassment*, *Enough with Catcalling* is a full-length documentary, filmed in the wake of #PrimeiroAssédio, that explores the phenomenon of male sexual aggression toward girls and women in Brazil. Like Paula Sacchetta, directors Amanda Kamanchek and Fernanda Frazão were journalists in their early thirties based in the city of São Paulo at the time the film was launched. Structurally-speaking, the two documentaries could hardly be more different: whereas the minimalist *Faces of Harassment* treats a wide variety of gender-based violence through an uninterrupted series of twenty-six different women who speak directly to the camera inside the featureless cocoon of Sacchetta's studio van, the crowdfunded *Enough with Catcalling* approaches the subject of street harassment by focusing on how it affects the lives of three very different women whose perspectives are complemented by talking heads interviews with feminist experts (including historian Margareth Rago, philosopher Djamila Ribeiro, and Think Olga founder Juliana Farias) as well as clips of a male moderator–led group discussion in which several men debate the topics.[10] The result is a rich, multi-perspectival treatment of the quotidian reality of women living in Brazilian cities. For all these differences, however, the two documentaries share at least three characteristics: they both adopt an intersectional lens, dialogue with social media, and constitute transmedia projects.

The centrality of intersectionality and social media in *Enough with Catcalling* is evident from the opening of the film, which begins with a panoramic shot of the São Paulo skyline pivoting to an overhead view of a city street, mostly empty except for a few buses. As the drone-operated camera slowly follows the street, an intersection comes into view, then another, cutting to overhead shots of two more intersections before cutting again to a panoramic shot of a favela perched on the side of hill and then to overhead shots of various other neighborhoods and eventually other parts of Brazil, including intersections of a dirt road in Lauro de Freitas, Bahia. The moving camera is accompanied by a voice-over in which a woman recites brief testimonies of street harassment:

> September 13, 2017. Yellow line, Paulista subway station. On my way home from work on a crowded subway car, I felt something warm on my pants. When I looked behind me I saw a guy with his zipper open. I started yelling and hitting him in the face. . . . I was screaming my head off . . . but no one helped me.

Similar testimonies by other women follow one after another until the voices start to overlap and transform into an indistinct chatter. Meanwhile, a lone woman appears on the screen crossing the second of these dirt road intersections and is immediately approached by a man before the camera cuts yet again to more overhead views of increasingly busy city intersections, the traffic serving as a visual counterpart to the cacophony of women's voices. As the camera zooms out and returns to the same opening shot of the São Paulo skyline, the women's voices fade away. The combination of overhead shots of multiple cities conveys the massive scope of the problem of street harassment but also its relative social invisibility, given that for the most part the camera's altitude renders it difficult to discern the human activities below. The very next scene, in which Frazão dons a pair of video glasses and steps out into the street to endure an onslaught of male sexual aggression, announces the film's intent to position viewers in the shoes of the 98 percent of Brazilian girls and women who report having been sexually harassed in the street, according to a study by Think Olga.

The imagery of traffic intersections that dominates the beginning of the documentary, and the wide range of neighborhoods shown (affluent, low-income, urban, small town), call to mind the key metaphors of maps and intersecting streets in legal theorist Kimberlé Crenshaw's writing and public talks on intersectionality, the Black feminist term she coined in the early 1990s to theorize how systems of oppression overlap and compound one another (1991, 2016). One of the experts featured in the film is Afro-Brazilian feminist philosopher Djamila Ribeiro, whose intervention stresses the importance of centering Blackness in discussions of sexual harassment in addition to serving the didactic function of introducing and defining the term *intersectionality*:

> The combination of racism and sexism has prevented Black women . . . from being seen as subjects, as people. At the same time, being a Black woman means resisting. As Black women who have long been excluded from political movements and

From Tweets to the Streets | 131

Figures 5.5., 5.6., and 5.7. Overhead shots of intersections in *Chega de fiu fiu* (screenshots).

demands for rights, we've been able to figure out ways of theorizing that account for our unique situation. So when we think in terms of intersectionality—which is a term developed by Black women—it means understanding that these oppressions [racism and sexism] intersect, they act in concert in such a way that for Black women they are inseparable.

Consistent with an intersectional sensibility, the film features three women who experience sexual harassment from very different social locations: Rosa Luz, a twenty-two-year-old Black trans woman from the outskirts of Brasília (Gama) who is a college student, visual artist, activist, and rapper; Raquel Gomes dos Santos, a twenty-nine-year-old queer Black woman who works as a manicurist while pursuing a nursing degree; and Tereza Chaves, a thirty-three-year-old white, upper-middle-class cisgender woman who works as a history teacher in São Paulo. Each woman appears in various contexts: sitting at home for a formal interview, walking or cycling in their cities at various hours of the day and night, using public transportation, and, in the case of Rosa, engaging in performance art in what appears to be a bus or subway terminal and rapping for the camera in the film's final scene.

Enough with Catcalling explores what it is like to move through Brazil's urban environments in each of the three women's bodies, emphasizing the under-recognized indignities and dangers confronted daily by Black, queer, and trans women in particular. Raquel is introduced in a scene in which footage of her riding a city bus is accompanied by a voice-over in which she describes how the intersection of race, class, and sizeism have impacted her life:

> I used to be much heavier than I am now, but I had to lose a lot of weight for college. I was embarrassed to leave my house because I couldn't fit through the turnstiles on the bus and the bus drivers would make a point of humiliating me by not letting me board through the main door. So yeah, I lost weight so I could get an education because otherwise it wouldn't have been viable for me to go back and forth for school. But I could care less if people stare at me and think I'm fat. I think I'm just fine and I don't have to measure up to anyone else's standards.

Rosa likewise notes that how a person is treated when they walk down the street is not about their actual body, but rather societal perception of their body:

Figure 5.8. Rosa Luz (screenshot).

Figure 5.9. Raquel Gomes dos Santos (screenshot).

Figure 5.10. Tereza Chaves (screenshot).

> After my transition everything changed. Men started looking at me differently and I started to feel uncomfortable walking down the street. Suddenly I was being treated like an object, harassed, honked at. It started happening all the time. When society saw me as a man, I had the privilege of being able to walk in the street without anyone bothering me. Even if society reads you as an effeminate gay man, you're still a man and have some privileges in a sexist and patriarchal society.

Most important, she points out that street harassment poses the most lethal threat to trans women, especially Black trans women like her.

As Sacchetta does with the twenty-six women featured in *Faces of Harassment*, Kamanchek and Frazão's film gives faces and voices to the flood of tweets that came out under the hashtag #PrimeiroAssédio via Rosa, Raquel, and Tereza. Yet *Enough with Catcalling* dialogues with social media in other ways as well. The string of testimonies in the film's opening scene are reminiscent of the stories Brazilians posted under the hashtag #PrimeiroAssédio in late 2015 and early 2016. Moreover, one of the participants in the talking heads interviews is Juliana Farias, who recounts the story behind the viral hashtag campaign. Images of several tweets are even incorporated into the film, showcasing other hashtags that emerged during the Primavera Feminista: #MeuAmigoSecreto (#MySecretFriend), #MeuProfessorAbusador (#MyAbusiveProfessor), #MeuMotoristaAbusador (#MyAbusiveDriver). Through the talking heads testimonies of Farias and others, Kamanchek and Frazão draw a straight line between #PrimeiroAssédio and the dozens of women's marches that took over Brazilian city streets between October and December 2015, reflecting the film's overall argument that a nationwide epidemic of street harassment denies Brazilian women their lawful right to occupy streets as pedestrians, cyclists, skateboarders, commuters, citizens, and protesters.

The documentary *Enough with Catcalling*, like *Faces of Harassment*, is a part of a transmedia project; however, whereas the latter started out as a documentary and eventually turned into a transmedia project after Sacchetta decided to post all 140 uncut testimonies on the film's companion website, the opposite is true for the former. *Enough with Catcalling*, which was the first film for both directors, grew out of Think Olga's homonymous online platform launched in 2014, consisting of a crowdsourced forum for collecting data on street harassment. The site made it possible for women to use their smartphones to type their denunciations (including a brief description of the offense along with the precise date, time, and location where it occurred) into an online form; the data from each report is published on a map with clickable "pins" akin to Yelp or other commercial services featuring interactive maps. The platform has the advantage of offering an anonymous outlet for women to ensure that the experiences of sexual harassment become part of the public record and are "counted" regardless of whether they choose to file a formal report with the police. It has proven to be a valuable tool for generating data and providing a clear, visual demonstration of the alarming scale of the problem. Kamanchek and Frazão's documentary grew out of the Enough with Catcalling campaign and was galvanized—but not initially inspired—by #PrimeiroAssédio.

So successful was Think Olga's activism and the #PrimeiroAssédio campaign in particular that they have been widely credited for the passage of recent legislation revising the Penal Code to include a new category of sexual violence: that of *importunação sexual* or sexual importuning, defined as "to practice against someone, without their consent, a libidinous act with the objective of satisfying one's own lust or the lust of a third party" (Presidência da República 2018). With the advent of this new category, there was finally an umbrella legal term for a range of other abuses that the law had not previously regarded as crimes. And while legal remedies alone are insufficient to eliminate sexual violence (and, indeed, can frequently have undesirable consequences themselves), the increased currency of the term *assédio* and the creation of the legal category of *importunação sexual* signal, according to Almeida, assert important "changes in [Brazilian] sensibilities concerning notions of violence that are also at the root of processes leading to the formation of Human Rights," especially the recognition of the personhood of women and girls (2019, 24).

Concluding Remarks

Faces of Harassment and *Enough with Catcalling* both represent emerging women documentarians' responses to epidemic levels of gender-based violence in Brazil. Whereas Kamanchek and Frazão focus on three different women, providing viewers a sense of what it is like to move through Brazilian cities in their bodies and revealing street harassment to be a denial of women's right to the city, Sacchetta selects twenty-six short, fragmentary testimonies that collectively declare the need for women to speak out about sexual violence, without dictating what form speaking out should take. Carrying forward a history of feminist filmmaking in Brazil dating back at least to the 1970s, these three documentarians herald a new chapter in this tradition characterized by a nascent intersectional feminist sensibility, synergistic relationships with social media, and exploration of transmedia projects. In this sense they are part of a global movement of digital-based feminist anti-harassment activism (Desborough 2018; Fileborn 2017).

Both documentaries take intersectional approaches by centering Black women, and particularly lesbian and trans women in the case of *Enough with Catcalling*. Yet all three women behind the camera in these two films are white, cisgender, middle-class journalists from Brazil's most prosperous southern city, revealing that the degree of change represented by this new generation of filmmakers remains limited, at least for now. The intersectional lens that they adopt represents a welcome shift in Brazilian cinema, yet it does not change the fact that women without the same privileges remain largely excluded from the national film industry. Although their presence is most evident in the realm of short films due to funding and other barriers, there is a growing number of talented young Black women directors in Brazil. If *Faces of Harassment* and *Enough with Catcalling* herald a new chapter in Brazilian women's feminist documentary filmmaking, it is a chapter yet to be fully realized.

Notes

1. One study found that the hashtag #PrimeiroAssédio (FirstAssault), along with #PrimeiroAbuso (First Abuse, a variation that is also popular), was tweeted and retweeted a total of 88,847 times by 35,266 discrete users in the six days following its launch; these numbers do not include posts on Facebook, where the hashtags also went viral (Perdigão 2015). Presumably, a significant portion of these users were women and girls who posted their own personal testimonies.

2. For a history of Brazil's Feminist Spring, see Medeiros and Fanti 2019.

3. The platform consists of an interactive map that allows users to denounce incidents of sexual harassment and violence on the spot, generating consultable data that also helps warn women about local "hot spots" in their cities. The resulting data can be leveraged to pressure owners of bars and other establishments where harassment occurs to take appropriate action. See https://thinkolga.com/projetos/chega-de-fiu-fiu/.

4. For a history of Brazilian women documentary (and fiction) filmmakers from the 1970s up to the early 2010s, see Marsh 2012.

5. As of this writing, Farias's tweets cited in this article can be found on Twitter under the @ThinkOlga handle.

6. Farias's original TED Talk can be viewed at https://www.youtube.com/watch?v=BpRyQ_yFjy8. It was posted on July 13, 2015.

7. Five days into the Twitter campaign, Think Olga tweeted that based on a sample of 3,111 tweets, the average age mentioned in testimonies posted under the hashtag #PrimeiroAssédio was 9.7 years old.

8. See Sacchetta's explanation of the story behind the masks in the interview included in this volume.

9. Given that the documentary consists entirely of a series of twenty-six unnamed women who give their personal testimonies of gender-based violence and for lack of a better option, I have opted to identify the participants in terms of their order of appearance, e.g., "Woman 17."

10. As noted in the film's opening credits, 1,219 people contributed to the crowdfunding campaign on the Catarse platform; donors received copies of a special cordel chapbook titled *Chega de fiu fiu (Enough with Catcalling)* by feminist *cordelista* Jarid Arraes. By all accounts the crowdfunding campaign was a huge success, reaching its stated goal in the first twenty-four hours and ultimately raising 322 percent of the amount requested.

Works Cited

Almeida, Heloísa Buarque de. 2019. "From Shame to Visibility: Hashtag Feminism and Sexual Violence in Brazil." *Sexualidad, Salud y Sociedad: Revista Latinoamericana* 33 (December): 19–41.

Arraes, Jarid. 2017. "Chega de fiu fiu." *Cordel*. São Paulo: Jarid Arraes.

Bluevision. 2018. "Conheça a história do documentário 'Chega de fiu fiu.'" September 19, 2018. https://bluevisionbraskem.com/desenvolvimento-humano/conheca-a-historia-do-documentario-chega-de-fiu-fiu/.

Crenshaw, Kimberlé. 1991. "Mapping the Margins: Intersectionality, Identity Politics, and Violence against Women of Color." *Stanford Law Review* 43 (6): 1241. https://doi.org/10.2307/1229039.

———. 2016. "The Urgency of Intersectionality" TED video. December 7, 2016. Los Angeles. https://www.ted.com/talks/kimberle_crenshaw_the_urgency_of_intersectionality?language=en.

Cuklanz, Lisa M., and Heather McIntosh, eds. 2015. *Documenting Gendered Violence: Representations, Collaborations, and Movements*. New York: Bloomsbury.

Desborough, Karen. 2018. "The Global Anti-Street Harassment Movement: Digitally-Enabled Feminist Activism." In *Mediating Misogyny: Gender, Technology, and Harassment*, edited by Jacqueline Ryan Vickery and Tracy Everbach, 333–51. Cham, Switzerland: Springer Nature.

Eiroa, Camila. 2016. "Projeto recruta mulheres em São Paulo para gravarem depoimentos sobre assédio." *Trip News*, March 4, 2016. https://revistatrip.uol.com.br/tpm/projeto-precisamos-falar-do-assedio-recruta-mulheres-em-sao-paulo-para-gravarem-depoimentos.

Fileborn, Bianca. 2017. "'Justice 2.0: Street Harassment Victims' Use of Social Media and Online Activism as Sites of Informal Justice." *The British Journal of Criminology* 57 (6): 1482–1501. https://doi.org/10.1093/bjc/azw093.

Kamanchek Lemos, Amanda, and Fernanda Frazão, dirs. *Chega de fiu fiu* [*Enough with Catcalling*]. 2018; ThinkOlga Online. https:thinkolga.com/ferramentas/documentario-chega-de-fiu-fiu/.

Marsh, Leslie L. 2012. *Brazilian Women's Filmmaking: From Dictatorship to Democracy*. Urbana: University of Illinois Press.

Medeiros, Jonas, and Fabiola Fanti. 2019. "Recent Changes in the Brazilian Feminist Movement: The Emergence of New Collective Actors." In *Socio-Political Dynamics within the Crisis of the Left: Argentina and Brazil*, edited by Juan Pablo Ferrero, Ana Natalucci, and Luciana Tatagiba. Lanham, MD: Rowman & Littlefield.

Perdigão, Luísa. 2015. "#PrimeiroAssédio: Uma breve análise sobre relatos e feminismo na rede." *LABIC (Laboratório de Estudos Sobre Imagem e Cultura)* (blog). November 6, 2015. http://www.labic.net/blog/primeiroassedio-uma-breve-analise-sobre-relatos-e-feminismo-na-rede/.

"Press Kit." 2016. *Precisamos falar do assédio* [*Faces of Harassment*]. Mira Filmes.

Presidência da República. 2018. "Lei Nº 13.718 de 24 de setembro de 2018." http://www.planalto.gov.br/ccivil_03/_ato2015-2018/2018/lei/L13718.htm.

Sacchetta, Paula, dir. *Precisamos falar do assédio* [*Faces of Harassment*]. 2016. São Paulo: Mira Filmes.

Serisier, Tanya. 2018. *Speaking Out: Feminism, Rape and Narrative Politics*. New York: Palgrave.

Chapter 6

Motherhood and Making Kin in Contemporary Brazilian Cinema

Jack A. Draper III

Brazilian families have often incorporated non-biologically related members since colonial times. Female domestic workers have been a common presence in elite and middle-class families, often developing close affective ties with family members—in particular a quasi-maternal relationship between nannies and their wards. Alternatively, the children of domestic workers have sometimes received a kinship status as godchildren (*afilhados/as*) of their parent's employers—a paternalistic and often, but not always, more distant (and certainly more unequal) relationship. Donna Haraway's (2016) theory of making kin can help us to consider the development of these forms of kinship as they have evolved and been represented in cinema in recent years. The evolving state of kinship ties between elite and middle-class nuclear families and their employees' families can be understood in this light as a *kinnovation* in which new practices of becoming family with each other are being established in contemporary Brazil. *Que horas ela volta* (*The Second Mother* [Muylaert, 2015]) and *Campo Grande* (Kogut, 2015) are two films by creative and skillful filmmakers with an acute sensitivity to kinnovation in today's São Paulo and Rio de Janeiro. The films follow two different trajectories of women and children making kin in the multi-class context of domestic employers and workers. *The Second Mother* traces the process of the empowerment of a nanny in relation to her employers' family through the catalyst of her own biological daughter's influence, a girl who had grown up outside the hierarchical relationships in the elite familial home. It is a dual process of becoming equal to adoptive kin and becoming mother to children, biologically related or not. An inverse process is established in *Campo Grande*, in which a middle-class mother must fill in for the absence of a former employee's daughter, looking after a poor boy and girl as they search for this woman, their biological mother. A rethinking of the Nietzschean terminology of "becoming hard" and "becoming soft" can help us to theorize what these processes look like in psychological-affective terms (Bull 2014, 143–47). While Val (Regina Casé) in *The Second Mother* must "become harder" in certain ways to achieve a more empowered identity as mother, Regina (Carla Ribas) of *Campo Grande* must "become softer" in order to make kin with the children who show up on her doorstep in need of her care. The general trend represented is a move toward more egalitarian forms of kinship, even as the characters continue to struggle with the postcolonial legacy of Brazil's social-class hierarchy.

The Second Mother: Kinnovating by Becoming Harder

A consideration of the character arc of Val (Regina Casé), the main protagonist of *The Second Mother*, will reveal a process of kinnovation relying on her personal development from a more dependent situation as a quasi-family member of her employer to a more autonomous situation in a household with her biological daughter and grandson. Val's work life is a common one for nannies in Brazil, requiring her to spend time away from her own child, Jéssica (Camila Márdila), to care for the child of a wealthy family. Also typical is the simultaneously close yet hierarchical relationship she has developed with her employers, Bárbara (Karine Teles) and Carlos (Lourenço Mutarelli), the parents of her ward Fabinho (Michel Joelsas). Likewise, she has developed a close, mother-like relationship with Fabinho by the time the main action of the film begins with Fabinho in his late teens. Her relationship with Jéssica, on the other hand, has suffered from their separation, as Val works in a different city and rarely sees her biological daughter. Largely for economic reasons, she is in a position of devoting more of her time and energy to being a quasi-family member in a wealthy household than she can devote to her own biological daughter. The "quasi" nature of the former familial relationship is emphasized over the course of the film through reminders of the social class divide that separates Val and her own daughter from her employers' family.

The figure of the nanny, particularly the Black nanny, has been an important one in Brazilian households and of interest to Brazilian and foreign artists since at least the nineteenth century. Even then, in the era of slavery, this was a contested figure. According to Lilia Moritz Schwarcz (2018),

> At times visual works conveyed a romantic and sentimentalised slavery. In these cases, painters emphasised the bonds of 'affection' that allegedly developed between enslaved nannies and the white children in their care. This was a kind of exotic and even official (and almost impossible) reality. These romantic and sentimental depictions existed in counterpoint to another type of image of black nannies at the beginning of the nineteenth century. These images used the same symbol as an example of the violence of slavery, using the image of this woman compelled to do mothering labour by force to denounce the internal horrors of the system. (983)

More recently, in the field of documentary film, Consuelo Lins's *Babás* (*Nannies*, 2010) emphasizes the continuing problematic legacy of this subaltern "mothering labor" in the hierarchical yet intimate relationships of working-class Black women with the children they care for and with their employers, the parents of said children. Lins goes so far as to capture her own family album photos from her childhood on film, as well as to include home video scenes, in order to demonstrate that her own nanny was always represented marginally by her family's photographers and videographers, at the edge of the images or excluded from them, despite the nanny's putative familial status. This twenty-first-century cinematic perspective and the divergent nineteenth-century paintings alike are in keeping with an anecdote oft repeated by Brazilian ex-president Luiz Inácio Lula da Silva, about a comment once made to him by the maid of a wealthy family. After the maid's employer said at dinner that she was like a member of the family, the maid said privately to Lula in the kitchen that if he wanted to know if she was really part of the family, he should ask her employer if she is mentioned in his will. Thus since before the beginnings of Brazil as an independent nation-state two hundred years ago, and up to the present day, we can find a tension over the role of poor, Black, or mixed-race women as employees in middle-class or elite families, a tension related to the perception of hypocrisy regarding the claim that they are members—or "almost" members—of the family.

With respect to the nanny in *The Second Mother*, director and screenwriter Muylaert takes the important step (in the same vein as Lins) of making her the central character, centering the story around a figure usually marginalized in elite and middle-class narratives. However, Val begins the story in a relatively dependent, disempowered position with respect to the family she is working for as a live-in nanny. Only by going through a process of reshaping her kinship ties, or kinnovation, does Val achieve a more autonomous, empowered status in her work and social life. This involves, simultaneously, a psychological-emotional process of "becoming hard" with respect to her preestablished, hierarchical kinship ties in her employers' family.

Val's process of kinnovation begins with the arrival of her young adult daughter Jéssica for a temporary stay in the household she works in. This introduction of a new element in a stable situation conforms to the first two parts of the three-part narrative structures Muylaert tends to rely on in her screenplays, in which, according to Leslie L. Marsh, "she pushes her protagonists out of their comfortable (but unfulfilling) routines, forces them to confront some new scenario that serves as the dramatic (and sometimes tragic) turning point and then lets these characters awaken in various respects to a new visibility or way of being" (2017, 166). The narrative of *The Second Mother* is no exception to this tendency, and no wonder, since it makes for a compelling plot structure about the empowerment of a woman of color who is in a subaltern position in her society in terms of class, race, and gender. In this film, there is a reversal of roles in terms of authority in that the daughter Jéssica shows the mother Val the way to become harder, more autonomous, and resistant to her employers' ambiguous and virtually unlimited affective demands, which come on top of the material requirements of housekeeping such as cooking and cleaning for the family.

Throughout the film, Muylaert emphasizes the restrictions of the built space and accompanying social borders within the bourgeois Brazilian household. Many of the ripples and waves introduced by Jéssica into the initially calm waters of the household's social dynamic are generated by the manner in which she shows very little regard for the hierarchical social rules which, by contrast, her mother and her employers have spent years reproducing in the class-coded areas of their common domestic space. One early example is how Val keeps to her own, small bedroom in the maid's quarters at night, where she also expects Jéssica to sleep when she comes to visit. Shortly after arriving, Jéssica notes that the house has an unoccupied guest bedroom, and she accepts to sleep there when the father of the family, Carlos, offers the room to her as a guest. This invitation also speaks to a gendered power dynamic between husband Carlos and wife Bárbara—Carlos feels free to bend the rules regarding social class barriers in his household without consulting with his wife, and Bárbara seems to feel that she must tolerate these rule violations to a certain extent, even if she doesn't agree with them. The financial dynamic of the household reflects this power dynamic, since Carlos later reveals that he is the primary source of the family's wealth due to his large inheritance.

The dividing line between the kitchen and the dining room is also one that is emphasized through cinematography, acting, and plot. As was the case with the sleeping quarters, the film establishes that Val "knows her place" as being in the kitchen, whereas the dining room is the space that belongs to her employers' family. Jéssica's behavior within the household once again breaks through this social barrier, undermining it in ways that create a high degree of anxiety for Val herself, as well as for her coworker, housecleaner Edna (Helena Albergaria). On her first full day staying in the house, Carlos is very friendly and welcoming to Jéssica, expressing enthusiasm for her studies in architecture and inviting her to eat lunch with him in the dining room to converse. Meanwhile Val cooks lunch for them and remains behind the kitchen door eavesdropping on her daughter and Carlos along with her colleague Edna. A stationary camera positioned near the kitchen sink captures the doorway to the dining room and how Val only crosses this threshold when called by Carlos to clear the dishes, even though her own visiting daughter is dining in the other room. On this side of the closed kitchen door, in the space designated for domestic workers, Edna and Val pantomime a wordless conversation with each other, both expressing their anxiety, even outrage, over the fact that Val's daughter is breaking all the social rules they thought had existed for the daughter of a working-class woman, simply by having a casual conversation with Carlos over lunch in the dining room (see figure 6.1). One other plot element regarding food and the kitchen involves Val's admonishment of Jéssica for eating "Fabinho's" ice cream. After discovering that Jéssica had been eating and wanted to eat more of this particular flavor, Val gives her daughter a stern warning that she should not eat "their" ice cream. Val knows that even if Carlos is lackadaisical about social class boundaries in Jéssica's case, the mother of the household, Bárbara, will be (at the very least) annoyed that Jéssica is eating Fabinho's special ice cream. The concern over how Bárbara perceives Jéssica's presence and actions in the household is well founded, as becomes obvious in the tension that arises over the space of the family's pool in the backyard.

Val demonstrates in the very first moments of the film, even before the title, that she considers the pool to be a space restricted to her employers' family and their guests. Indeed, the swimming pool has become something like a metonym of bourgeois respectability and conspicuous consumption in twenty-first-century Brazilian and Argentine cinema, in films from Heitor Dhalia's *À deriva / Adrift* (2011 [2009]) to Marcelo Piñeyro's *Las viudas de los jueves / The Widows of Thursdays* (2010 [2009]) and Lucrecia Martel's *La ciénaga / The Swamp* (2015 [2001]) and *La mujer sin cabeza / The Headless Woman* (2009 [2008]). In all of these films, some form of contamination of the middle-class swimming pool occurs, which signals a disruption or corruption of the norms of everyday bourgeois life. At the beginning of *The Second Mother*, the pool appears to be an idyllic place for the young child Fabinho to play, but Val refuses to get into the pool with him, even though he asks her to, and she is the only other person around. The pool is thus established as a space that is hierarchically coded before anything else in the film, as a place not for the help but only for

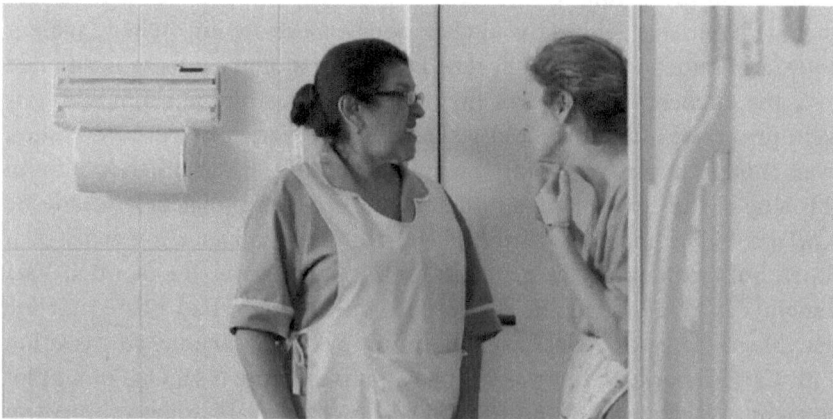

Figure 6.1. Val (Regina Casé) and Edna (Helena Albergaria) listen at the kitchen door to Val's daughter's conversation with Val's employer over lunch. (Courtesy Anna Muylaert)

the members of the household and their guests, who we can assume are considered as part of the same social class. After this prefatory scene about ten years before the main action of the film, the narrative jumps to the present day, when Jéssica comes to visit the household for the first time, after having been raised in the home of relatives in the northeastern city of Recife.

On her first tour of the house, which occurs at night, Carlos makes a point of turning the pool lights on for her to admire the swimming pool. Later in the film, Carlos and Bárbara's son Fabinho is splashing around in the pool with his friend. He pushes Jéssica into the pool as a joke, and she begins to splash around with them. Again, this scene of breaking social barriers is upsetting to Val, who has no wish to see her daughter break these barriers. However, Bárbara's reaction to seeing Jéssica in the pool takes the tension to a new level. Up to this point, she has not openly expressed her resentment of Jéssica's relative freedom of movement within the house, but shortly after this pool scene, Bárbara claims that she saw a "rat" in the pool and must have the pool entirely drained of water (incidentally, the amount of water usage that Bárbara feels entitled to because of her bigotry is shocking, considering the fact that the action is contemporaneous with major droughts in the São Paulo area).

This kind of obsessiveness about the cleanliness of pools is most akin to that displayed by a middle-class mother in one of the Argentine films mentioned above, *The Headless Woman*. The character of Josefina (Claudia Cantero) maintains a running monologue about the cleanliness of the pools that her family swims in, including her worry about a turtle swimming in one of them. Her concern about contamination is indirectly connected to the violent death of a lower-class, Indigenous boy. In the case of Bárbara, her perception that a working-class body in her pool represents a contamination is even more obvious, albeit with less deadly connotations. After ordering the pool to be drained, Bárbara also takes a more direct step of requesting that Val isolate—perhaps "quarantine" is the more appropriate word—Jéssica to the servants' quarters, including at night when she should sleep in the maid's quarters with Val. When Val tries to get Jéssica to accede to this request, the tension between Jéssica's desire for equal treatment and Val's desire to not challenge the status quo in her employers' household comes to a head. Jéssica feels betrayed by her mother and decides to leave to look for a place to stay with friends.

Jéssica's departure becomes a turning point for Val. The Nietzschean conceptions of weakness and strength of will, and the related behavioral tendencies of becoming soft and becoming hard (Bull 2011, 143–47), are helpful in understanding the transformative process Val goes through here. Jéssica's criticism of her mother's loyalty to her employer's rules over her love for her daughter strikes home, forcing Val to make a choice between compassion and love for Jéssica on the one hand and maintaining the status quo–affective politics in Bárbara and Carlos's home on the other. Her will to change is weakened by her long-standing habit of catering not only to the material but also to the emotional demands of her employers' household, so she must harden herself to these demands as she maintains or increases her compassion for her daughter, opening herself to a future relationship with Jéssica free of the social constraints of her bourgeois domestic workplace. Val becomes hard toward her employers' family to the point of achieving a leveling, wherein her own family is at least as important as her employers'. Importantly, it is not a reproduction of the power dynamic of the elite family, thus not reaching the level of a Nietzschean will to power since it does not create and reproduce its own subclass as her employers' family did. Further, although Val chooses to retire from her career as nanny and housekeeper at film's end to set up a household with Jéssica, even if she were to remain with the same family or work in a different household, the affective dynamics would be fundamentally changed. The scene that clearly marks this change is when Val decides to jump in the pool herself and splash around (in the shallow water when it is being refilled) while leaving a message for Jéssica, in order to prove her solidarity with Jéssica's rule breaking and thus her loyalty to her biological daughter over her employer (see figure 6.2). She has now established a boundary and a sense of proportion for the affective labor she would be willing to dispense on behalf of her employers' family. It is to this extent and in this interclass context that she has "become harder," while in a different relational vector she has become softer, more compassionate, to her own biological kin—daughter Jéssica and infant grandson Jorge. By establishing a household with the two, she hopes to be able to help her daughter avoid the economic necessity of living away from her child that she herself experienced after giving birth to Jéssica. In this sense she seeks to break the younger generations of her family out of the "global care chain," which entraps so many caretakers and domestic workers globally, in which "their oppression enables better conditions for more privileged women, who avoid (some) domestic work and pursue demanding professions" (Arruza, Bhattacharya, and Fraser 2019, 37).

Motherhood and Making Kin in Contemporary Brazilian Cinema | 147

Figure 6.2. Val finally rebels against the class-segregated spaces in her employer's house by climbing into the refilling pool. (Courtesy Anna Muylaert)

It is in this light that we can understand the pleasure Val takes, having moved into her own apartment, in serving coffee to Jéssica in her kitchen with her black and white coffee set. Originally Val had given this set to Bárbara, but the latter had no desire to use it, perhaps finding it tacky. Val then reappropriated the set for her own household (an act of "theft," which she brags about to impress and amuse her daughter). Acting and dialogue reveal Val's fascination for this coffee set, for its "beautiful," "modern" look and most importantly for the fact that the design of the set involves placing black cups on white saucers and vice versa. Val adores that this makes the coffee set, in her words to Jéssica, "different, like you" (see figure 6.3). We can also find a dual symbolism in the mixture of black and white cups, which likely appeals to Val on some level, or at the very least, which resonates with the film's larger narrative. Firstly, the racial overtones of black and white and the equal measure of each color placed on top as a cup and on the bottom as a saucer (three of each combination) suggest a leveling of social status between the races. At the same time, the duality of white and black as opposed to some in-between color does not confirm the traditional, nationalist conception of Brazil's essentially mixed racial identity. The social hierarchy revealed in the film does not allow for an affective sexual overcoming or mitigation of said hierarchy. (Indeed, when the wealthy heir Carlos surprises Jéssica—a young woman his son's age and his domestic servant's daughter—by proposing marriage, she laughs at the idea, assuming it's a joke.) The coffee set is also "modern," then, in the sense that Brazil's capital city Brasília is "modern"—it represents a utopian, republican impulse in Brazil, the country of the future, forever.

Here I will focus more closely on Haraway's concept of kinnovation mentioned above in order to illuminate Val's evolving relationships with her families, both biological and professional, and to anticipate how kinnovation is also evident in a different multi-class and multiracial constellation of characters in the next film I will discuss, *Campo Grande*. Haraway states that the purpose of her theory

> is to make "kin" mean something other/more than entities tied by ancestry or genealogy. The gently defamiliarizing move might seem for a while to be just a mistake, but then (with luck) appear as correct all along. Kin making is making persons, not necessarily as individuals or as humans. I was moved in college by Shakespeare's punning between kin and kind—the kindest were not necessarily kin as family; making kin and making kind (as category, care, relatives without ties by birth, lateral relatives, lots of other echoes) stretch the imagination and can change the story. . . . I think that the stretch and the recomposition of kin are allowed by the fact

Figure 6.3. Val admires her "modern" coffee set and brags to Jéssica (Camila Márdila) that she "stole" it from her employer, Bárbara (Karine Teles). (Courtesy Anna Muylaert)

> that all earthlings are kin in the deepest sense, and it is past
> time to practice better care of kinds-as-assemblages (not species
> one at a time). Kin is an assembling sort of word. All critters
> share a common "flesh," laterally, semiotically, and genealogi-
> cally. Ancestors turn out to be very interesting strangers; kin
> are unfamiliar (outside what we thought was family or gens),
> uncanny, haunting, active. (102–3)

Through distance enforced by economic necessity, Val's daughter became somewhat estranged from her. This is an inversion of the process of making kin, demonstrating that the bond of genealogical kinship can be weakened if left unnurtured. The film then reveals that Val has "made kin" with the boy (Fabinho) who she is employed to care for as a nanny, becoming very close to him in a mother-like relationship. We see in this relationship and in the broader power and affective dynamics between Val and her employers' family that some forms of kinship (in this case non-genealogical) may have problematic elements and reflect inequality in society. Women like Val in a subaltern position in a global care chain must struggle to maintain and strengthen their kinship ties (in this case biological) beyond the affective obligations and restrictions placed on them by their employer(s).

Campo Grande: Kinnovating by Becoming Softer

On the other hand, *Campo Grande* more directly demonstrates a process of kinnovation between those unfamiliar with each other, making new kin and finding a way toward both true kindness and kinship between those who had been strangers. The film begins with a boy and a girl whose mother (anonymous, though we learn her name is Ana [uncredited] at film's end) leaves her children on the doorstep of a middle-class woman, Regina (Carla Ribas). This is an action in the tradition of the *roda dos enjeitados* (literally, the circle of the abandoned/rejected) described in Brazil as early as Henry Koster's *Travels in Brazil*, published in 1816. Koster describes the roda dos enjeitados thusly:

> An infant is frequently during the night laid at the door of a
> rich person; and on being discovered in the morning is taken
> in, and is almost invariably allowed to remain: it is brought up

> with the children of the house (if its color is not too dark to admit of this), certainly as a dependent, but not as a servant. (Koster 2016 [1816], 226–27)

Revealingly, even this altruistic act of noblesse oblige is qualified by the race of the abandoned infant. The expectation that the child will be taken in as a dependent reveals a traditional, hierarchical form of making kin, even as the possibility that the child will be rejected as too Black reveals the racism and classism of the white elite.

Unlike in *The Second Mother*, Regina and her own daughter Lila (Julia Bernat) do not have a quasi-family relationship with their family's former maid Maria, who has passed away and was mother to Ana and grandmother to the two abandoned children. Maria is not well-remembered, and Regina does not realize the connection between her former maid and the children initially. In fact, rather than serving as the ideal proponent of noblesse oblige by immediately taking in the children, Regina takes a number of actions to drive them away and/or place them elsewhere. She also attempts for a time to recruit her current housekeeper as a caretaker of the children, in the same vein as Bárbara in *The Second Mother*. However, in a parallel to the character Dora in Walter Salles's *Central do Brasil / Central Station* (1999 [1998]), Regina gets to know the children while attempting to return them to their family or drop them at an orphanage and develops an emotional connection to them along with her daughter Lila.

Unlike the stable situation at the start of *The Second Mother*, in this film Regina and her household are in a transitional state for almost the entire course of the film, since she is planning to move after a divorce or separation. Her character's arc is one of becoming softer, opening up her heart to the children as she gets to know them, and it may well be that being in a transitional phase of her life makes her more open to kinnovation with the children. The encouragement of her own daughter Lila, also a young woman influencing change in her mother like Jéssica in *The Second Mother*, is paramount. The journey of becoming softer toward the children left with Regina parallels her overcoming of an emotional distance from her daughter, who is seeking more love and caring from Regina in the wake of her parents' separation—both for herself and also for the small children that have been left in their household. Ultimately, Regina and Lila themselves are brought closer together as they care for and make kin with the two children, forming new, non-biological kinship ties even as their nuclear family has broken apart.

Motherhood and Making Kin in Contemporary Brazilian Cinema | 151

After the children first arrive, we see a similar class topography of the middle-class apartment as seen in *The Second Mother*, with the children initially restricted to the maid's quarters and kitchen or, alternatively, disciplined for coming into the living room and making a mess (see figure 6.4). However, this is less emphasized, all the more so because this is a household in transition, with all the furniture and belongings prepared for a move. The fact that Regina is moving resonates with the transitional state that she and her family are in. She has relatively recently separated from or divorced Lila's father, while Lila herself is a young adult and has very recently moved out of the household herself. Being in this transitional state of their lives seems, ultimately, to leave both Lila and Regina more open to becoming softer and making emotional room for the preadolescent siblings Rayane (Rayane do Amaral) and Ygor (Ygor Manoel) who arrive on their doorstep. As with her previous film *Mutum* (2007), Kogut made the neorealist choice to cast nonprofessional actors to represent the children in the film, while balancing this choice by having them trained by renowned acting coach Fátima Toledo.

Both of the women in the family, mother Regina and daughter Lila, have scenes with Ygor revolving around music, which reflects the emotional development of the characters as they make kin with each other. Lila is more open to forming an emotional bond with Ygor, and consequently her musical scene with him comes first and involves a more active role

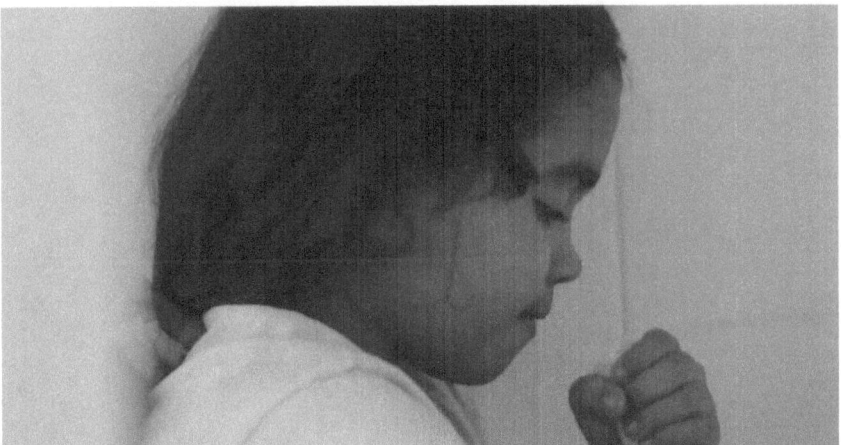

Figure 6.4. Rayane (Rayane do Amaral) finds a private moment for a snack under the kitchen table. (Courtesy Sandra Kogut)

on her part, in that she actually plays a song of her choice on the piano for Ygor. The song she chooses to play for him is John Lennon's "Love." The lyrics resonate perfectly with the process of softening and becoming emotionally available as kin to one another: "Love is feeling, feeling love / Love is wanting to be loved / Love is reaching, reaching love / Love is asking to be loved." As Lila sings, Ygor stares in rapt attention with a look of fascination and joy on his face in close-up.

In a later scene, Ygor is eating lunch with Regina at a restaurant in a mall (see figure 6.5). In this case, the music they hear is played by the restaurant for its customers. Ygor recognizes it as "Talismã/Talisman," a song in the *sertanejo* genre by Leandro and Leonardo. The song recalls Ygor's familial relationship to Regina's former maid, since he comments that it was a favorite of his grandmother Maria. The song's lyrics reference romantic love, as did the John Lennon song, but in this case the words also mention that the singer misses the distant lover. Ygor begins to sing the song to Regina, bringing a smile to her face. Again, music helps to both communicate and stimulate emotional attachment between this adult and child forming a kinship relationship. Further, several other phrases in the lyrics themselves resonate with emotional changes in the characters. The words "your fragile way" resonate with the softening of Regina's affect toward Ygor and even her own daughter, while the reference to "saudade," or missing an absent loved one, is echoed in the dialogue of the char-

Figure 6.5. Ygor (Ygor Manoel) eats lunch with Regina (Carla Ribas) while they listen to a *sertanejo* love song. (Courtesy Sandra Kogut)

acters in this latter part of the film, such as when Rayane mentions her saudade for her brother while she is living alone at the orphanage. The film's narrative arc resolves itself in this general atmosphere of emotional expressiveness and connection.

An important distinction to address between the characters of Ygor and Rayane and that of Jéssica in *The Second Mother* is their difference in age. Since Jéssica is a young adult, and indeed a mother herself, her autonomy is inherently less in question than that of Ygor and Rayane, who are eight and six years old, respectively—though it bears reemphasis that Jéssica's autonomy and agency are impressive and have a large impact on her mother's changing perspective and consequently her ability to adapt and realign her kinship ties. Despite their much earlier stage of emotional development, the two preadolescent children in Kogut's film are portrayed as far from helpless, especially the older Ygor. On multiple occasions, Ygor sets out on his own as he seeks to discover the whereabouts of his mother while leaving his sister waiting for him in a safe place (first in Regina's home and then in an orphanage). The children also resist being placed in an orphanage without being told in advance, initially running away and then agreeing to leave six-year-old Rayane there temporarily while Ygor continues to search for their mother.

At the same time, in keeping with her portrayal of children in her earlier film *Mutum*, director Kogut makes a clear effort to focalize the perspective of the children. In her analysis of *Mutum*, Rocha (2014) states that Kogut

> prioritize[s] poor or marginalized children's relationship with the maternal or feminine as a dialogical (and subversive) relationship . . . resorts to multiple focalizers so as to avoid depicting the child protagonist as an object of the gaze . . . [and] strives to provide the child's perception of his own story, thus imbuing him with a subjectivity that closely presents him as a subject. (5)

In *Campo Grande*, Kogut continues this careful approach to representing marginalized children's subjectivity in a dialogical relationship with the maternal and the feminine. The film's cinematography treats the children as equals to the adult characters, often positioning the camera at their level, taking their points of view, and/or focusing on their faces in close-up. Kogut's script, cowritten with Felipe Sholl, provides ample scenes for viewers to get to know the children on their own terms, when they are alone or with each other in various private or public spaces they have sought out for themselves in which to eat, play, converse, or rest. These scenes of Ygor and Rayane alone or with each other include a quiet moment on the floor under a kitchen table; a moment of sister awaiting her brother at the window, hands and face pressed against the glass; a moment of raucous sibling play in the laundry room of Regina's apartment; and a conversation between the siblings while perched atop a statue pedestal, free from adult supervision in a public plaza. Over the course of the narrative, the children, especially Ygor, open up to a new kinship relationship with Regina and Lila, cooperating with the latter in a softening (and subversion) of the lines of class and biological descent that initially divide them.

Unlike in *The Second Mother*, in the narrative of *Campo Grande* there is no issue of the biological mother resenting the adoptive mother; instead Regina is obliged to help the children when their mother Ana intentionally leaves them with her. The general relational dynamic is of one mother filling in for another, with some help from her young adult daughter, and little to no participation of the fathers. When Ana returns to seek out her biological children again in the final scene of the film, we see that her desire for her children to make kin was a coping strategy to deal with a crisis in her life. While we do not know the exact nature of this crisis, the fact that she has given birth to another child in the interim may indicate that she was unable to provide financially or otherwise for her older children at the time of the birth of her third child. Thus Ana relies on an interclass act of solidarity from a mother in a higher social class to get her family through this difficult time, and in doing so she effectively expands her kinship network.

However, as suggested above, Regina must go through a process of becoming soft to become an adoptive mother figure to these children. A significant part of this emotional process is symbolized by Regina and Ygor's physical journey from her middle-class neighborhood to the poorer neighborhood of Campo Grande in Rio's West Zone. Ironically this is initially because Regina is trying to get rid of Ygor by finding his family and returning him. The fact that Regina recognizes a clear class difference between her own neighborhood and Ygor's is revealed when she forbids her daughter Lila from going to Campo Grande where "these people" live. Even though these two neighborhoods exist in the same city, the distance traveled by car and Regina's difficulty finding a residence in

Campo Grande emphasize the divide between the poorer and the wealthier classes in Rio de Janeiro.

There are many parallels here between *Campo Grande* and a 1998 film I mentioned briefly above, *Central Station*. The scale is smaller since Regina and Ygor are traveling between neighborhoods rather than regions of Brazil as Dora and Josué do in *Central Station*, but otherwise the situations are quite similar. In each film, a middle-aged woman travels with a young boy to an unfamiliar place in order to find the boy's family and return him to them. Also in both films, the physical journey overlaps with an emotional journey, such that the woman in each film progresses from simply wanting to help the boy return to his family and thus relieve herself of responsibility for him to a real motherly affection for the boy and a concern for his future. One major difference is that in *Campo Grande*, unlike in *Central Station*, there is no idealized family waiting for Ygor to take him in when they reach his neighborhood. Regina discovers from a local waitress that Ygor and Rayane's grandmother passed away and his mother no longer lives there. The absence of house or home for the children in this place is underlined by the fact that the piece of land they used to live on is walled in behind a billboard announcing an upcoming luxury apartment building. The phenomenon of real estate speculation is referenced here, along with the difficulty for many of Brazil's urban residents to find affordable housing within a reasonable distance of their workplaces.

One can imagine Regina's former domestic employee Maria having to travel this same extensive urban trek countless times as her regular work commute, a journey Regina herself was apparently blissfully ignorant of when Maria was working for her. Thus this journey gives her the opportunity to better understand the life experience of Maria as well as that of her grandchildren. When she discovers that Ygor and Rayane have no place or people to return to in their old neighborhood, and after going on this surprisingly long journey through her own city to that neighborhood with Ygor, she has clearly developed a closer emotional connection to him. Subsequent scenes not only emphasize this character development but demonstrate a more general emotional softening, which affects Regina's relationship with her own daughter as well. As they await the expected arrival of Ygor and Rayane's mother Ana (who ultimately does not show up), Regina and adult daughter Lila have some quality time together as they share a sandwich and sleep together in the same bed. When Ygor finds out that his mother is not coming to find him as had been promised, he runs off on his own. At this point we see Regina's concern for him, as she seeks him out and promises to bring him to see his sister. This act demonstrates her increasing concern for the boy and desire to care for him in his mother's absence, and her desire to at least reunite him with his sister, even if their mother remains absent.

Conclusion

Although a comprehensive analysis of filmic representations of domestic workers per se falls outside the limits of this chapter, a consideration of these two films as well as Sandra Kogut's subsequently released *Três verões / Three Summers* (2019), in tandem with a number of other twenty-first-century Brazilian films, indicates that film narratives centering on women who are domestic workers (and their evolving kinship networks) constitute a significant cinematic trend in Brazil. This trend has involved portrayals of the situation of domestic workers from varying subjective perspectives, and at least some progression in terms of representing the voices and subject positions of domestic workers themselves. Val and Jessica are obvious examples of central characters in this vein in *The Second Mother*, and Val's role has been analyzed elsewhere specifically as representative of the domestic worker in Brazilian households (Sá 2018). Further, though the domestic worker character is deceased in *Campo Grande*, it is her prior tie of employment to Regina that helps determine the fate of her grandchildren, since her daughter assumes that Regina will feel some kind of obligation to care for her former employee's grandchildren when they are left on her doorstep.

The theme of trans-class solidarity and kinnovation, introduced in *Campo Grande* with this trust of a domestic worker (and her daughter) placed in her former employer, and then by Regina's relationship with Ygor and Rayane, returns in a somewhat different configuration in Kogut's *Three Summers*. Like the children in *Campo Grande*, the elderly man Lira (Rogério Fróes) finds himself in a vulnerable situation requiring care, which opens up the possibility of a close relationship with someone of a different social class, a woman named Madá (played by Regina Casé, the same actress who played Val). However, in this case it is the domestic worker Madá, the caretaker of a wealthy family's vacation home, who is in the more typical position of caring for Lira, the grandfather of said family. Lira expresses his gratitude for her care, and his appreciation for the formation of something akin to father-child kinship ties with her that are closer than those with his own biological son, by helping Madá in various entrepreneurial ventures and ultimately by bequeathing her his apartment in Copacabana.

Beyond these seminal fictional feature films of Muylaert and Kogut, we can take note of the innovative approaches taken in several documentaries to understand some other key developments in the representation of women domestic workers as protagonists/subjects in Brazilian cinema. Several of the directors of the documentary films in this area are also women, including Consuelo Lins and Karoline Maia, whose films I will mention briefly here alongside that of Gabriel Mascaro. At the beginning of the 2010s, Lins's *Babás / Nannies* (2010) addressed the exploitative yet often invisible legacy of the nanny's relationship to the family and its history going back to the period of slavery in Brazil, while Gabriel Mascaro's *Domésticas / Domestics* (2012) began to engage with maids and nannies as subjects who directly address the camera and the middle- and upper-class gaze by supplying the children in the households cameras to film them. As Rachel Randall (2018, 275) puts it, "Lins's and Mascaro's documentaries indicate the ways that colonial slave-owning relationships continue to weigh uncannily on modern-day domestic labour arrangements." Finally, a film shot in 2019 but not released as of this writing, Karoline Maia's *Aqui não entra luz / Here no light enters*, reportedly takes a step further in representing the subject position of the domestic worker, in that filmmaker Maia herself is the daughter of a maid. Maia made the film to explore her mother's and her own experiences in the household of her mother's employers, in light of the same postcolonial history laid out in Lins's and Mascaro's films (Veiga 2020). Meanwhile, in their films analyzed in this chapter, Muylaert and Kogut feature protagonists who generally appear to be more of European descent (though at least one domestic worker depicted by Kogut is played by a Black Brazilian actress, Mary Sheila). This being the case, one element that all the documentary directors mentioned here reveal more clearly than Muylaert and Kogut is the often racialized dynamic of domestic worker–employer relations, since women of color and in particular women of African descent have been overrepresented in the roles of maids and nannies since the period of slavery up to the present and most often have been employed by Euro-Brazilians in a higher social class.

Finally, we can return to the notion of making kin to highlight the unique focus of Anna Muylaert and Sandra Kogut on the formative role of women in shaping and renovating kinship ties. Above, I suggested a parallel between Regina's and Ygor's physical-emotional journey and that of Dora and Josué in Walter Salles's *Central Station*. A final major distinction from that earlier film and *Campo Grande* is that the figure of the biological father is relatively unimportant. In Salles's *Central Station* and indeed in his oeuvre as a whole, even in his absence the father figure looms large as a theme. Here the mothers simply help one another and do not even discuss seeking aid from the fathers. Ultimately the picture of making kin we are left with is a fairly flexible one that relies on neither biological parents nor a nuclear family. The tendency is to portray a shifting web of matriarchal solidarity, something shared with the resolution of Muylaert's film in the household of a mother and daughter, if not its initial setting in a nuclear family household. The improvisation of these relational webs in both films is akin to Haraway's (2016) description of the string figure game, which "is about giving and receiving patterns, dropping threads and failing but sometimes finding something that works, something consequential and maybe even beautiful, that wasn't there before, of relaying connections that matter" (10). Muylaert and Kogut are both fine contemporary examples of Brazilian women filmmakers' interest in, and sensitivity to, strong and emotionally adaptive female characters. They portray characters who form connections that matter because they sustain and empower themselves and their loved ones.

Works Cited

Arruza, Cinzia, Tithi Bhattacharya, and Nancy Fraser. 2019. *Feminism for the 99 Percent: A Manifesto*. London: Verso.

Bull, Malcolm. 2011. *Anti-Nietzsche*. Verso: London.

Dhalia, Heitor, dir. *À deriva / Adrift*. 2011 [2009]; Universal City, CA: Universal Studios Home Entertainment. DVD.

Haraway, Donna J. 2016. *Staying with the Trouble: Making Kin in the Chthulucene*. Durham, NC: Duke University Press.

Koster, Henry. 2016 [1816]. "The Free Population." In *Keen's Latin American Civilization: Volume One: The Colonial Era*, edited by Robert M. Buffington and Lila Caimari, 222–31. Boulder, CO: Westview Press.

Lins, Consuelo, dir. *Babás* (*Nannies*). 2010. Available at http://portacurtas.org.br/filme/?name=babas.

Marsh, Leslie L. 2017. "Women's Filmmaking and Comedy in Brazil: Anna Muylaert's *Durval discos* (2002) and *É proibido fumar* (2009)." In *Latin American*

Women Filmmakers: Production, Politics, Poetics, edited by Deborah Martin and Deborah Shaw, 164–85. London: IB Tauris. E-book.
Martel, Lucrecia, dir. *La mujer sin cabeza/The Headless Woman*. 2009 [2008]; Culver City, CA: Strand Releasing Home Video. DVD.
Martel, Lucrecia, dir. *La ciénaga/The Swamp*. 2015 [2001]; New York: Criterion Collection. DVD.
Piñeyro, Marcelo, dir. *Las viudas de los jueves/The Widows of Thursdays*. 2010 [2009]; Buenos Aires: Cameo. DVD.
Randall, Rachel. 2018. "'It Is Very Difficult to Like and to Love, but Not to Be Respected or Valued': Maids and Nannies in Contemporary Brazilian Documentary," *Journal of Romance Studies* 18 (2), 275–99.
Rocha, Carolina. 2014. "Can Children Speak in Film?: Children's Subjectivity in *Mutum* (2007) and *O contador das histórias* (2009)." In *Screening Minors in Latin American Cinema*, edited by Carolina Rocha and Georgia Seminet, 3–18. Lanham, MD: Lexington Books.
Sá, Lúcia. 2018. "Intimacy at Work: Servant and Employer Relations in *Que horas ela volta? (The Second Mother)*," *Journal of Iberian and Latin American Studies* 24 (3), 311–27.
Salles, Walter, dir. *Central do Brasil/Central Station*. 1999 [1998]; Culver City, CA: Columbia TriStar Home Video. DVD.
Schwarcz, Lilia Moritz. 2018. "Black Nannies: Hidden and Open Images in the Paintings of Nicolas-Antoine Taunay," *Women's History Review* 27 (6): 972–89.
Veiga, Edson. 2020. "'Quartinho de empregada é a senzala moderna' ['The Maid's Room is the Modern-Day Slave Quarters']," *Deutsche Welle*, November 20, 2020. https://www.dw.com/pt-br/quartinho-de-empregada-%C3%A9-a-senzala-moderna/a-55665011.

Chapter 7

The Many Mirrors of Maria Augusta Ramos

Landscape, Institutions, and Everyday Lives
in Contemporary Brazil

Paula Halperin

The opening scene is a high pan of endless commercial and residential buildings and skyscrapers crowding the skyline covered in a blanket of fog. After a few seconds, a familiar Brazilian landscape emerges: São Paulo, the country's largest city with its 12 million people, and the setting of documentary filmmaker Maria Augusta Ramos's *Futuro Junho* (*Future June*, 2015). Ramos's camera wanders through the urban space following four men in their daily activities at work and at home during the prelude to the World Cup, from mid-June to mid-July 2014. Alex Cientista, Alex Fernandes, Anderson dos Anjos, and André Perfeito—a car factory worker, a subway union leader, a motorcycle courier, and a financial analyst—are closely observed by Ramos's film, which draws a thick portrait of urban life amid the dramatic political transformations that surrounded the soccer event that year.

Ramos (hereafter referred to as MAR) delves into the nationalist feelings that the World Cup elicited in a large majority of Brazilians, while also covering the discussions and massive protests triggered by the event regarding the public spending choices made by different levels of government. The event itself generated distinct consequences in the lives of the four men, highlighting class, race, and gender differences that cut across Brazilian society. Alex Fernandes commands a subway strike as the

Figure 7.1. *Future June*, 2015. (Courtesy Maria Augusta Ramos)

city prepares to host the opening match of the World Cup. Alex Cientista works in a car factory that faces production surplus and an imminent wave of layoffs. Anderson dos Anjos roams the city delivering packages and renovates his recently bought house in one of the city's populous favelas. André Perfeito, a wealthy financier, preaches about the benefits of hosting the World Cup, since for him it puts Brazil in a privileged global position that promises to end the inferiority complex that has historically ravaged the country.

MAR's camera is present in many of the intimate spaces these individuals traverse (family dinners, work activities, bar gatherings), but she paradoxically dedramatizes these moments leading up to the World Cup. While the experiences of these four individuals are undeniably intense, her camerawork and lack of both voice-over and nondiegetic music create a distance while the film brings the characters closer to the audience to encourage reflection. She is not interested in what people say but what people do. Doing is much more revealing of who these figures are and what they want. Their daily actions take place in spaces the filmmaker's camera and editing identify as emblematic: the subway, the street, a karaoke event, a doctor's appointment. People's experience and subjectivity closely interlace with their landscape, defining the raw material of MAR's films.

In this chapter, I analyze MAR's work primarily through the tensions that surface in the interaction of space and characters. Following her vision that artistic creation is an incessant recreation, I will examine how MAR's fragmented narratives are the result of her characters' experiences relating to distinct interconnections with their environments. Her work explores menial aspects of daily life, but through character building, dramatization, and mise-en-scène, she transforms the common and simple details into an unusual and complex portrayal of contemporary Brazil. Her work, nevertheless, does not aim to reveal an alleged national identity, an imagined community developing in material spaces that individuals or groups journey across. As in much of contemporary Brazilian cinema, MAR's work portrays space as an ever-changing component in which people coexist, creating and recreating their subjectivities and daily experiences (Da Silva and Cunha 2017).

MAR is best known for her trilogia da justiça (trilogy of justice): *Justiça* (*Justice*, 2004), *Juízo* (*Judgment*, 2007), and *Morro dos prazeres* (*Hill of Pleasures*, 2013), as well as her highly acclaimed, award-winning (and in the first twenty most-watched films of that year) *O processo* (*The Trial*, 2018). But she has mastered an original style (within a robust Brazilian documentary scene) in all of her films, including *Future June*. Her work is characterized by the subtle interaction between the impersonality of public spaces, the overwhelming power of state institutions, and the characters who circulate throughout both. Her sharp look at the structural elements present in Brazil's political and social spheres is softened by and contrasted to the action of her multidimensional subjects and the way they navigate harsh circumstances in their lives.

MAR and the Brazilian Documentary Tradition

Part of a vibrant documentary scene in Brazil, MAR occupies a singular place in the nation's cinema. Born in the capital city of Brasília in 1964, the filmmaker left for the Netherlands around thirty years ago but never lost the organic connection she had with her homeland, as Brazil has been the protagonist in almost all of her films.[1] With one foot in Brazil and another in the Netherlands, she looks at her own very familiar culture from a certain distance that becomes evident in her camera work.

She does not belong to any of the consolidated film gangs—neither the one in the Rio–São Paulo axis nor those of Pernambuco, Minas Gerais, or Rio Grande do Sul. Her work, even if in dialogue with Brazilian documentary style, distances itself from the well-established local conventions, which privilege the interview as a narrative resource, as seen in Eduardo Coutinho's films (Barroso 2019, 20); the use of voice-over and self-referentiality, emblematic in the documentaries of João Moreira Salles; or the chronicle of central historical characters, as seen in Silvio Tendler's work. For many of the younger generations in the métier, the overt political dimension of documentary has taken on new significance in recent years, as seen in the adoption of different conceptual frameworks and evidence-based explanatory models (i.e., the use of voice-over and a narrator who guides viewers through what they are seeing and hearing) (Mesquita 2010, 77–88).

Embracing form over content points to the multiple ways that MAR abandons all *dispositifs* used in the so-called 1960s and 1970s sociological documentary that looked for archetypes to help build a political thesis. Her actors' daily interactions with their surroundings highlight the power that certain structures exert over people and the spaces that benefit from those structures. In MAR's films, life is a complex game of circumventing daily tensions that are inseparable from local surroundings, and thus a myriad of different subjects (formed by structural circumstances as well as by individual experience) live and interact with space differently.

A former musicology major at the University of Brasília, MAR has opposed the use of music as a means of generating emotions and feelings that do not come directly from the action on-screen. Her work privileges the sounds of the surroundings in her cinematic spaces. Natural noise, loud settings, and moments of deep silences are crucial sound elements that enable her to articulate a unique filmic language (Couret 2019). For MAR, if music is inserted, it becomes an outsider to the action and serves as an imposed commentary. As she has said multiple times, in particular when *The Trial* was released, "Faço um tipo de cinema documental que é altamente formal, isso significa que o público é consciente desse formalismo. Os filmes deixam claro (através da forma) que são uma 'representação' da realidade e não a 'realidade' concreta que está sendo filmada" ("I make documentaries that are highly formal; the public is aware of this formalism. The films make it clear (through form) that they are a 'representation' of reality and not the 'reality' being filmed") (quoted in França and Avellar 2013, 96).

Evidently, Brazilian modern documentary has changed significantly since its inception in the late 1950s. Film historian and critic Paulo Emílio Salles Gomes has described Brazilian documentary films up to the 1950s as "rituals of power," as they portrayed, spoke the language of, and served the elites. After 1950s, Brazilian documentaries were produced by a generation of filmmakers linked to national cinema renewal, making films that emphasized popular imagery and politics, such as the struggles of impoverished fishermen (Mario Carneiro and Paulo César Saraceni's *Arraial do cabo* [*Village on the cape*, 1960]), the experience of rural migrants coming to the big city (Geraldo Sarno's *Viramundo* [*World turning*, 1964]), and the political alienation of middle-class people in the Rio de Janeiro post–coup d'état (Arnaldo Jabor's *Opinião pública* [*Public opinion*, 1967]) (Holanda 2006).

During the 1960s and 1970s, at the height of the authoritarian military government (1964–1985), the possibility of recording direct sound led to a rampant use of interviews by documentarians, and the interviewee's speech came to be called the voice of the experience (Rodrigues 2016). This mechanism created the illusion that the veracity of what was said by the documentary subject was indeed unquestionable. In the 1980s, as Ismail Xavier has pointed out, a new documentary style emerged, in part as a response to the political opening that began in the late 1970s. Although there was a dilution of experimental concerns with the dismantling of the mechanisms of filmic language, during this period each documentary remained as a personal vision of the director in relation to the world (Xavier 2014). The filmmaker was not afraid to take a stand before the documented object. Documentary filmmaking further developed as a mode of reporting on the revival of popular movements, reflecting the political openness the country was experiencing.

Still during this period, and despite cinema being a male-oriented field, documentary filmmakers such as Helena Solberg, Ana Carolina, Sandra Werneck, Suzana Amaral, Regina Jehá, Kátia Mesel, Eliane Bandeira, Inês Cabral, Iole de Freitas, Eunice Gutman, and Lygia Pape, among others, heavily participated in the métier, either as directors, producers, or directors of photography. And unlike their male counterparts, these filmmakers chose a subjective point of view when telling stories that mostly referred to the multiplicity of the female experience. Karla Holanda, filmmaker and film historian, notices that with the feminist struggle for equity gaining strength in the country in the mid-1970s, the production of documentary directed by women was guided by themes that addressed their situation in a patriarchal society (Holanda 2015).

MAR, somehow, does not appear on the lists of directors who paved the path of an open feminist cinema. In several of her films, especially the ones that address power relations, many of the protagonists are effectively women (*The Trial*, *Justice*, and *Judgment*). The filmmaker does not necessarily speak to themes specific of the feminine condition, but her voice as an artist could be considered historically feminist, especially in terms of the trajectory of Brazilian documentary, as she avoids adapting an assertive voice—whether it is the voice of a narrator or her own voice as both an interviewer and an active participant of the story—and favors a plurality of voices.

Space, Coexistence, and Conflict

In one of the first scenes of *Future June*, a crowd awaits the arrival of the subway. The diegetic sounds of the overflowing station provide a sense of familiarity with the scene immediately. The subway arrives and passengers push out of and into the car. This scene depicts a new normal in the morning commute in São Paulo's metropolitan area. Going to and coming back from work every day has become a major task for millions of Brazilians living in big cities, as public transportation is precarious, inefficient, and expensive. The event in its familiar but brutal routine sets the scene for a major conflict between the subway workers and the state government. It is in the crowded and disputed space of the subway that Alex Fernandes is introduced to the audience.

Figure 7.2. *Future June*, 2015. (Courtesy Maria Augusta Ramos)

Minutes following this scene, metalworker Alex Cientista is shown focusing with precision on assembling a car door. Car ownership is a symbol of middle-class status in Brazil, and it is also a major hurdle in the difficult task of organizing the flow of urban transit in the country's big cities. Even if São Paulo enjoys the largest subway extension lines in the country (and probably in South America), its constant congestion leads to an excess of circulating cars in the city.

The two sequences are not edited sequentially. They are in fact interspersed with domestic scenes and the introduction of other characters. It is almost impossible, however, not to mentally stitch them together, due to the symbolic load that crosses them. In addition to the very strong class undertones associated with the use of public transportation or car ownership, the two professions delineated here, subway worker and metalworker, refer to two highly combative sectors within the national labor movement and supporters of the Workers' Party, which at the time had secured Brazil's presidency again with the reelection of the country's first female president, Dilma Rousseff.

Since her first documentary, *Brasília, um dia em fevereiro* (*Brasilia, a Day in February*, 1997), MAR has created a screen world that relies on specific formal principles. Her notion of space is drawn with wide-angle shots that are usually distant from her subjects, avoiding the intimacy and subjectivity of close-ups but never so far that audiences are unable to

Figure 7.3. *Future June*, 2015. (Courtesy Maria Augusta Ramos)

recognize the experience of the characters and the centrality that landscape plays in the configuration of such an experience. *Brasília* indeed opens with a wide-angle shot showing three people coming from opposite sides of a vast green zone that seems to be a rural area. The saturated urban diegetic sounds (car horns, buses, loud conversations) are disorienting and feel artificial, disjointed from the image. The three characters cross each other for a second in the middle of the frame, but they immediately disperse to carry on with their lives. Soon after, there is another wide-angle shot of a less anonymous, more identifiable place, a Praça dos Três Poderes (Three Powers Square), a monumental modernist symbol intended to project harmonious forces that foster coexistence at the heart of Brazil's capital city. A man carrying multiple mirrors crosses the frame from one side to the other, quickly disappearing.

MAR's statement is an ironic consideration of the making of the nation's capital city. This first shot seems to suggest that Brasília, built in 1960, is nothing but an artificial experiment imposed on a piece of land in the middle of nowhere. This almost political assertion, however, has its foundation in the aesthetic principles chosen by MAR that distances herself from several previous political documentaries on the subject, which have established a repeated pattern of utterances about the city through interviews and voice-over.

And yet, a planned city like Brasília that is so expansive that it cannot be walked through, as some of the characters complain, prompts MAR to

Figure 7.4. *Brasilia, One Day in February*, 1997. (Courtesy Maria Augusta Ramos)

show how people appropriate their spaces, circulate through them, and live valuable experiences regardless of the daily difficulties they face. Even in the monumental capital that lacks public transportation and enhances its highways, spaces of collective sociability exist. A bar, a bus terminal, the main stairs at the university entrance, and Three Powers Square (that will be portrayed under a totally different lens in *The Trial*) are front and center in the everyday experiences of Letícia (a college student), Maria Cristina (the wife of a diplomat), and Valdir (a mirror peddler). What these two women and one man have in common is simply the fact of living in the same city, which despite being so widespread allows unaware encounters between individuals as they move through the same spaces.

The desire to capture apparently uneventful moments with a camera that avoids exuberant aesthetics and adopts austere editing also informs and produces MAR's perception of space. Her biggest accomplishment as a filmmaker is creating a minimalist mise-en-scène that works as a key reference point for understanding the little actions of her characters. Sounds and images seen and heard by the audience are inconspicuous. Common, average events acquire profound relevance through her eyes. The profound political statement of her films lies in the certainty that symbolic and material spaces shape people's lives and their interaction with those places every day.

From her first documentary feature until the more recent *The Trial*, she has displayed similar principles of formal selection of the resources used to define her cinematic space. Thinking about Henri Lefebvre's ideas regarding representational space as a system of symbolic representations, what constitutes MAR's space in her films comprises a certain set of formal elements. The austerity of both her filming and editing methods, with a camera that accompanies characters from a distance but approaches them in apparently uneventful moments, reveal the social and the mental worlds displayed in the landscape (Lefebvre 1991).

In doing so, the images incorporate or signify the physical space of the actual human experience; her construction of landscape places human affairs and interaction in a representational world and not in a previously existing space. Space is revealed in the interaction between the material world, the characters, and the subjectivity of her camera. It is her camera that gives an actual sense of testimony, a close presence, and a witness in either open or secluded areas. Her documentary language is, thus, devoted to uniquely displaying an almost pro-filmic space and the activity that follows in it, reflecting the para-fictional style of Frederick

Wiseman. MAR combines this observational and distant shooting style to emulate narrative continuity by means of careful editing.

The vastness of Brasília contrasts with the crowded public and private areas in the city of São Paulo. MAR edits snippets of congested spaces throughout *Future June*: the bird's-eye shot of a crowded soccer stadium in one of the games played by the Brazilian team (and attended mostly by men and women of an affluent middle class) is presented in opposition to a popular demonstration that denounces the use of public funds for the sporting event, instead of directing funds toward pressing issues such as public health and transportation. The yellow of the stadium (including shirts worn by the players and the crowd with the color of the Brazilian flag) contrasts with the vibrant red of the Workers' Party flags. While one crowd calls for national unity around a dubious event, the other calls for social justice and the end of police brutality. As in *Brasília*, all of these characters live in the same city riddled with social differences.

We also see Anderson dos Anjos taking his epileptic son to the public clinic. There he is told by the emergency doctor that he needs to look for a specialist, and we see Anderson's desperation. None of the scenes mentioned are sequentially edited together. At the end of the film, however, a correlation has been established between the lack of basic services for the needy population and the protection of the most privileged sectors of the Paulista society, who enjoy beautiful restaurants, luxury cars, and expensive shows. The film does not engage in metaphors but rather provides a stark chronicle that exposes the irrational aspects of an overpopulated city in a country with evident issues deciding priorities. A masterpiece, *Future June* leaves pedagogical rhetoric aside to lay bare the economic imbalances affecting contemporary Brazil by observing the daily experiences of these specific characters in a brief span of time.

Previous to *Future June*, MAR made for Dutch TV HOS *Rio, a Day in August* (2002) about the boys who live along the tracks of the main Rio de Janeiro train station Central do Brasil. The film won the GNT/Brasil Documenta award at the É Tudo Verdade (It's All True) festival in 2003. By the time she released the first film in her justice trilogy, the award-winning *Justice* (Best Film at the international documentary festival Visions du Réel 2004 in Nyon, Switzerland; La Vague d'Or Award for best film at the International Women's Film Festival in Bordeaux, France; and the Best Documentary at the Taiwan International Documentary Festival), MAR was gaining visibility in the male-oriented documentary scene in her country. *Justice* achieved extensive audience recognition, as well as positive criticism among both specialized critics and the mainstream media. The film was also praised in the legal sector, as multiple newspaper articles reproduced magistrates' and lawyers' praise for the film's ability to make the Brazilian public aware of the complexities of the judicial system. Today, both *Justice* and the following *Judgment* are assigned in law school classes throughout the country (Werneck 2004).

These three documentaries that comprise MAR's justice trilogy propose an in-depth examination of the state institutions in Rio de Janeiro (courts of law, police, juvenile detention centers), adopting an observational approach along with reenactment and dramatization of real-life situations. She examines the day-to-day mechanisms and devices that allow these institutions to effectively exist and the roles that lawyers, judges, prosecutors, and inmates play within them. Her films discover a theater of justice in its complex links with the poor populations of the favelas and the peripheries of Rio de Janeiro. The three films question the functioning of these institutions by examining their daily practices and their participation in the construction of a definitive otherness through small-scale and large-scale processes. MAR's gaze reveals how notions of citizenship, gender, and racial archetypes intersect with the violence generated by the social abyss and the criminalization of poverty fundamental to the theater of justice and repression.

The trilogy offers a detailed portrait of Brazilian society through the close observation of a determined space and the clashes that take place there. In *Judgment*, MAR shows more than institutional violence, open racism, and the abuse that minors are subjected to and their daily suffering in the juvenile detention centers. As in her previous film *Justice*, *Judgment* also highlights how the court itself becomes a performative space, which has harmful consequences for the minors tried there. The sermons of judges and prosecutors are portrayed as reifying the stereotypes that stigmatize these same minors. Authority and power reinforce the officials' words and actions during these proceedings, and the minors are only formally heard. Defense lawyers' arguments are almost always dismissed. The outcome is known in advance. These boys and girls are labeled as morally weak individuals, lacking honesty and perseverance.

The reification of the popular classes' stereotypes is also explored in MAR's final installment in her trilogy. *Hill of Pleasures* chronicles the day-to-day of a favela of the same name located in Rio de Janeiro, one year after the installation of a communitarian police (the Pacifying Police Unit [UPP]) in 2006. As usual, MAR does not interact with the subjects on camera nor does she interview them. The camera accompanies both the police and the residents in their actions, who once again interact in a space of intense social and symbolic dispute. The UPP's formal objective is to combat and dismantle organized crime in charge of drug trafficking in communities (the formation of the police force was the result of a strategy taken jointly by the municipal, state, and federal governments in 2000s Brazil). Different police officers spell this out throughout the documentary. Speeches by the UPP addressing the community, at first glance, unfold as radically different from the ones delivered by the different judges and/or prosecutors in MAR's two previous films. Crime, drug trafficking, and the violent behavior attributed to the poor are not the primary sources of concern in these police diatribes. They instead focus on community police work, the importance of understanding the real needs of residents, and the central presence of female (police) in the "pacification" process, highlighting how their gender allows a broader acceptance by residents of the Hill. MAR, however, captures scenes of violence and harassment against people in the community, showing a pulsating tension throughout (Halperin 2018).

Her lack of blatant didacticism and distant approach to the conflicts staged in those spaces make MAR a difficult artist to openly embrace by part of the radical documentarian scene devoted to denouncing police brutality and injustice. *Autos de resistência* (*Police Killing*, 2018) is a remarkable documentary codirected by Natasha Neri and Lula Carvalho that appears more explicitly aligned with this radical stance. The film narrates the Rio de Janeiro police killings practiced as so-called self-defense acts. It follows people who deal with these deaths in their daily lives, showing how Brazil's government responds to these cases, from the police investigations to the courtroom hearings. In many ways, MAR's filmmaking addresses the same material and radical critiques displayed in *Police Killing*, albeit through arguably more indirect means.

Her films move away from the representation of the extraordinary violent event that bursts on a daily basis, a tempting and common gesture for documentarians dealing with situations centrally concerning the abuse of power. In *Morro*, MAR resists showing the ostensible acts of violence resulting from the confrontation between traffickers and the BOPE (Battalion of Special Operations), which have been saturating the mainstream media for decades and are presented in other iconic films on the subject (e.g., Kátia Lund and João Moreira Salles's *Notícias de uma guerra particular / News from a Personal War*, 1999) and fictionalized in José Padilha's two *Tropa de elite* (*Elite Squad*) films of 2007 and 2010.

Certainly, the films by Padilha and Moreira Salles and Lund influenced MAR's project, but in *Hill of Pleasures*, drug trafficking, an omnipresent element in those communities, is not the main object she is interested in observing. Instead, she aims to portray the personal and collective experiences of the people inhabiting those spaces beyond the stereotypical images projected on those communities by arbitrary (and external) powers. The sense of landscape in MAR's work is profoundly impacted by the community's perceptions of time.

The Unpredictable Length of Time

There is something unique in *Brasilia, a Day in February*'s rendering of time. As its title clearly states, everything we see happens in the span of just twenty-four hours. Letícia has her photo taken (she is probably applying for a job), goes to class, talks to her fellow students about the uncertainties of growing up and seeing a therapist, goes home, shares a meal with her family, and meets her boyfriend in the evening. Valdir, the peddler, strolls all over the city carrying his mirrors, talking to different people, and bargaining the price of his merchandise, finally ending his journey in a bar having beers with a friend. Both complain about the harshness of daily life, longing for a prosperous and stable past that no longer exists.

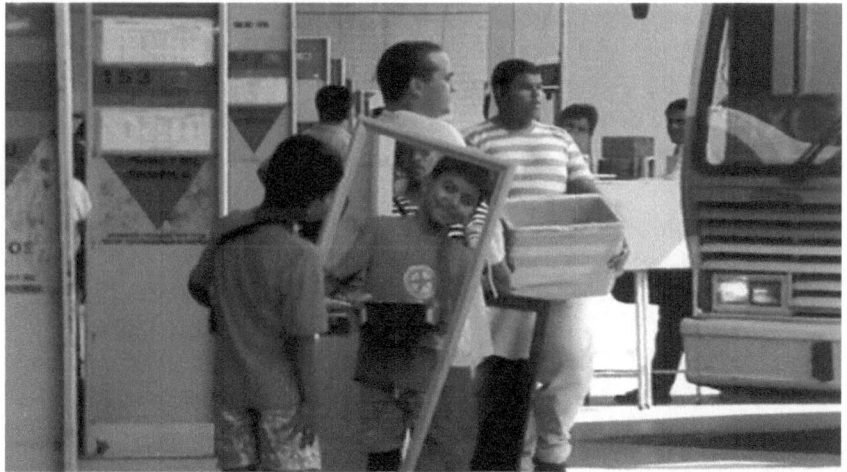

Figure 7.5. *Brasilia, One Day in February*, 1997. (Courtesy Maria Augusta Ramos)

Time is a recurrent resource and preoccupation in MAR documentaries. Precisely defined in some of her films or purposively indeterminate in others, it plays a key role in portraying different dimensions of experience in the characters' daily lives. She does not attempt to highlight the monotony of everyday life, even though many of her characters sustain hard and difficult lives. Alex Fernandes loses his job due to his union activity, but he goes home to an amorous pregnant wife in *Future June*. Valdir walks the city incessantly and does not sell a mirror, but he nonetheless jokes and genuinely smiles at everybody. Elma, the mother of Carlos Eduardo, accused of stealing a car in *Justice*, takes care of his wife and newborn.

Elma, like all the relatives of the kids in *Judgment* and the adults in *Justice*, waits. Whether patiently or despairingly, she experiences the arbitrary timing of justice as something both foreign and intrinsically constitutive of her daily life. It passes quickly during Carlos Eduardo's trial and the sentence that sends him to prison. In her final conversation with his lawyer, the possibility of a never-ending, almost infinite waiting for his release becomes blatant. The same experience of the lingering of time is expressed in the multiple daily conversations minors hold in *Judgment* about what they will do when they leave the institute—an imprecise, blurry, and never specified date to come.

The construction of time in her films is plastic and malleable, and it is deployed to allow the characters to emerge in all their complexity and multiplicity. Time is no longer a variable depending on different notions of space but rather a crucial component in MAR's notions of social experience. Even if time is shown as fragmented and nonlinear (as her editing style presents it), the viewer nonetheless is able to apprehend its profound relation to people's heterogeneous and in many cases irreducible experience of the quotidian. The viewer, through MAR's films, internalizes a broader notion of time and its multiple dimensions.

A comparable sense of time can be seen in *Seca* (*Drought*, 2015). MAR's camera follows a water delivery truck through the drought-stricken Brazilian landscape of Pernambuco. The truck driver delivers water to urban and rural areas, simultaneously witnessing the multiple activities people perform in their everyday lives. The characters work, meet, and chat, and the time of these daily tasks seems to be defined by the need to find and/or use water. The arrival of the truck, the expected rain that often does not fall, and the multiple digging expeditions to the desert looking for natural springs all reveal not only the strength and endurance of these communities but how culture can be shaped by a different experience of time length.

The Many Mirrors of Maria Augusta Ramos | 175

Figure 7.6. *Drought*, 2015. (Courtesy Maria Augusta Ramos)

MAR does not position her work within an empty cultural relativism but openly disarticulates previous stereotypes built by the mainstream media (but also by the political cinema of the 1960s) regarding this particular region, its communities, and its residents. In those depictions, spatial context (the desert) and the temporal (a supposed precapitalist) dimension of their daily experiences have been determinant in the portrayal of these populations and have attributed to them a backward and traditional character. As in the rest of her oeuvre, in this film MAR interlaces multifaceted representations of space, time, power, and experience to portray different aspects and places of Brazilian contemporary society without editorializing.

Spaces of Power: *The Trial*

The articulation of aesthetics and formal resources analyzed above finds its best expression in MAR's film *The Trial*. MAR opens it with a wide drone shot that reveals (once again) the Praça dos Três Poderes in Brasília, while multitudes gathered to watch the House vote on President Dilma Rousseff's impeachment live on giant screens. The landscape is visibly divided into two halves opposing each other: one side of the crowd dressed in yellow in favor of the impeachment and the other side in red in support of Rousseff and against the parliamentary coup. In an almost prophetic way, the scene echoes the less confrontational crowds portrayed in *Future June*.

Figure 7.7. *The Trial*, 2018. (Courtesy Maria Augusta Ramos)

The film premiered in February 2018 at the 68th Berlin Film Festival, was screened at the It's All True festival in São Paulo and Rio de Janeiro in April of the same year, and was released commercially in May. Successful and critically acclaimed (and on a list of several documentaries to deal with the topic), *The Trial* has the aesthetic features present in MAR's previous works. Here MAR is an observer in the strict sense, and despite the difficult circumstances present in the topic she addresses, she resists interfering with the flow of events, interjecting explanations, or recreating situations, as has been her trademark.

What interests the director most are the procedural rituals Rousseff's opponents in Congress carried out with zeal, appealing to the Constitution and the rule of law even if they rampantly had ignored and openly broken it before, during, and certainly after. A vast majority of these white male representatives indeed faced investigations or charges for corruption, slavery, and even murder. The congressmembers' dramatic performances in this political theater, replayed in the documentary, seem to veil more serious reasons behind the impeachment, motives MAR unambiguously gestures toward from the beginning of the film. "In October 2014, Dilma Rousseff was reelected president of Brazil, potentially extending to 16 years the consecutive rule by the left-wing Workers' Party," the screen reads at the beginning of the documentary. MAR seems to suggest conservative political forces and elite economic interests could not afford and did not want one more Workers' Party administration.

Well-crafted cinematography and skillful editing characterize *The Trial*. As in her previous films, MAR wanted to register how people interacted with others, in this case within the Brazilian Senate in preparation for the impeachment trial after Congress voted in favor of it. She did not know anyone before the making of the film—there were no preproduction planning meetings—and her decision to focus on the Senate was the result of former house speaker Eduardo Cunha refusing to give her authorization to film in the House. Cunha, previously allied with Rousseff's government, was the main instigator of Rousseff's impeachment. He was incarcerated for corruption shortly after the vote in Congress.

MAR focuses on the multiple meetings of the Workers' Party senate caucus, where senators discussed defense strategies and reviewed the technicalities of Rousseff's alleged crimes. As spectators of MAR's film, we feel it is pure theater being performed in front of our eyes, in which all the protagonists with vast experience and long political careers already knew their roles and how to present themselves in front of the cameras. MAR's focus on their gestures was more revealing than their political speeches (Dennison 2020).

She composes the scenes masterfully, conveying the polite but palpable tension present in the proceedings. It becomes obvious that, despite the efforts of Rousseff's allies and the fact that the accusations against her had no real weight, all opposition parties and interests were committed to removing her. Nothing Rousseff's articulate lawyer or senators of the Workers' Party could argue would influence a final result that, in the vein of Franz Kafka's *The Trial* (1925), had been decided since the beginning.

As with MAR's other work, the film avoids gross didacticism. She does not identify groups or players by name; there is (once again) no voice-over. The film is self-explanatory, and what matters most is the dynamics of the game that unfolds before spectators' eyes. In one of her briefings to the Senate, Janaína Paschoal—the conservative lawyer who coauthored the petition for Rousseff's impeachment—screams and gesticulates, her face twitching, her frenzied movements a bare imitation of an Evangelical church pastor's performance. Gleisi Hoffmann, then-senator for the state of Paraná and president of the Workers' Party, stares at her serenely. The scene is an unconcealed contrast between the two women and what they represent, and in many ways it is a profound consideration of female politicians, the complexities in the articulation between gender and power, and the public perception of such a link. After all, these two women are on opposite sides of a conflict whose epicenter is another woman.

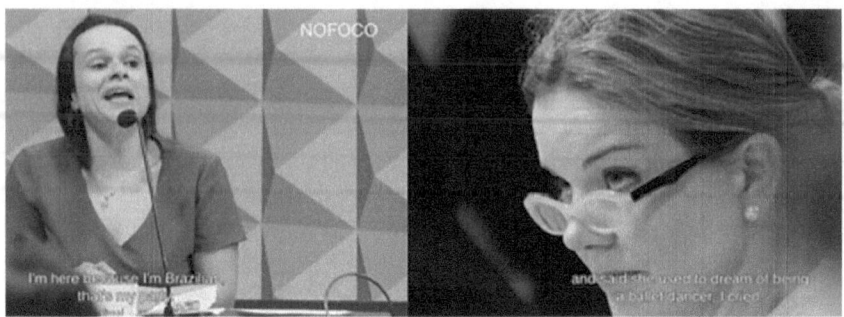

Figure 7.8. *The Trial*, 2018. (Courtesy Maria Augusta Ramos)

The Trial generated debate in the mainstream media due to the proximity of the events it narrates and the tense political climate during 2018, a year of national elections. The Brazilian mainstream press, which supported the parliamentary coup against Rousseff, acknowledged that MAR's position regarding the President's overthrow was expressed through the pathetic behavior eloquently displayed by the President's political enemies (Miranda 2018; Araújo 2018). It is clear, nevertheless, that MAR's political choices and formal style do not align with the mainstream local taste regarding documentary aesthetics. Praised by blogs and specialized critics, *The Trial* did not receive the same praise as other documentaries similar in scope released around the same time did (Halperin 2019). The subtlety embedded in her style and approach make MAR a recognized but peripheral artist in the Brazilian documentary scene.

Concluding Remarks

The portrayal of the political dispute in her recent work, with its rituals essentially embedded in space and time, is no different from the depiction of other spaces in the director's previous films. Without defining people's experiences as mere scripts determined by the material conditions of power and the institutions that represent and enforce them, MAR creates a constellation of symbolic cinematic landscapes that allows audiences to absorb the complexities of the relations that humans establish with their surroundings and how that determines and is defined by specific experiences of time. There is always something elusive, deliberately unfinished in all of these places, experiences, and characters that MAR chooses to reveal.

The complexity of those experiences emerge yet again in her most recent work, *Não toque em meu companheiro* (*Don't touch my fellow worker,* 2020), a documentary that explores the experiences of a group of bank employees and union members of the state bank Caixa Econômica Federal who reunite to remember the layoffs of over a hundred employees fired by the neoliberal government of Collor de Mello in 1991. The unions reacted and thousands of the bank workers organized and created the movement Não Toque em Meu Companheiro (Don't Touch My Fellow Worker), whose tenacious struggle led to the rehiring of the workers one year later.

The footage of those past events (an unusual stylistic choice for MAR), provides a historical dimension to the documentary and is contrasted to the emotional and almost intimate stories told by those men and women, their political and personal struggles, their solidarity, and the mystique that allowed them to keep going. MAR uses political propaganda of the early 1990s to establish a clear profile of Collor de Melo, comparing his fierce neoliberalism to the ideas and practices of the current protofascist president, Jair Bolsonaro.

As in the vast majority of her films, she does not intend to portray exceptional and/or extraordinary characters, even in *The Trial* where all the faces shown are part of the drama of political theater and familiar to the audiences. In all of her work, including the 2018 film, MAR lingers on the certainty that through her camera's close and in-depth observation of these subjects' personal interactions and gestures, power disputes could be unveiled, without further explanation. She has decided, since the making of her first film about her hometown, to be the portraitist of worlds in tension and that the complexities of reality are not predetermined material her camera should capture.

All of her spaces are saturated with previous lived experiences and memories, influencing the ways peoples circulate in them. However, MAR's individuals persistently modify that memory and that history. The landscape of *Drought*, impregnated with meaning drawn from decades of media imagery, is recreated and reimagined with the lively characters the film portrays. The city of São Paulo, oftentimes portrayed as the monstrous and impersonal urban metropolis, is presented through the solidarity of its workers, their daily lives, their affective relationships, and their moments of leisure.

Overall, MAR composes these spaces overtly avoiding the illusion of homogeneity, coherence, and thus unified identity. The query of unveiling a national ethos is out of the question. It becomes evident that that would be a convoluted and futile task to pursue by her cinema. And yet, she still identifies a palimpsest of voices of a nation immersed in a severe structural crisis of the state, its institutions, and the political system as a whole. The mechanisms of justice, radically politicized and crossed by ideology, are shown, in her films, to be highly inefficient. Today, they are being questioned by a large part of the nation's civil society and the media. Criticism of state institutions and the parliamentary regime are part of a debate between a wide range of ideological positions, but the radical right, in power throughout the country, has used them as a platform to loudly voice its antidemocratic positions.

MAR's aesthetic and political choices and her craftsmanship throughout her films are an essential reference in public debate to show the density of political and social tensions in these current times. Her current project on Brazil's convoluted and multilayered corruption probe, known as the Operação Lava Jato (Car Wash), attests to that. Her work is not only important—it is politically urgent.

Note

1. For more on the biography and approach to filmmaking of Maria Augusta Ramos, see her interview with Jack A. Draper III, Cacilda M. Rêgo, and Gustavo Procopio Furtado in chapter 4 of this volume.

Works Cited

Araújo, Inácio. 2018. "O processo, de Maria Augusta Ramos, se arrisca em percurso exaustivo." *Folha de São Paulo*, April 15, 2018, 42–43.

Associação dos Magistrados do Estado do Rio de Janeiro. 2004. "A justiça que queremos." *Jornal do Brasil*, June 12, 2004, 4.

Barroso, Cecília. 2019. "Um olhar aos invisíveis. O cinema de Maria Augusta Ramos." In *Mulheres atrás das câmeras. As cineastas brasileiras de 1930 a 2018*, edited by Luiza Lusvarghi and Camila Vieira da Silva, 219–39. São Paulo: Estação Liberdade.

Couret, Nilo. 2019. "Due Process: A Conversation with Maria Augusta Ramos." *Film Quarterly*, 72 (3) (Spring): 52–58.

Da Silva, Antônio Márcio, and Mariana Cunha. 2017. *Space and Subjectivity in Contemporary Brazilian Cinema*, 1–19. Cham: Springer International Publishing.

Dennison, Stephanie. 2020. *Remapping Brazilian Film Culture in the Twenty-First Century*, 57–76. New York: Routledge.

França, Andrea, and José Carlos Avellar. 2013. "As imagens silenciosas e os corpos em desajuste no cinema de Maria Augusta Ramos," *Devires* 10 (2) (July/December): 90–109.

Guimarães, Victor. 2011. "Da política no documentário às políticas do documentário: notas para uma perspectiva de análise." *Revista Galáxia* 22 (December): 77–88.

Halperin, Paula. 2018. "Ele te chamou pra roubar? E tu foi. Tá gostando agora?" Justiça e alteridade em três documentários de Maria Augusta Ramos. *Latin American Research Review*, 53 (4): 831–38.

———. 2019. "We Will All Be Judged by History: Political Upheaval in Brazil." *NACLA*, August 27, 2019. https://nacla.org/news/2019/08/27/bolsonaro-brazil-political-upheaval-documentaries.

Holanda, Karla. 2015. "Documentaristas brasileiras e as vozes feminina e masculina." *Significação* 42 (44): 339–58.

———. 2006. "Documentário brasileiro contemporâneo e a micro-história." *Fênix* 3 (1) (January/March): 1–12.

Lefebvre, Henri. 1991. *The Production of Space*, 68–168. Oxford: Blackwell.

Mesquita, Claudio. 2010. "Retratos em diálogo. Notas sobre o documentário brasileiro recente." *Novos Estudos* 86 (March): 105–118.

Miranda, André. 2018. "Escolhas políticas." *O Globo*, May 17, 2018, 6.

Nagib, Lúcia. 2012. "Além da diferença: a mulher no cinema da retomada." *Devires*, 9 (1) (January/June): 14–29.

Rodrigues, Flávia Lima. 2016. "Uma breve história sobre o cinema documentário brasileiro." *CES Revista* 24 (1) (April): 61–73.

Xavier, Ismail. 2014. "A teatralidade como vetor do ensaio fílmico no documentário brasileiro contemporâneo." *Aniki* 1 (1): 33–48.

Werneck, Alexandre. 2004. "Cinema e justiça no banco dos réus." *Jornal do Brasil*, June 20, 2004, 4–5.

Chapter 8

Interview with Petra Costa

Petra Costa (PC) and Jack A. Draper III (JD)[1]

Figure 8.1. Petra Costa. (Photo credit: Diego Bresani)

Petra Costa began her career in the 2000s with a moving short film about her grandparents' relationship, *Olhos de ressaca / Undertow Eyes* (2009). Over the last decade, she has directed two acclaimed feature-length documentaries—*Elena* (2012) and *Democracia em vertigem / The Edge of Democracy* (2019)—and codirected another with Danish director Lea Glob, *Olmo e a gaivota / Olmo and the Seagull* (2014). Her earlier films tend to play with the boundaries between fiction, memoir, and documentary, while also exploring memory and emotion through film narrative and voice-over. In these films, she developed a recognizable personal film style based in creative cinematography and editing, and a "haptic visuality" (see Marks 2000), which we discuss in the interview. Her most recent, Oscar-nominated film *The Edge of Democracy* is her most political in the formal sense, dealing with the recent Brazilian political crisis including the impeachment of Brazil's first woman president, Dilma Rousseff, and the controversial arrest and imprisonment of her predecessor, former president Luiz Inácio "Lula" da Silva (since released from prison as he appealed his convictions, which were eventually overturned by Brazil's Supreme Court). Critics on the left, not all of them from Dilma and Lula's Workers' Party, have interpreted these events, along with the so-called Car Wash federal corruption investigation, as part of a parliamentary-judicial-mediatic coup, which effectively removed the Workers' Party from the presidency after it had won four consecutive presidential elections (substantial background evidence for such a claim had been published in investigative journalistic reports since 2015 regarding the actions and communications of various opposing forces in Congress, the executive branch, and the judiciary). During this interview, we discussed the development of Costa's directorial voice over the course of her career thus far, her perspective on the current state of Brazilian cinema, on women's cinema or feminist cinema, and on her focus on women protagonists in most of her films, from members of her own family to President Dilma Rousseff. The interview took place on March 2, 2019, on the campus of the University of Missouri. At the time, Petra Costa was visiting Columbia, Missouri, for the annual True/False Film Fest, at which she would screen *The Edge of Democracy*.[2]

JD: Beginning with *Undertow Eyes* through *The Edge of Democracy*, how do you see the development of themes, of narratives, and of your style in your films?

PC: It's something that I am discovering as I do it. In a certain way it's as if the lens is opening out—in *Undertow Eyes* I began with a lens restricted to a very intimate and specific theme, which is the loving relationship of two people who have been together for seventy years, my grandparents, and it also has the intimacy of their gaze, but looking only at that. The relationship of the two as they get older.

And later in *Elena* [2012], the lens remains more or less restricted. I think it opened up a bit—it was the family of my mother, three people—in an intergenerational relationship but also focused on the intergenerational relationship of the three, without looking much at issues relating to the nation, to politics, but more to intimacy, to sexuality, to artistic life, and to mourning and guilt.

And then *Olmo* [*e a gaivota / Olmo and the Seagull*, 2014] continued on but displaced itself to a family that was not mine, as if it were a displacement of 180 degrees, from a gaze inwards to a gaze outwards, but remaining very intimate.

And in this film [*The Edge of Democracy*, 2019] the lens widens, and I try to look at the whole country. And in a way that even, somehow, seems an impossible film in the moment, to take account of so many things; a recent but very intense historical process that happened in such a way that when we had barely begun elaborating the film—still in relation to the country—I felt that the film was much bigger than I was. The others, they fit in my hand in a sense, and in this one I was swallowed up a bit [laughter] by the course of events.

And the question of language, I think it remains, at least in the case of *Elena*—and also in *Olmo*—they are essayistic films and make use of a lot of montage with voice-over, so they have that freedom in a way, of having a voice-over narrative that makes sense of things, that places things—sort of knits everything together. And also this cinematographic language itself—I think there is something in common in all of them that is more, the camera that searches, a camera that is seeking out, a camera that has to transmit a point of view. It's not a stationary camera, static; it's a camera always in movement, seeking, seeking.

JD: You said the word *intimacy*. Do you think that this might be a line of development—a growth, a journey from more private spaces to more public ones? I would not say more political, but in a certain way they are; we see a more of obvious politicization.

PC: Yes, there is that dislocation, indeed, from an intimate space to a public space. I had not thought of it in that way, but certainly, this film is made, almost the entire time, in public spaces, about public decisions that were made, and the street as a public space, the Congress as public space. Yes, it has those dislocations of course—it moved from the intimate space of *Undertow Eyes*, [in which] I was looking at my grandparents' sheets, to public spaces. And even taking up again the theme of family itself, which had been portrayed in *Undertow Eyes* and *Elena* but from a completely different point of view; there I did not deal with the issue of the construction company, my grandfather—even though it was the same grandfather. Nor in *Elena* [did I deal with] the issue of how much that break that my parents made with the family, with the way of life of the family, led to the diversified agenda that follows in the film *Elena*. I find interesting the idea that one could make a thousand films about my family that would be quite different!

JD: There is perhaps an inversion in emphasis between *Elena* and this film [*Edge*], because in *Elena* you have that part in the beginning which has to do with living underground during the dictatorship and afterwards the story of Elena, and here the emphasis lies on the political side of the current situation in Brazil. There is also that continuity of speaking about your mother, your grandparents. How, in terms of the continuation of themes from the first films, do you see *The Edge of Democracy*?

PC: What continued?

JD: Yes, in terms of your family and the connection with the larger history of Brazil.

PC: Right. Continuity is the right word. The exploration of familial history continues but looking at it within a political and historical context and not just in the context of familial intimacy—of the issues of the more intimate fetish—but more the history of the family with the history of the country.

JD: In terms of cinema, I wanted to ask about your perspective on the current scenario of Brazilian cinema. First, I have three questions: about national cinema in general, about documentary specifically, and about the situation for women filmmakers.

PC: Well, it's very difficult to know what will happen with Brazilian cinema currently, because there is a dismantling [of policies] going on. We are still seeing the impact of public policy, with five to six films in Berlin, three films here [in the True/False Film Fest of Columbia, Missouri], perhaps for the first time.

JD: Yes, for the first time. I think there was never more than one before. So this would be a result of policies from five years ago, of Dilma?

PC: Yes, exactly. It is a policy from 2002 until recently. And what will happen with national cinema is difficult to predict, but I think there will be a decrease. We are in a very rich moment that is perhaps reaching its end, at least of this phase. I hope not, I hope that it will be possible to continue by other means but . . . how I see national cinema independent of this, in terms of production?

JD: Yes, sure, you can talk about that as well.

PC: I think there is a small paradigm shift going on in national cinema perhaps, in the sense that I think that Brazil has undergone a cultural revolution since 2013 in that many people have become politicized, repoliticized—politics was resignified throughout the country, but I see this in cinema with many films about the high school activists, [as] a very important movement; *The Second Mother* itself, which has the perspective of a small familial revolution of the children of domestic workers enrolling in university; all of the debate stimulated by Daniela Thomas's film [*Vazante* (*Wetland*, 2017)] about racism. The debate was very interesting—what is being debated a lot in Brazil today is the *lugar de fala* [place of speaking, or standpoint], which has been a discussion in the United States for a long time but in Brazil is more present now, that is, who are you to speak about slaves?

JD: We have that discussion in the presidential elections, the primaries, since many people don't want a white man again as president.

PC: Yes, that discussion is very present in the United States because the Black movement here is stronger, and the feminist movement, too. So I think the question of "Who are you to represent the other?" has been much stronger for a much longer time, since the 1970s I think it has been on the agenda—while in Brazil, it arrived in force a little while ago. So we have a lot of films by white men representing the favela and women, and now the time has arrived that Blacks are asking, "Who are you to represent us?" and women are asking, "Who are men to represent women?" I think this theme is causing a real paradigm shift in speaking about and representing the other in Brazil.

JD: For *Edge*, you also spoke [at the True/False Film Fest] about how you are going to release the film on Netflix in Brazil, and there is that debate or discussion about video on demand (VOD) in Brazil. How do you see this situation, will cinema shift to VOD? Is that a concern? Will we see a fall in the number of movie theaters in Brazil? Here [in the US] we avoided this perhaps through blockbusters, 3D films, for people who want to see a spectacle, or through film festivals.

PC: I think that VOD brings a good opportunity to cinema, which is, when could a documentary like mine be seen by 100 or 90 million people? Not that it will be seen, but that they have the opportunity to see it. Also, the resources that they have, that are coming now, are producing a lot more films—in Brazil they are making twelve series now, Netflix. So, it is stimulating a lot of production. I hope that the experience they had with *Roma* [2018], a theatrical release in various countries, allows more and more for them to combine the two forms, even when it is watchable on the platform. Because if not, I'm afraid cinema will cease to exist and it will become an individual experience, or of just one family watching TV, and will cease to be that experience that is something of the sacred, of being shared in the space, in the best form. I'm concerned about that.

JD: In terms of State policy, it's not very clear if it will support the exhibition of Brazilian films in the theaters there, correct?

PC: The situation worsened recently, yes, in a drastic way. . . . Now they are declaring that Petrobras cannot invest in films, only in children's education. And there are other funds that are ceasing to invest in independent productions and only investing in big commercial productions. So there is less and less money to make independent film in Brazil . . . the idea has been going around recently that the Rouanet Law, which . . . supports principally theaters, shows, entertainment, was paying artists to suckle on the teat of the State, the idea that the State should stop investing in art. Indeed, in an interview I did with [then-Congressman, now-President Jair] Bolsonaro, he says that there should be no State money in cinema, including for those who go to Cannes, the Brazilians. He says, "Eh,

[Brazilian films] don't even go to the Oscar[s]," but they had just gone to Cannes. And he says, "They've got to stop." To stop investing in culture. [Made public in the press afterwards by Petra Costa, this interview, cut from the final film, shows Bolsonaro saying, "Which film is competing in Cannes to win the Oscar? Or whatever it might be?" Ironically, it was the film that Petra Costa was making in that very moment that later would compete to win the Oscar, nominated for Best Documentary in 2020.] Every time that an artist would come along and defend a public policy, or a politician would defend it (Dilma or Lula), [Bolsonaro] would say, "It's because of the Rouanet Law."

JD: Yeah. It's a return of the neoliberal policy of the early 1990s, isn't it?

PC: Yes, it is!

JD: It just so happened that they only produced two films in 1992. I hope things to do not return to that point.

PC: Same here.

JD: You spoke a bit about this in terms of a feminine sensibility in cinema. There are some women directors that say they can identify a feminine gaze watching a film, identify that it was made by a woman through the style of storytelling, of treating the characters. What do you think about that?

PC: I think there is a more feminine way of making cinema but that there are certain male directors who are more feminine. Let's say there is a way of making feminine cinema, a feminine becoming, and that it can exist in men just as much as in women. I think there are male directors that are much more feminine than certain women directors in their form of filmmaking. And that feminine becoming . . . I observe it in diverse forms. Among these, a greater attention to the body, to dance, to movement; to the more emotional, empathetic side of the characters, be it in a fictional or documentary film, in which you try to connect with the emotion of the characters, not just to their actions. I think perhaps men's forms focus more on the actions and women's more on the emotions of the characters. And I think that this autobiographical question comes also from an impulse that is perhaps feminine, of speaking about oneself, more uterine in that way, of connecting, of being honest, that it is a personal point of view . . . to give oneself over as an author and to unveil oneself as an author in the process and not to hide behind a fictional process. Because fiction, in many cases, hides, doesn't it? It hides the director. I think that the more autobiographical [a film is], the more directors tend to strip themselves bare in the process.

JD: In *Elena* you said that you chose the emphasis on the women of the family. Would that be a feminist option or a feminist decision, to choose the story of the women?

PC: Yes, I think it is. Definitely. In *Elena* they asked me why I didn't talk about her boyfriends or the father. In a certain sense, *Elena* is taking *Hamlet* and rewriting it from the perspective of Ophelia, because she really always fascinated me. Ophelia is an extremely secondary character but who conceals many riches about the secrets of the soul. And I always wanted to look more to Ophelia.

JD: Yes, it's a feminist version of Tom Stoppard, isn't it, who focused on two marginal characters in the story.

PC: Rosencrantz and Guildenstern.

JD: Right. We can close with this idea of haptic style, which has to do with the exploration of the other senses beyond vision: touch, hearing, etc. In your films, especially before *Edge*, I see an exploration of the senses beyond vision—for example, in *Elena* there are shots of hands exploring a fabric or your own face, the emphasis on the act of breathing too, of listening to the conch, which has a connection to memory and emotion as well, or even of your mother feeling the sun on her face. Would you connect this more to that part [of your work] that explores intimacy, and we have less of that in *Edge* because it is more about public spaces?

PC: I think there was no time, you know?

JD: In a "vertigo" [reference to the word *vertigem* in the Portuguese title] it's difficult [laughter].

PC: Yes, when you're falling, you can't breathe, there's no time to feel, to connect with yourself.

JD: I think that you felt yourself lost, it has that feeling. Would those be ways of finding oneself or discovering oneself in a different way?

PC: Yes, I think so. Maybe if I were to make this film ten years from now, I could be figuring out those gestures. I think for me it has to do with connecting to the pain of this moment now, and how I elaborated that pain, but at the time it was more trying simply to take account of the trauma while it was happening and retell it in that way. I think that the listening to the conch, the hand on the chest, the sun, that is also when one is already in the future remembering—I think it is connected to memory.

JD: Memory, yes. I don't remember because I only watched the first version [in the offices of the Buscavida Filmes production company in August of 2018] of *The Edge of Democracy*, is there some scene in which you show your hands?

PC: No, there is one in which I show my feet, walking.

JD: During a protest there?

PC: No, it's when I am talking about the wall. That my family would all be there on the right side of the wall but for a small mutation in 1964. And then I say, "I don't know how I can tell that history" and then I tell about my grandfather. But there are no hands, just those feet. [In the scene, one sees Petra's feet, in boots, walking on a sidewalk on the edge of the grass—in the context of the narrative, we suppose that the location is Brasília, close to the area of the temporary wall separating the two groups of opposing protesters, for and against the impeachment of Dilma Rousseff—and it looks like the scene was filmed in Super 8 to fit better in a montage, in the middle of archival footage in the sequence. In Costa's previous films, she had already utilized a Super 8 camera for scenes associated with the past and memory.]

JD: Thinking about Dilma Rousseff as an important protagonist in the latest film, *The Edge of Democracy*, how much does her story represent a larger story of Brazilian women? And/or what did you learn about that issue in your time filming her?

PC: I think that the film reveals, at least very specifically in the way that one sees Dilma, Dilma in a manner that they had never seen before, in which she is freer.

JD: More intimate?

PC: Freer, more spontaneous, perhaps more—speaking a little about her intimate life as well, which, when she was president, I think she was not.

JD: In this context, it was a situation in which she had to be in a defensive posture.

PC: Right, she fought from that posture. And I think it had to do, certainly, with the context of a *machista* country in which a woman, in order to be respected in politics, has to hide her emotions. For that reason I find very inspiring what I read about that mayor of Barcelona [Ada Colau] who is affirming now a more feminine way of doing politics, and that more feminine way of doing politics for her is to work more through empathy.

JD: She is younger, right? She is something like forty years old . . . so there is perhaps a generational difference?

PC: Yes, no doubt.

JD: Because Dilma is more or less from the same generation of Hillary Clinton, for example. In terms of foreign policy, [Clinton] wanted to present a strong policy, "masculine," to avoid the attacks of being weak as a woman.

PC: Yes, yes.

JD: Did you see that with Dilma as well?

PC: Yes, I did see it.

JD: Is the question more or less sui generis? You have a woman president who's in the process of impeachment, defending herself, or is there something more universal there, in the story? There were people who were criticizing the situation in which they were yelling, "Bye, sweetie" during the process in the Congress, right?

PC: Yes, the process was very chauvinist from the beginning to the end. She made mistakes, many, but the process was one of white men retaking power—without any scruples, without any shame. There was a great deal of discomfort about a woman serving in that position. And I've been watching this since that way they reacted to her at the World Cup [of 2014 in Brazil], saying, "Hey, Dilma, shove it up your ass!" up through the "Bye, sweetie" and the expressions, the stickers of her that they put on cars with her legs spread in the middle, where you put the gas. The way that she did not hug people, did not go out to drink whiskeys, did not chat, did politics in a more formal way. It has been centuries, you know, that politics has been done in a bar among men smoking cigars. And so there was a divergence . . . between how all those men on the other side did politics and how she did politics, and it was a discrepancy of gender as well. And more shocking, I think, is the way in which suddenly they lose all sense of shame and decide to take her out at all costs. And that was in plain sight for the camera to capture: the way they sang songs, the way they entered the hallways as soon as she left power. One of the strongest scenes for me was to film May 12, when the Senate was voting on impeachment until five in the morning. At ten o' clock, Dilma had to make a speech.

JD: Seated there in front of everyone?

PC: No, leaving the Planalto Palace [presidential offices], going to the Alvorada Palace [presidential residence] where she would remain imprisoned, really imprisoned [during the months in advance of the Senate trial, when the Brazilian Constitution says an impeached president's duties must be suspended]. Four, five hours later, Temer and his ministers took the [Planalto] Palace, which is that scene in the film in which I show that the rules of the Palace were suspended, and the owners took the halls full of thirst in that way, after years of having to ask permission to walk through them. That's what it was, a horde of men retaking that palace. The scene went so far as to be operatic—the one of them taking the palace back.

Notes

1. Preface and translation from the Portuguese by Jack A. Draper III.
2. This interview has been edited for reasons of length and clarity and to conform with the format of the other interviews in this book.

Work Cited

Marks, Laura. 2000. *The Skin of the Film: Intercultural Cinema, Embodiment, and the Senses*. Durham, NC: Duke University Press.

PART 3
INTERSECTING IDENTITIES

Chapter 9

Conditions for a Twenty-First-Century Black Woman Cinema in Brazil

The Politics and Aesthetics of Yasmin Thayná's Audiovisual Practice

María Mercedes Vázquez Vázquez

In the years leading to the preparation of her acclaimed short film *Kbela*, Afro-Brazilian filmmaker Yasmin Thayná had become acutely aware of the fact that Brazilian cinema was overwhelmingly produced by white male directors despite the fact that 52 percent of Brazil's population was of African descent (Thayná 2016). Moreover, according to an often-cited study by the Universidade Federal do Rio de Janeiro's Group of Multidisciplinary Studies of Affirmative Action (*Grupo de Estudos Multidisciplinares da Ação Afirmativa*), a strong influence on Thayná (Candido et al. 2014), there was no film directed or scripted by Black women in Brazil among the 218 highest grossing fiction films produced between 2002 and 2012. Thirteen percent of the directors in this selection of films (the most viewed in Brazilian theaters in that period) and 26 percent of the scriptwriters were women, but all of them were white (Thayná 2016). A more recent study by the same research group covering a larger period of time shows an even more dire state of the industry with 98 percent of male directors and only 2 percent of women directors (Candido et al. 2017). It must be pointed out, however, that these statistics are produced on the basis of studies focusing on fiction features with highly successful results at the box office, a type of film that does not represent the work produced by

Black Brazilian filmmakers, both men and women, which are mostly short films. As Janaína Oliveira points out, "É no universo dos curtas-metragens que a produção de filmes de diretoras (e diretores) negras(os) tem se desenvolvido" ("The production of films by Black filmmakers, both men and women, belongs to the short-film genre") (Oliveira 2019, 45).[1]

The pervasive race and gender inequality in Brazil's film industry is obvious not only on the gender and racial composition of film crews but also in representations of the population on the screen (Smith, Choueiti, and Pieper 2015). Calls to redress this gender and racial imbalance by national and international agencies resulted in the promulgation of laws that may have become ineffective after the impeachment of President Dilma Rousseff in 2016. The conservative president Jair Bolsonaro has positioned himself against what in his circle is pejoratively named "the ideology of gender" and has reduced dramatically the power of film and cultural institutions to continue supporting public initiatives for gender and racial equality since he became president in 2019.[2] In their investigation on gender representation in Brazilian films, Stacey L. Smith, Marc Choueiti, and Katherine Pieper warned,

> After decades of legal and institutional improvements in minority rights and gender equality, Brazil is now crossing a rather turbulent period, with serious risks of regression in the terms of gender equality. The current Federal Chamber of Deputies, elected in 2014, is the most conservative since the return of democracy in the 1980s. . . . Above all, evangelical representatives have been very active in fighting what they call "gender ideology," which is . . . basically the inclusion of . . . gender equality concerns in law making and public policy. (Smith, Choueiti, and Pieper 2015, 39)

Awards to promote gender and racial equality face an uncertain future now that the Ministry of Culture has shrunk to the status of Secretaria Especial da Cultura (Special Secretariat for Culture) of the Ministry of Tourism. Such awards include the Carmen Santos Award of Cinema launched in 2013 by the Secretariat of Audiovisual Activities of the Ministry of Culture and the Secretariat of Women's Policies of the Presidency of the Republic of Brazil, and the program Curta Afirmativo: Protagonismo da Juventude Negra na Produção Audiovisual (Affirmative Short: Protagonism of Black Youth in Audiovisual Production), also created by the Ministry of Culture in 2012 on the National Day of Zumbi and Black Consciousness.

In the case of women filmmakers of African descent, official figures show that there was only one Black female director who solo-directed a feature-length film in Brazilian cinema up to 2020 (Adélia Sampaio's *Amor maldito / Damned Love*, of 1983, would be the first and Viviane Ferreira's *O dia de Jerusa / Jerusa's Day*, the second).[3] This alarming statistic is due to the fact that Afro-Brazilian women filmmakers suffer a double discrimination. As Marcia Rangel Candido et al. (2017, 5) have denounced, "Elas sofrem uma dupla exclusão, de gênero e de raça—fenômeno que a literatura especializada denomina interseccionalidade" ("They suffer a double exclusion, of gender and race—a phenomenon denominated intersectionality in academic publications").

Yasmin Thayná's racial and gender awareness grew stronger at a time when class discourses where prominent in Brazil as fit the successive governments of two presidents from the Workers' Party (Partido dos Trabalhadores) such as Luiz Inácio Lula da Silva and Dilma Rousseff. When she was initiating her filmmaking career, the Brazilian government was implementing measures to reduce social inequalities at federal, state, and municipal levels, and Thayná benefited from these as well as educational reforms in the 1980s that led to the creation of public secondary schools called Centros Integrados de Educação Pública (Public Integrated Schools). Part of her studies and extracurricular activities at this school involved investigating her surroundings, and this is how she got attracted to film school, where she produced shorts, as is required for starting filmmakers. Although Thayná's filmmaking career is short, her work is proof of the positive effects of left-wing cultural policies for the advancement of diversity, and the impact of her work is a sign of a new sensibility in Brazilian filmmaking and society at large toward race and gender. Thayná deserves close attention as she is not only a filmmaker but also a cultural activist and intellectual who seeks to understand cultural processes regarding the Black presence in Brazil's audiovisual industries.

This chapter is concerned with the study of the aesthetics and politics of Thayná's short film *Kbela* (2015) from a film and cultural studies perspective, combined with the scrutiny of the industrial dynamics that enabled Thayná to become a relatively well-known filmmaker despite not having produced a feature yet. Of special interest are the innovative strategies that she employs to exhibit and promote not only her films but also those of other Black filmmakers. In Brazil, as in most countries, feature fiction or documentary films are often primarily identified with their director and measured in terms of the success obtained after their postproduction at film markets or film festivals. Film scholars tend to focus more on the finished product than on the (often) long process that allows the film to come into being and its reception. In her manifesto on approaches to study women's filmmaking, Deborah Shaw (2017), however, recommends examining the industry's constraints suffered by women working in cinema in particular, as well as the opportunities afforded to them. Taking Yasmin Thayná's short filmmaking career as a case study, such an approach will help to better understand the opportunities afforded to, and constraints faced by, contemporary Afro-Brazilian women filmmakers and the innovative strategies they employ in the field.

This research also draws inspiration from Stephen Hart's (2015) analyses of Latin American Cinema through the prism of technology, focusing on technologies of circulation linked to aesthetic, social, and ideological transformations rather than filmmaking technology. Juliana Vicente, Afro-Brazilian filmmaker and director of the production company Preta Portê Filmes, for instance, speaks of the importance of distributing films made by Black filmmakers (Vicente 2017), while film scholar Janaína Oliveira denounces the invisibility of films made or written by Afro-descendant women in Brazilian cinema (Oliveira 2019). Understanding how women filmmakers innovate in order for their films to become visible is therefore essential for understanding their work.

In the pages that follow, I will first situate Thayná's trajectory in its context to better understand the significance of her audiovisual production and her activism. It is important to reiterate that the increased visibility of Afro-Brazilian filmmakers was boosted by the springboard of left-wing cultural ideologies and democratic governmental practices during the governments of Lula da Silva and Dilma Rousseff. We ought to acknowledge this success, because since the impeachment of President Rousseff in 2016, what some have perceived as a negative attitude toward artists and cultural officers by the ensuing governments has resulted in a gradual destruction of preexisting platforms for cultural development that had been successful in promoting Brazilian filmmaking and, to a limited extent, women and Black filmmaking.

Various laws were passed between 1995 and 2014 to promote diversity in Brazilian media and film production. One of them was the Federal Law 12.288/10 of July 20, 2010, called Estatuto da Igualdade Racial (Statute of Racial Equality), based on the Law Project no. 3.198/2000 proposed by Senator Paulo Paim in collaboration with the Black movement. This Statute prohibits ethnic discrimination and promotes equal opportunities for Black actors and technicians in films, commercials, and other media. Although, as Marcia Rangel Candido et al. (2014, 7) point out, the Statute constituted an important advancement but its effectiveness was hindered by the lack of precise quotas. In fact, according to the same researchers, many laws for the promotion of racial equality passed at the time are expressed in equally vague and unspecific language with regard to the promotion of equal opportunities.

Moreover, most laws of this type do not affect commercial cinema but are aimed at independent cinema. Spcine in São Paulo is a good example of this as well as a program with quotas that might prove more effective. Directed by the female filmmaker Laís Bodanzky since 2019, Spcine is one of the few remaining public offices with affirmative action policies toward gender equity. Operating at the state level for only five years in the center of Brazil's economy (São Paulo), Spcine is a public company of the city in charge of the audiovisual incentives in cinema, television, games, and new media. Its remit is to implement mechanisms to promote diversity in all the funding-seeking opportunities. To develop these strategies, Malu Andrade, Spcine's director of Development and Audiovisual Policies, drew from similar audiovisual policies in Sweden and the United Kingdom. The institution set targets such as achieving 50 percent of women directors in feature and film series projects and 25 percent of people of African descent in film direction or ownership of audiovisual companies. To reach these targets, the film and audiovisual institution also offers educational opportunities according to the needs of the audiovisual labor market. Within Spcine, women filmmakers of African descent can opt for public financing and receive priority attention in educational programs related to creation, business development, and networking. According to Andrade, at the moment, Brazil maintains an average of 20 percent of films directed and scripted by women, but she hopes that Spcine's affirmative actions will yield good results and this percentage will increase in the coming years, at least in São Paulo (Malu Andrade, email communication with author, January 20, 2020).

One of the directives followed at Spcine is the institutionalization of the requirement for a diverse composition in film commissions, selecting projects whereby a proportion of fifty-fifty between male and female members of different ethnic groups and sexual orientation must be maintained. Another significant development is the launch of an online film streaming platform one year ago called Spcine Play, which has become a new platform for the circulation of works by women and Black Brazilian directors. Spcine's advancements are impressive, particularly when taking into account the current federal government that is unfriendly to any measures toward gender and racial equality, and when compared with similar institutions operating in other major Brazilian cities, such as Rio de Janeiro, where Thayná is based.

At the national level, Ancine, the national film agency, used to have a commission to promote diversity in film and audiovisual production led by the producer Débora Ivanov[4] (whose term was from 2015 to 2019), but after her departure and that of other managers also invested in addressing gender, ethnic, and social class inequalities, it is likely that these affirmative action initiatives will be stalled for a long period.

Yasmin Thayná's Media and Intellectual Endeavors

It is in this national context that Yasmin Thayná develops her work as a filmmaker, an intellectual, and a cultural activist. Born in 1993 in the periphery of the state of Rio de Janeiro in the municipality of Nova Iguaçú (Baixada Fluminense), she has authored more than twenty productions including short films, web series, and clips, the most successful of which is her short *Kbela* produced in 2015. Despite its huge box office success during its premiere at the Odeon cinema theater, *Kbela* was initially rejected by Brazilian film festivals. However, it was later sought out by festivals following its selection for the prestigious International Film Festival Rotterdam (IFFR). Incidentally, IFFR is a film festival known for its support of Latin American independent filmmakers, particularly through the Hubert Bals Fund. Sadly, *Kbela*'s shifting reception in its national context points to the continuation of an attitude that requires overseas legitimation, owing perhaps to the country's colonial past.

As mentioned before, in addition to producing short films, Thayná has sought to provide more visibility to Black filmmakers, producers, scriptwriters, and other film crew, probably because her own career owes much to socially committed educators and politicians. In 2003, the prominent Brazilian musician of African descent Gilberto Gil took a position as Minister of Culture during Lula da Silva's first presidential term. Thayná's life was transformed by the public programs of the Partido dos Trabalhadores government to promote education among the less-privileged youth and to address the extreme social and racial inequalities still persistent in Brazil at the beginning of the twenty-first century.

Yasmin Thayná studied in public schools and was in secondary school during the time when the cultural policies of a government taking part in Latin America's leftist wave, the Pink Tide, were being implemented. The new cultural policies were followed after a process of democratic consultation and profound intellectual reflection. Gilberto Gil's transformative approach toward cultural promotion tried to avoid the pitfalls of previous governments, such as understanding State support merely as a resource whereby individuals can apply for funding for particular projects. In Gil's own words, "Nós recusamos a enxergar o financiamento público como mero recurso ao qual se pode recorrer para a realização de projetos particulares" ("We refuse to conceive of public financing as a mere resource to produce personal projects") (Gil 2006).

Instead, Gil's cultural policies were devised after broad public consultation with national and international intellectuals. Among other measures, Gil proposed the organization of seminars debating four major topics, one of which was "Populações e territórios: o global, o nacional e o local no agenciamento de identidades e na diversificação da cultura" ("Populations and territories: global, national, and local considerations in the agency of identities and cultural diversification") and claimed "A incorporação da diversidade em nossos corações—e em nossas instituições—é o reconhecimento de que diferenças culturais são positivas, mas desigualdades sociais não são e não serão jamais" ("The incorporation of diversity in our hearts—and our institutions—is the recognition that cultural differences are positive but social inequalities are not and will never be") (Gil 2007).

This mode of cultural promotion in which decisions are taken democratically and researchers from all over the world are invited to contribute to cultural developments produces more long-lasting effects than the subvention of particular projects among the underprivileged because it provides creators with the tools to multiply those efforts, as the case of Thayná demonstrates. From sixteen to seventeen years old, Yasmin Thayná frequented the Escola Livre de Cinema de Nova Iguaçú (Free Film School of Nova Iguaçú), linked to the municipal Culture Secretary, which was a result of such an approach. In this municipality, public policies for cultural development were engineered by representatives of the popular sectors, some of whom were female educators and thinkers of African descent. These progressive educators were aware of the fact that "historicamente, as mulheres negras brasileiras têm vivenciado a interseção do racismo, do sexismo e da desigualdade social nas práticas cotidianas, na produção de conhecimento e, principalmente, nas representações dos meios de comunicação" ("historically, Black women of African descent in Brazil have experienced the intersection of racism, sexism, and social inequality in the spheres of everyday life, knowledge production, and, more importantly, in mass media representation") and aimed to address these inequalities through municipal policies in line with those of the federal government (Ferreira and de Sousa 2017, 175). Therefore, Thayná enjoyed public policies that enabled her to gain self-confidence and imagine that she could attend a university such as the Universidade Federal do Rio de Janeiro, despite this institution being three hours away from her home and Thayná not having completed the university-entrance exams (*vestibular*).

Furthermore, Thayná's desire to critique the stereotyping of audiovisual constructions of the place where she lived—a community marked by high levels of violence—produced by mainstream mass media is reminiscent of Gil's seminars about the self and the city. At the Escola Livre de Cinema de Nova Iguaçú, in addition to learning filming techniques, students were learning *o direito à cidade* (the right to the city). She participated in an educational program that covered not only scriptwriting, cinematography, or film directing but also ways of looking at the city, methods for understanding the country, and methods for reflecting on the associations between the body, the memory, and the city. The combination of scholarship and film circulation is a characteristic strategy of Black film circulation in Brazil and has been used by other Black filmmakers such as Zózimo Bulbul (through the Centro Afro Carioca de Cinema) and Viviane Ferreira (one of the founders of the Associação de Profissionais do Audiovisual Negro [Professional Association of Black Filmmakers]). Film exhibitions are often tied to scholarly seminars.

The pedagogical approach adopted in her school connected with Thayná's rising awareness of ancestral knowledge under the strong influence of Mãe Beata de Yemanjá, a religious leader of the Afro-Brazilian religion Candomblé, a writer, and a human rights activist. Stela Guedes Caputo and Mailsa Passos, who have studied the intersections of culture and knowledge in Mãe Beata's community practice, claim that the stories narrated by Mãe Beata introduced young generations to a fundamental and structural element of the Afro-Brazilian cultural-religious universe: *ancestralidade* (2007, 105). This ancestralidade is a major characteristic of the work of new women filmmakers such as Thayná and Viviane Ferreira. Ferreira is the first Black filmmaker who, following in the footsteps of

Adélia Sampaio (the first Black woman filmmaker of Brazil who made a feature-length film), solo-directed a feature-length fiction film.

The acknowledgment of the community in Thayná's intellectual and creative method is paramount (Yasmin Thayná, Skype interview with author, February 29, 2020). In addition to Mãe Beata, Thayná acknowledges the great influence of Raul Fernando, her scriptwriting teacher from the Escola Livre, and Zózimo Bulbul, the pioneer Afro-Brazilian filmmaker and Cinema Novo actor (*Alma no olho / Soul in the eye*, 1973) and her participation in the enormously successful film education project Projeto Cine Tela Brasil (Project Cinema Brazil) led by the filmmaker Laís Bodanzky and her partner Luiz Bolognesi. This program aimed to promote film viewing and filmmaking in peripheral communities. In the program's first ten years, 407 short films were created by young people who might not have enjoyed this opportunity otherwise. In fact, one of Thayná's current projects as of the time of this writing (August 2020) is to open an Escola Afroflix de Imagens (Afroflix School of Images) in Nova Iguaçú, Baixada Fluminense (Rio de Janeiro), to study images and narratives with Afro-diasporic epistemologies. More opportunities for learning appeared in the form of film clubs. Nova Iguaçú was full of cine clubs where films were viewed and discussed and ideas were circulated.

Another major influence in Thayná's trajectory has been Adélia Sampaio, the first woman filmmaker of African descent, who started as a telephone operator in productions by well-known filmmakers such as Glauber Rocha and Leon Hirszman. Before producing her first feature film in 1984 (the first ever produced by a woman filmmaker of African descent in the history of Brazil), she directed a short and worked as a film and theater producer, as well as performing other roles in the industry. Funding for this first feature, about a lesbian woman accused of her partner's death titled *Amor maldito* (*Damned Love*), followed a method of *ajuntamento*, a kind of crowdfunding of the time that has been inspirational for other Afro-Brazilian filmmakers.

Overall, the teaching methodology used by Thayná's teachers and predecessors is one that promotes a way of filmmaking that seeks to understand the artist's reality. Thayná's process of artistic creation, of learning by creating and inheriting from her community, recalls the views of Vietnamese scholar and filmmaker Trinh T. Minh-Ha:

> To listen carefully is to preserve. But to preserve is to burn, for understanding means creating. . . . The world's earliest archives or libraries were the memories of women. Patiently transmit-

ted from mouth to ear, body to body, hand to hand. In the process of storytelling, speaking and listening refer to realities that do not involve just the imagination. The speech is seen, heard, smelled, tasted, and touched. It destroys, brings into life, nurtures. Every woman partakes in the chain of guardianship and of transmission. (Minh-ha 1989, 121)

The act of audiovisual creation as a way to better understand and feel with images and narratives is combined with Thayná's journalism and scholarship. In addition to participating in film festivals, Thayná is an audiovisual researcher at Rio de Janeiro's Institute of Technology and Society (Instituto de Tecnologia e Sociedade do Rio de Janeiro) and has conducted academic presentations on the meaning of experimental Black cinema in Brazil and racism and police violence at international conferences in the United States and Switzerland, as well as in Brazil (Itaú Cultural). She was a columnist at *Nexo Jornal* until February 2018 and founded Afroflix, a platform for the distribution of audiovisual content produced by Black professionals (at least one of the major crew members must be Afro-descendant).

The film context in which Thayná's productions exist is inserted into the broader context of the United Nation's International Decade for People of African Descent, 200 million of whom live in the Americas. In addition to the growing scholarship to unveil the hidden contribution by Brazilians of African descent to the audiovisual panorama (rather than the industry), there is an explosion of new directors producing important shorts that have now become visible such as Thayná, Viviane Ferreira, Carmen Luz, Lilián Solá Santiago, and Juliana Vicente, among others. Janaína Oliveira (2019, 46–47) describes how this current generation was nurtured by a number of initiatives in the recent past.

In the next section, I will focus on *Kbela* to analyze the imprint left by this learning path and these creative methodologies in the rich text. At the same time, I will situate this short film in its filmic and social contexts, which are more intimately related in Black women filmmaking than in other filmmaking modes, as many of these films are feminist and anti-racist.

Kbela's Aesthetics and Politics

From an aesthetic perspective, Yasmin Thayná stands out as an experimental filmmaker among the generation[5] of new Black women filmmakers. More specifically, two aspects of Thayná's short films call for attention: her focus on the representation of the collectivity and the filming of performances. In terms of production and circulation (distribution, exhibition), the film not only achieved national success and gained international legitimation by its selection in prestigious international film festivals in Europe (official selection at IFFR 2017, award of the public at Vitoria in 2016) and Africa (FESPACO) but also went beyond this typical path with promotion on scholarly and media networks and filmmaking affiliations on the web. With the later practice, Thayná is taking advantage of a strong global trend toward film streaming that substitutes or complements theatrical performances, introduced globally by Netflix and strengthened by the COVID-19 pandemic of 2020.

Experimental filmmaking is practiced throughout Thayná's trajectory, which confirms the director's predilection for this mode. From the short produced in 2011 at film school, titled *Guia da periferia afetiva* (*Guide of the affective periphery*, 2011), to the more recent visual essay *Programa convida: Yasmin Thayná* (*Program Invites: Yasmin Thayná*, 2020, the Moreira Salles Institute) filmed nearly a decade later, her inclination for experimental filmmaking and attention to the body can be observed. An experimental style allows Thayná to subvert stereotyped representations of Black women and Afro-Brazilian heritage on the screen. There are two scenes in *Kbela* that illustrate this effect particularly well.

The nonnarrative twenty-two-minute film is a montage of apparently disconnected scenes that start with a (trans?) woman with a partly covered tattoo on her chest that seems to read *no se nace mujer, se hace* (Simone de Beauvoir's famous phrase "One is not born a woman, but rather becomes one"). This first woman who opens the film eats some black jelly, and from there the film moves to a montage of short scenes with other women in isolation (or fragments of their bodies) undergoing cosmetic hair treatments or suffering with their faces and upper bodies trapped in bags, shortly interspersed with bright mouths in intense makeup uttering an uninterrupted speech (direct intertextual references to Samuel Becket's *Not I*, also an uplifting self-realization story). The whole film moves from these agonizing scenes to images of women dressed in African attire and sitting on thrones (*seu trono de rainha* or "her queen's throne," words from the diegetic song being played as the images are shown), which provides a narrative progression and structure to this montage and the long climax scene.

After the first series of short agonizing scenes comes a liberating one in which a woman who had earlier been seen crying removes the white paint from her face and neck and becomes herself, that is, Black (which explains why it is said that the film is about "uma experiência audiovisual sobre ser mulher e tornar-se negra" ["the audiovisual experience of being a woman and turning Black"]). A musician dressed in white and located in a room with natural light (which contrasts with the darkness of the previous scenes) serves as a transition to scenes of undressed women outdoors in a circle, happily applying white mud to each other's bodies. This is the first illustrative scene mentioned above where an experimental aesthetics serves "to disrupt, unhinge or gesture beyond normative incarnations of gender and cinema" (Lindner 2018, 1). In it, the upper bodies of women are shot in close-up or medium close-up shots with a camera that, rather than circling around them, moves around the female characters in a way that appears to join the party.

This contrasts markedly with mainstream cinematography of the female body as an object to be looked at, as studied by Laura Mulvey (1975). Although her argument that the cinematic apparatus itself is scopophilic has been refined by herself and other scholars in recent years, it was and still is extremely useful to understand how the audience is invited by the camera to adopt a male voyeuristic perspective toward the female body represented on the screen. This short film (*Kbela*) is constructed around images of women, some naked, but the unusual position of the camera invites viewers to adopt unusual perspectives as opposed to mainstream views. In addition to the example just provided, there is another shot in

Figure 9.1. *Kbela*, 2015. (Creative Commons License)

the central scene of the film when a woman is having her "self-defining" Afro haircut and is naked, but Thayná's experimental style produces a non-racist and non-chauvinist viewer. When the haircut is finished, we can see the satisfied woman smiling at the mirror, which is the camera, from a superior position. In a way, the mirror/camera is entangled in her body, inviting the viewer to participate in the woman's satisfaction.

The group scene of the women applying white mud to each other prompts another important reflection on Thayná's collective mode of filmmaking and promoting Black cinema. The film was collectively funded by 117 people through the web, not through public funding. The five thousand Brazilian reais in the budget paid for renting the film set for two days (Oliveira 2016, 194), and the rest was the collective work of fifty people who formed the crew. The hard drive and computer where the first version of the film was saved were stolen, so Thayná had to secure the collective support of her enthusiastic crew to film it again. Referring to the film's tagline that describes it as "uma experiência audiovisual sobre ser mulher e tornar-se negra" ("the audiovisual experience of being a woman and becoming Black"), Oliveira claims,

> Na verdade, não é o processo de construção e afirmação da identidade da mulher negra que vemos em *Kbela*, mas das mulheres negras, juntas, coletivamente trabalhando para um processo de fortalecimento mútuo, na batalha da superação das dificuldades da sociedade em que vivemos.
>
> (In fact, it is not the process of constructing and affirming the Black woman's identity what we see in *Kbela*, but of Black women's identities, together, collectively working in the battle to overcome the difficulties of the society in which we live.) (2016, 194–95)

This collective audiovisual perspective is not exclusive to Thayná but can actually be identified as one of the trademarks of contemporary Black women filmmaking of shorts in Brazil. It owes to centuries-long traditions of ancestralidade, of collective support and understanding, and also to Cinema Novo's less-acknowledged undermining of mainstream films with plots led by characters who fight for individual advancement and social commitment through film, albeit by white middle-class males who often spoke for their subjects. Thayná´s filmmaking method likewise agrees with Trinh's description of "speaking together," understanding that "speaking nearby or together with certainly differs from speaking for and about" (1989, 101).

The second fundamental feature of this short is its design as a performance in two main ways: as a theatrical genre and as the philosophical performance of genre. The film pays homage to Priscila Rezende's performance in *Bombril* in the scene where a woman washes a saucepan with her hair. The soundtrack of this scene, in which the hair sounds like a scourer cleaning a pot, and the close-up of the well-dressed woman invite emotional identification through the senses with a Black woman who is at the same time performing self-identification and acknowledging her ancestors' slave past as well as contemporary social class (since many members of Brazilian's precariat are Afro-descendants). The rich resonance of this hybrid gesture of using negative stereotypes to one's own advantage can be compared to Oswald de Andrade's 1928 Manifesto Antropófago (Cannibalist Manifesto) and its fruitful application to the 1960s–1970s Cinema Novo productions, among which stands Nelson Pereira dos Santos's *Como era gostoso o meu francês* (*How Tasty Was My Little Frenchman*) of 1973.

As is well-known in film history, the cannibalism in this film serves to subvert the dominant view of the colonizer and associate cannibalism with Indigenous empowerment and self-recognition. Cleaning pots with the African hair, which has become a symbol of Afro-Brazilian women's fight for equality and visibility, performs in *Kbela* and *Bombril* a similar function to that of cannibalism in Pereira dos Santos's and Andrade's texts. There is a mechanism in place that subverts the negative connotations attached to domestic service whereby the Black woman appropriates her negative image as a cleaner or a slave to turn it into her source of pride.

On the other hand, *Kbela* is a performance of gender and race. It is enlightening to look at the presentation of women in *Kbela* through Judith Butler's theory of gender performance. Butler explains how "the very subject of women is no longer understood in stable or abiding terms" (2006, 2); rather, "gender is a performance" (190). *Kbela*'s configuration as a series of performances, both artistic and of a personal nature, points to a redefinition of Black women through the screen. Regarding this point, in her overview of feminist theory from counter-cinema to film as an event or political act, Ana Maria Veiga (2019, 272) has noted how Teresa de Lauretis considers self-definition a fundamental feminist question. Moreover, de Lauretis proposes an epistemology of women's cinema that extends beyond the text:

Conditions for a Twenty-First-Century Black Woman Cinema | 211

> I have suggested that the emphasis must be shifted away from the artist behind the camera, the gaze, or the text as origin and determination of meaning, toward the wider public sphere of cinema as social technology: we must develop our understanding of cinema's implication in other modes of cultural representation, and its possibilities of both production and counterproduction of social vision. (de Lauretis 2007, 34)

To close this chapter, I turn to a consideration of Thayná's circulation practice. Thayná's relative success in the Brazilian film scene despite not having won important awards, nor even having made a feature-length film, relies on her innovative marketing and exhibition strategies. For instance, the director makes use of the Internet and licensing through creative commons to make some of her work accessible to all. This choice can be linked to one of Gilberto Gil's earliest initiatives as Minister of Culture: starting a partnership with Creative Commons. Thayná's award-winning short, *Kbela*, has a Creative Commons license that allows users to copy or modify it, a possibility that certainly distances her from commercial filmmaking.

In addition, Thayná devised communication strategies from the start of *Kbela* because as a graduate in the field of social communication, the promotion and dissemination, as well as the possible circuits and networks of distribution, were in her mind throughout the film's creation. This young filmmaker's work clearly differs from the trajectories of earlier generations of women filmmakers in Brazil as described by Leslie L. Marsh (2012, 4). Thayná did not start as an actress, as was usual among pioneer Brazilian women filmmakers.

Well after *Kbela*'s successful exhibitions in Brazil and rejection by national film festival organizers, in January 2019, *Kbela* was invited to take part in a series of Black Brazilian cinema at the 48th IFFR. This was an initiative by Afro-Korean curator Tessa Boerman, a Dutch independent documentary filmmaker whose films deal with issues of representation, diversity, and inclusion.[6] Boerman wanted to make a series of Negros Rebeldes (Black Rebels) where Thayná was presented alongside important figures, despite the meager five thousand Brazilian reais budget of *Kbela*.

After this success, her trajectory as a filmmaker and researcher has continued. One of her most representative recent works is *Fartura* (*Abundance*, 2019), a short that she produced as part of her film studies at Pontifícia Universidade Católica do Rio, a prestigious private university attended largely by students from affluent families. Even though the film's title suggests being full, not hungry, in a country where millions suffer hunger, she wanted to use food as an excuse to reflect on community practices around food. Thayná's use of filmmaking as a medium for understanding reality and expressing identity continues in this work. Beyond *Fartura*, Thayná has created web series and is currently scriptwriting for Netflix and producing her first feature.

Concluding Remarks

Thayná's filmmaking practice intertwines theory and practice and is firmly rooted in both the past and the present. Her reliance on and appreciation of ancestral practices do not exclude attention to new trends in viewing styles. Young filmmakers around Latin America often rebel against the new Latin American tradition of the 1960s and 1970s, to which they claim they are not indebted. Instead, they have grown up watching American blockbusters, even in a country like Cuba, and feel more identified with a global filmmaking community than with the major filmmakers of their own countries. In contrast to this, Yasmin Thayná's evocative power and uniqueness rely on her capacity to connect the past with the present and prepare us for the future.

Another aspect to consider with the aim of understanding the significance of Thayná's contribution is the formation of a growing audience that identifies with films produced by diverse filmmakers and not only by white males from the middle class. Ana Paula Alves Ribeiro (2019, 168) has noted the changes in audience composition and behavior in the case of films produced by Afro-Brazilian filmmakers, such as the shorts *Elekô* (produced by the collective Mulheres de Pedra) and *Kbela*. In fact, innovative circulation of films and ideas is one of Thayná's strengths. She designed and directs the important website Afroflix, a platform that houses films in which at least one of the technical or artistic areas is directed by a person of African descent (at the moment Afroflix is open only to Brazilians but may open its subscription up to other nationalities).

The positive effects of public filmmaking support on underprivileged filmmakers such as Thayná demonstrate the need for public film financing programs (currently under threat) targeting specific sectors of the population, while the director's experimental exhibition strategies point to changes in modes and platforms of spectatorship beyond the cinema theater that are becoming increasingly popular, particularly among young audiences.

Acknowledgments

I would like to thank Malu Andrade, Natália Christofoletti Barrenha, Karla Holanda, Marina Cavalcanti Tedesco, Luiza Lusvarghi, and especially Yasmin Thayná for the help provided in writing this chapter.

Notes

1. Unless otherwise noted, all translations are mine.
2. See Cacilda M. Rêgo's chapter in this volume for further discussion.
3. Viviane Ferreira's *O dia de Jerusa* was first released as a short in 2014, and although some sources indicate that the feature-length version was released in 2016, the fact is that the date of release is unclear. In early 2020, the film was making the festival rounds and some databases situate its date of release in 2020.
4. In the Maria Augusta Ramos interview in chapter 4 of this volume, she discusses the importance of Debora Ivanov's role as director of Ancine.
5. One of the scholars who has devoted more efforts to the study of this new group of filmmakers, Janaína Oliveira, refers to them as a generation. The new Black women filmmakers that have entered Brazil's audiovisual scene in recent years may not be a "generation" yet in terms of a characteristic style such as the one proposed by the earlier movement Dogme Feijoada, which was following the European Dogme 95. They are a diverse group but have a clear political stance—an awareness that, regardless of their narrative, their films are political in a sense different from the 1960s–1970s Cinema Novo.
6. For more on Zózimo Bulbul, see Reighan Gillam's chapter in this section.

Works Cited

Alma no olho. 1973. Zózimo Bulbul.
Amor maldito. 1983. Dir. Adélia Sampaio.
Butler, Judith. 2006. *Gender Trouble: Feminism and the Subversion of Identity*. New York: Routledge.
Candido, Marcia Rangel, Cleissa Regina Martins, Raissa Rodrigues, and João Feres Júnior. 2017. "Raça e gênero no cinema brasileiro: 1970–2016." *Boletim GEMAA*, no. 2: 1–22.
Candido, Marcia Rangel, Gabriella Moratelli, Verônica Toste Daflon, and João Feres Júnior. 2014. " 'A cara do cinema nacional': Gênero e cor dos atores, diretores e roteiristas dos filmes Brasileiros (2002–2012)." *Textos para discussão GEMAA*, no. 6: 1–25.

Caputo, Stela Guedes, and Mailsa Passos. 2007. "Cultura e conhecimento em terreiros de candomblé—lendo e conversando com Mãe Beata de Yemanjá." *Currículo Sem Fronteiras* 7 (2): 93–111.
Como gostoso era o meu francês. 1971. Dir. Nelson Pereira dos Santos.
Fartura. 26'. 2019. Dir. Yasmin Thayná.
Ferreira, Ceiça, and Edileuza Penha de Sousa, eds. 2017. "Formas de visibilidade e (re)existência no cinema de mulheres negras." In *Feminino e Plural. Mulheres No Cinema Brasileiro*, 175–86. São Paulo: Papirus Editora.
Gil, Gilberto. 2006. "Uma gestão para a cultura e o pensamento." *Folha de S. Paulo*, January 18, 2006. http://cultura.gov.br/272138-revision-v1/.
———. 2007. "Hegemonia e diversidade cultural." *Biblioteca Diplô*, January 12, 2007. https://diplo.org.br/2007-01,a1481.
Hart, Stephen. 2015. *Latin American Cinema*. London: Reaktion.
Kbela. 23'. 2015. Dir. Yasmin Thayná. http://kbela.org.
Lauretis, Teresa de. 2007. *Figures of Resistance. Essays in Feminist Theory: Teresa de Lauretis*. Urbana and Chicago: University of Illinois Press.
Lindner, Katharina. 2018. *Film Bodies: Queer Feminist Encounters with Gender and Sexuality in Cinema*. London: IB Tauris.
Marsh, Leslie L. 2012. *Brazilian Women's Filmmaking: From Dictatorship to Democracy*. Urbana: University of Illinois Press.
Minh-Ha, Trinh T. 1989. *Woman, Native, Other: Writing Postcoloniality and Feminism*. Bloomington: Indiana University Press.
Mulvey, Laura. 1975. "Visual Pleasure and Narrative Cinema." *Screen* 16 (3): 6–18.
Oliveira, Janaína. 2016. "*Kbela* e cinzas: O cinema negro no feminino do 'Dogma feijoada' aos dias de hoje." In *Encrespando. Anais Do I Seminário Internacional: Refletindo a Década Internacional Dos Afrodescendentes (ONU, 2015–2024)*, 175–98. Brasília: Brado Negro.
———. 2019. "Por um cinema negro no feminino." In *Mulheres Atrás Das Câmeras. As Cineastas Brasileiras de 1930 a 2018*, 37–52. São Paulo: Estação Liberdade.
Ribeiro, Ana Paula Alves. 2019. "Mulheres negras no Rio de Janeiro. Cidades generificadas e racializadas." In *Mulheres de Cinema*, 159–74. Rio de Janeiro: Numa Editora.
Shaw, Deborah. 2017. "Latin America's Women Filmmaking: A Manifesto." *Mediático* (blog). December 18, 2017. http://reframe.sussex.ac.uk/mediatico/2017/12/18/latin-american-womens-filmmaking-a-manifesto/.
Smith, Stacy, Marc Choueiti, and Katherine Pieper. 2015. "Cinema and Society: Shaping Our Worldview Beyond the Lens. Investigation on the Impact of Gender Representation in Brazilian Films." *Geena Davis Institute on Gender in Media*. Geneva: Oak Foundation.
Thayná, Yasmin. 2016. "Yasmin Thayná. Diálogos ausentes (2016)." Instituto Itaú Cultural, São Paulo, October 2016. https://www.youtube.com/watch?v=1SBD6P3sDdA.

Um dia com Jerusa. (Short). 2014. Dir. Viviane Ferreira.
Um dia com Jerusa. (Feature). 2020. Dir. Viviane Ferreira.
Veiga, Ana Maria. 2019. "Teoria e crítica feminista: Do contracinema ao filme acontecimento." In *Mulheres de Cinema*, 261–78. Karla Holanda. Rio de Janeiro: Numa Editora.
Vicente, Juliana. 2017. "Juliana Vicente: Diálogos ausentes (2016)." Presented at the Diálogos Ausentes, Instituto Itaú Cultural, São Paulo, May 3, 2017. https://www.youtube.com/watch?v=BsgJZOE-5bw.

Chapter 10

Afro-Brazilian Women Creative Workers Speak

Juliana Vicente's Standpoint Cinema
(Cinema de *O Lugar de Fala*)

REIGHAN GILLAM

In a video created in alliance with Itaú Cultural Institute and its *Diálogos Ausentes* (*Absent Dialogues*) series, Juliana Vicente faces the camera and discusses her work. She introduces herself as a "director, producer, scriptwriter, and ninja master at Preta Portê Films. I do a little of everything" (0.23). Indeed, Vicente, an Afro-Brazilian female filmmaker, founded and runs the production company that creates short- and feature-length films, documentaries, and fiction as well as music videos. Toward the end of the ten-minute interview, Vicente discusses the importance of Black people occupying spaces of power. She says, "In the moment you start to occupy the same space, you start to bother people, understand? But I have been trained for this. I have been bothering people since I was born." She then goes on to note that Black people have to strengthen their own self-esteem and make space for evolution, which other people do not have to undergo. She ends the interview, "We can't wait for others to open this space for us to talk. That won't work. We really break in, foot in the door" (9:10). In this narrative Vicente describes the importance of Black people and specifically Black women occupying spaces of power and the challenge of disturbing the status quo once such space is obtained. When one's presence in spaces of power disturbs the status quo, it requires fortification of self-esteem and strengthening the sense of self to withstand such conditions. Yet, according to Vicente, this space is not readily handed over, which requires one to force their way into it. By presenting this small excerpt of her own life story and experience, Juliana Vicente provides an important window into the lives of young Black creative workers in contemporary Brazil, in a segment of the work force often represented and imagined as white.

The presentation of statements or life stories from marginalized groups has offered an important tool for countering invisibility and illuminating the contours of different groups' experiences. Daphne Patai interviewed, recorded, edited, and presented in translated and written form the life histories of ordinary Brazilian women. She notes that the "image of women is most likely to be formed from the representations of privileged artists and scholars, usually male, for it is they who have had access to the public arena" (1988, 3). She aimed for the stories of the women she interviewed to add complexity to the image of women in Brazilian society. In a similar vein, Ricardo Santhiago (2009) undertook oral history interviews with Black women musicians who did not sing samba to uncover the experience of transcending expressive categories of music assigned to Black people. Finally, Haroldo Costa (2009) presents narratives from Afro-Brazilians in *Fala, Crioulo: O que é ser negro no Brazil* (*Speak, Crioulo: What it means to be Black in Brazil*) to express the experience of Blackness for a variety of Black Brazilians. Life stories, testimonies, and statements of experiences of different categories of people—women, Afro-Brazilian non–samba singing women, and Afro-Brazilians—construct bodies of recollections, memories, and experiences that communicate the complexity of these different groups. Djamila Ribeiro (2017) explicated the idea of *lugar de fala*, or place of speaking, from her work as a journalist and from her study of philosophy, building on the work of Black feminist scholars like Patricia Hill Collins, Beatriz Nascimento, Sueli Carneiro, and Jurema Werneck. Ribeiro has spoken publicly about how historically and structurally silenced groups, in a society where white, heterosexual men dominate, have not had access to speak publicly. She argues that everyone has the right to a voice and asks, if minoritized or marginalized groups do not speak, what kind of society is being built? Her articulation of the lugar de fala is to open a space for others to speak and insists that marginalized groups tell their own stories.

In this chapter, I interpret Juliana Vicente's videos in the *Afronta!* (*Face it!*) series through the idea of the lugar de fala or the place of speaking, developed and made popular by Djamila Ribeiro. Juliana Vicente filmed a series of interviews with young, predominately female-identified cultural producers in São Paulo and fashioned them into a series of videos, each between eleven minutes and fifteen minutes long, of various cultural producers reflecting on their life experiences, their work, and their identity as a Black person. These short videos in the *Afronta!* series constitute short life stories, narratives, or testimonies about one's life and work, and they voice the life experiences of a particular group of young Black female workers in the cultural industries. By recording their statements, editing the content, and presenting the videos together, Vicente brings into view a group of cultural workers who have little representation in Brazil and in ways that Black women are rarely seen: young Black women who work in the culture industries and pursue their interests through music, style, acting, filmmaking, and dance. This generation of women accessed college education through scholarships or other means, mostly came from working-class families, and honed their talents of artistic production for economic support and visibility. Ribeiro's idea of lugar de fala encompasses the right of minoritized groups or those previously silenced to define themselves and speak for themselves. Vicente's videos depict the places from which young Black female cultural producers speak through their own descriptions of their life and work. These audiovisual narratives might resemble what Michael Chanan calls *cine testimonio*, in which a group is able to make its point of view public and bring greater awareness of itself (2003, 209). Vicente's videos provide her interviewees with a publicly accessible platform from which to project their ideas and present their narratives. Vicente renders a picture of a group to which she also belongs, and in doing so, amplifies the visions and voices of Black women.

Black Women in Audiovisual

Afro-Brazilian women are disproportionately underrepresented in front of and behind the camera. When considering commercially released feature-length films between 1970 and 2016, Black women have not held the role of director or scriptwriter (Candido et al. 2017, 3). Recent census totals found that 55 percent of the population identified as Black or brown, making the absence of Black people in those roles quite striking (Saraiva 2017). White Brazilians continue to dominate the roles behind the camera in national cinema, despite making up less than half of the population.

Cinema's images of Black women have been the subject of considerable critique. In *Tropical Multiculturalism: A Comparative History of Race in Brazilian Cinema and Culture*, one of the few book-length studies of racial representation in Brazilian film, Robert Stam notes that "the most striking absence within Brazilian cinema is that of the black woman" (1997, 342). Indeed, Black female actresses fill 2 percent of the roles in cinema, while brown actresses fill 3 percent (Candido et al. 2017). Yet, when Black women are represented they tend to assume stereotypical roles in the film and remain as marginal characters. João Carlos Rodrigues found that archetypes of Black womanhood prevail in cinema through the form of various types that he delineates in *The Black Brazilian and Cinema* (1988). To Rodrigues' list of archetypes, Candido and Feres Júnior (2019) analyzed a selection of feature-length films from 2002 to 2014 and found that Black women appear through such stereotypes as the favela woman, maid, or evangelical. While Black male actors have also had to negotiate their place in Brazilian national cinema both historically and today, Black women have to confront a dearth of opportunities to appear on-screen and a lack of complex roles (Hirano 2019; Ferreira 2017). Cinema is no exception to the problems with race and Brazilian media in general, which include the dominance of whiteness, the exclusion of discussions of racism, and the prevalence of stereotypes regarding Blackness (Araújo 2000; Sovik 2004; Heise 2012).

These stereotypes are harmful in that they naturalize the place of Afro-Brazilian women as subordinates, thus contributing to racial inequality. Afro-Brazilians generally inhabit a lower socioeconomic status and struggle with disproportionately low political representation, limited access to education, and poor health outcomes (Paixão 2004; Telles 2006). Racial inequality takes on gendered formations in contemporary Brazil when "it is socially expected and accepted that Afro-Brazilian women will be servants, sexual objects, or social subordinates" (Caldwell 2007, 57). Afro-Brazilian women are also disadvantaged by an aesthetic hierarchy that values white features and casts features associated with Blackness, such as full lips, wide noses, and coarse hair, as ugly or less desirable (Hordge-Freeman 2015; Jarrín 2017). Visual images of Black women delimit them to stereotypes or erase them completely, thus reinforcing their subaltern position as a normal and given part of the social hierarchy.

A few feature-length films, such as *Casa grande* (*Big House,* 2014), do present more complex and progressive images of racialized and gender dynamics in Brazilian cinema (Warren 2017). The film *Casa grande* "problematizes the contemporary iteration of the master class" by focusing on the relations between an upper class family in Rio de Janeiro and their non-white employees and associates (Warren 2017, 20). For example, access to private schools and college exam prep classes is depicted as facilitating the possible entrance into college for the children of the wealthy family, rather than their hard work and intelligence. This calls into question common arguments that position affirmative action as non-meritocratic by illuminating the inequalities embedded within educational access. Moreover, Jasmine Mitchell (2009) argues that the film *Antônia* (2006), directed by Tata Amaral, articulated a hip-hop feminist politics in its portrayal of an all-Black female musical group and their lives in the periphery of São Paulo. The film centers Black female voices and depicts the triumphs and tribulations of making a living through hip-hop music. The characters resist gender norms and patriarchal standards of behavior by working to reach beyond the constraints placed on female artists. They insist on being seen beyond the image of a sexual object, controlling their own image by choosing a particular look, and striving to maintain a sense of independence in the area of romantic relationships. In pursuing creative work and advocating for themselves, the Black female characters in *Antônia* present an image of Black womanhood outside of the norms of maid or service worker typically found in Brazilian cinema. Films such as *Antônia*, among other films, remain exceptional to the general tendency to feature white casts and avoid discussions of racism, yet they contribute to a growing tradition of media that confronts racial issues head on and centers Black actors and characters in these films.

Cinema Negro

While underrepresented in national Brazilian cinema, Afro-Brazilians have forged a space from which to speak and express themselves through cinema production (Dennison 2020). In cities around the country, Black film collectives, individuals, and students access the resources, training, and equipment necessary to make their own short and feature-length films. They form cinema screening and discussion circles, organize festivals, and invite presenters to discuss film aesthetics and filmmaking techniques. Film scholar Tatiana Heise (2012, 133) characterizes this cinema as alternative, which she describes as films that "point out the often profound problems faced by Brazilian society, but they do so from the perspective of those social groups who identify themselves primarily in terms of race, ethnicity, social class, and gender." This Black alternative film scene takes place in São

Paulo through production companies, film screenings and premiers, and lectures. As founder of a production company located in Vila Madalena, Juliana Vicente is one of the key participants in this film sector.

Historically, Zózimo Bulbul (1937–2013) contributed to the formation of cinema negro by advocating for the expression of Black culture through film (Carvalho 2012). He gained his start in film as an actor in Cinema Novo (New Cinema) films. Eventually, he directed the short film *Alma no olho* (*Soul in the eye*) in 1973, which recounted the historical trajectory of Black people in Brazil. He also made the film *Abolição* (*Abolition*), a documentary released in 1988, the centennial of slavery's abolition, which made the argument that little had changed from abolition to the then present day. In 2007, he founded the Centro Afro Carioca de Cinema (Black Carioca Film Center) and, along with it, the Encontro de Cinema Negro—Brasil, África e Caribe (Black Cinema Meeting—Brazil, Africa, and the Caribbean) film festival to showcase films by Black directors both inside and outside of the country. While Bulbul is credited as one of the founders of cinema negro, it is important to note that Adélia Sampaio was the first Afro-Brazilian woman to direct a feature-length film. The daughter of a domestic worker from Belo Horizonte, Sampaio worked for a film distributor and learned filmmaking by working in various roles of production. In 1984, she released the film *Amor maldito* (*Damned Love*). The film explored a lesbian relationship during a time when such material was uncommon. She had directed other feature-length films, documentaries, and short films. After years of erasure, recent actions to recover her legacy have resulted in interviews with Sampaio, and in 2017 a section of the Festival Palmares de Cinema (Palmares Cinema Festival) was named for her. The festival section seeks to highlight the work of Black female film directors.

Today, local Black filmmakers in São Paulo produce films that center Black actors and actresses and tell their own stories. For example, Jeferson De founded the project Dogma Feijoada in protest of films that center whiteness in Brazil. He has gone on to produce feature-length films such as *Bróder* (*Brother*, 2010), which explores the friendship of three men from a peripheral working-class neighborhood. Viviane Ferreira is the head and founder of Odeon Films, a production company that centers Afro-Brazilian culture and politics through filmmaking. Ferreira directed and wrote the short film *O dia de Jerusa* (*Jerusa's Day*, 2014), which centers on two Black female protagonists. The film presents the conversation between two Black women, Jerusa (Léa Garcia), an older Black woman in her Bixiga neighborhood home, and Silvia (Débora Marçal), a young woman conducting a survey on attitudes regarding a particular soap. Every time the younger woman asks a question as part of her survey, Jerusa is prompted to think of her past and she answers through her recollections and memories. The film constructs an image of Black female identity expressed through multigenerational encounters and memories of the past (Souza and Santos 2016). Many times advertisers do not consider Afro-Brazilians to be legitimate consumers due to their lower socioeconomic status, regardless of the fact that they have to purchase products such as soap that would be considered necessities. By making Jerusa the focus of consumer opinions, the film casts Black women as central agents of consumption and people whose opinions should be considered. Renata Martins, another Black female filmmaker in São Paulo, founded a group called Empoderadas (Empowered), which is working to raise the profile of Black women by documenting their lives. Martins and Ferreira are two Black female film directors and contemporaries of Juliana Vicente. Together they constitute a group of Black women taking the camera into their own hands to tell their own stories. Black women have been central figures in the Black cinema scene as directors, actresses, scriptwriters, and other roles.

Face It!

Juliana Vicente is the founder and head of Preta Portê Films. Vicente grew up in the interior of São Paulo, the daughter of a middle-class family. She studied cinema at the Fundação (Foundation) Armando Alvares Penteado and literature at the University of São Paulo. After experiencing a variety of different programs of study, she settled on cinema because it appeared to be a medium through which she could work with various themes. During college she made the short film *Cores e botas* (*Colors and boots*, 2010), which focuses on a Black girl protagonist named Joana who is rejected during a tryout for a position as one of Xuxa's backup dancers. Xuxa is a white, blond female entertainer who hosted a popular children's program. The centrality of Xuxa, and the similar-looking white young women who surrounded her on the show, centered whiteness, thus evidencing a visual barrier to entry that a Black girl would not be able to cross (Simpson 1993; Dennison 2013). After college she worked for different production companies to learn how they operated and, eventually, opened her own production company. The name, Preta Portê, is a play on the term *prêt-a-porter* in French, which means "ready to wear." The word *preta* refers to the color black. One of the first projects by Preta Portê was to film Hip-Hop Week in Diadema, a municipality in São Paulo. The production company deals with socially conscious material about marginalized communities and individuals, and it serves as a conduit through which Vicente has brought her own and others' visual projects to fruition.

The experiences of Black women are a central subject matter, although the company makes films and visual material that work with other themes. The logo for the company visualizes the silhouette of a Black woman, which aligns with the name of Preta (black) in the title. The silhouette has a white circular outline of what appears to be an Afro hairstyle, which signifies her Blackness. She also wears large hoop earrings, and a multicolored panel provides the backdrop. Many of Vicente's projects bring Black women to the center, as the logo communicates. The director is currently working on a documentary film on the life of Ruth de Souza, an iconic Black actress, whose career spans work in the Black Experimental Theatre of the 1940s through roles on television and mainstream film. In 2014, she made the documentary *As minas do rap* (*The women of rap*) focusing on Afro-Brazilian women in the male-dominated space of hip-hop. Although this is not the only theme she works with, many of her films and projects focus on the lives and experiences of Black women.

The *Afronta!* (*Face it!*) episodes feature videos of different Black youth narrating their own life experiences. All of them are filmed in a confessional tone, where an individual person sits, facing the camera, and recounts their experiences and perspectives. The individual's voice is the only one heard during the scene, and the videos also contain clips of the artistic endeavor with which they are involved. All of the people appear to be in their twenties or thirties, and they are all pursuing careers in the creative industries, including music, visual culture, style, acting, and filmmaking. While the first season depicts five men and eight women, the second season includes only female or femme-identified people in thirteen episodes. Taken together, this series deploys filmed life narratives that forge an image of Black female participation in the creative economy rarely seen in other venues in Brazil.

Each video opens with the same introductory montage. After about a one-minute excerpt of the filmed interview, a quick series of images show Juliana Vicente in the process of having blond lock extensions attached to her hair. The scenes zoom into a close-up of the locks and show the hands installing the locks in her hair. A musical sequence plays with a voice saying, "*Afronta, então*" or "Face it, then," which echoes. As scenes of people walking in the street and hair styling continue, the phrases "It's now" and "Our encounter is healing" are spoken. The montage ends with the whispered words "*Descoloniza seu pensamento*" ("Decolonize your thinking"). The words "Afronta!" ("Face it!") command the viewer to encounter the stories of the interviewees. The other words suggest that recounting their stories and encountering one another is healing and is a pathway to decolonize one's thinking or gain access to alternative ways of understanding the world. The montage of Vicente's hair being styled in locks points to the importance of hair and Afro-Brazilian women's identity. All the women in the videos wear their hair in what appear to be natural hairstyles, such as Afros or synthetic braid extensions. These styles resist the valorization of straight hair, often expressed through the label of "good hair" bestowed upon straight hair that undulates or waves in the wind. According to this aesthetic hierarchy, coarse or kinky Afro hair is constructed as ugly and has subjected Black women to a great deal of pain due to their inability to achieve the dominant aesthetic (Caldwell 2007). Thus to embrace one's natural texture, or hair without chemical straighteners, resignifies the value of one's natural hair texture.

The videos of the interviews are to be taken in orally and visually, making the voice and subjectivity of the interviewee more immediately accessible. Daphne Patai (1988) describes the challenges of converting an oral narrative to a written narrative, including transcribing interviews, rearranging them for coherence, and altering the dialogue to conform to language norms (15–17). Filming life stories is not without manipulation, as the videos were edited for length and the interviewee responded to a series of prompts. Yet the video enables access to the oral character of the testimony and the actual voices of the interviewees. Additionally, the viewer can see the interviewee and their clothing choices, hand gestures, facial expressions, and comportment.

The interviews take a similar form and generally include information about the subject's early life, including descriptions of their city of birth, family of origin, and schooling. Then they move on to college education and movement into creative work. Along the way, they recount experiences with racism or current struggles as Black women in their industry. All the interviews end with the interviewee's ideas about Afrofuturism. The interviews together present a complex portrait of young Black women who are creative workers in contemporary Brazil.

Many of the interviewees appear to be based in São Paulo, yet they come from different cities and states, including Salvador da Bahia, Pernambuco, Belo Horizonte, Rio de Janeiro, and Araraquara (a city in the interior of São Paulo state). All the interviewees discussed their family backgrounds, coming from a mixture of economically stable and precarious families. Juliana Luna, a yoga teacher and healer, mentioned that her father was the first Black graduate of the Centro de Cultura Anglo-Americana (CCAA) English language school and worked as an industrial chemist for an international company. She grew up in various Latin American countries in which her father worked. Her parents provided her with ballet lessons, private school, and other enriching activities. Tássia Reis, a singer, attended private school for one year. After that, her father lost his job at a factory and the family struggled to make ends meet. They could not afford to send her to college, yet she managed to earn a scholarship to access higher education. Additionally, some interviewees came from families primarily of Black people, while others came from interracial parental relationships. Yasmin Thayná, a filmmaker, as well as Raquel Virgínia and Anelis Assumpção, both singers, had a Black parent and a white parent. Yasmin Thayná had a Black mother and white father, and her father and his family raised her. She mentions being called a little Black girl (*neguinha* or *pretinha*), in a loving way, by her family. While she was looking at a picture that depicted slavery, her aunt mentioned that Yasmin was lucky to be born today because otherwise she would be fanning her aunt, thus marking the distinction between Yasmin and her white family. While her family may not have meant to harm her, their comments frame her description of growing up as a Black person in a white family: "If you live with white people, you're still not white." The interviewees came from diverse family backgrounds, demonstrating the variety of family formations, influences, and economic status that Afro-Brazilians can have.

Many of the interviewees talked about experiences of racism or observations about how racial dynamics affect them. Many discussed sensing that their color and facial features were not valued and felt that they were not beautiful. School emerged as one of the principle spaces of racism. For example, Raquel Virgínia, a singer, discussed studying history at the University of São Paulo (USP). She describes USP as "a space that is very, very, very white." She emphasizes the whiteness of USP through multiple uses of the word *very* and by adding space in between each word. She says she was "bewildered by the bibliography" due to its lack of Black authors. She describes the knowledge at USP as an "erudition that does not want to expand its mental horizons. And because of this we know more." Despite not seeing Afro-Brazilians in spaces of power as professors or authors, Raquel Virgínia came away with the knowledge that Black people can know more precisely because their knowledge is not included. Several of the interviewees mentioned experiences of differential standards. "They always demand more from us," stated Magá Moura, an Instagram influencer and show host. After noticing that white classmates with worse résumés received jobs that she did not get, Moura realized that racism informed her difficulty in acquiring employment. Others mentioned the inability to make mistakes, as they were judged more harshly for any missteps. Erica Malunguinho, activist, student, and politician, believes that if she "wasn't a Black person, [she] would be 30,000 times much farther ahead. Because what we see the most are mediocre white people occupying spaces." She attributed their mediocrity to their achieving positions through their privilege. The interviewees mentioned racism as a force that affected them from childhood, through adolescence, and into their adulthood and career.

The interviewees discussed their entrance into creative careers and reflected on their work. Moura told a story about working at a men's clothing store after graduating from college. At first she wore her hair in black synthetic braids and, while working at the store, began a private blog. As her work situation deteriorated due to the impending closure of the store and her coworkers losing their jobs, she made her blog public. She also had her hair braided with pink synthetic hair, which people made fun of in Brazil. During a trip to London, fashion week attendees complemented her on the pink braids, finding them attractive and interesting. Using English, Moura recounts that people reacted to her pink braids by exclaiming "Oh, my God!" Street photographers took her picture, and it began to circulate online. Eventually, *Elle* magazine invited her to be on the cover. Magá Moura appears on the May 2015 edition of *Elle Brasil* wearing yellow synthetic braids in her hair. The braids are styled as pigtails on either side of her head and fashioned into large braids that cascade past her shoulders. The publicity led to sponsorship from an eye glasses company and to invitations to give lectures. Another interviewee, the singer Liniker, grew up in Araraquara and recalls studying tap dance in school and participating in community theater classes and performances. She traveled to São Paulo to take classes at a high school for the performing arts. Upon returning to Araraquara, she joined a band that became an overnight success when their music video went viral the day after it was filmed. Eventually, she left school to perform and tour full time. The interviewees receive different amounts of fame and recognition, yet they are all pursuing creative work, taking advantage of opportunities, and honing their crafts to sustain themselves.

By including trans Black women, Vicente expands on the category of women and embraces current movements for queer visibility and acceptance. Trans identities are not new to Brazil, as Don Kulick (1998) previously examined in his work with trans prostitutes. However, Liniker, Raquel Virgínia, and Erica Malunginho are not sex workers. Rather, they work in the creative industries as singers and activists. In the beginning of her interview, Raquel Virgínia says that "being transgender is an overwhelming process. It's a free-for-all. Once you come out as trans, anything can happen." Having to manage people's reactions and anticipate the potential for violence enacted against trans women can wear on a person. Toward the end of the interview, she also notes the difficulty for a trans woman to get a job. Erica Malunginho identifies herself as a trans activist and the founder of a Black community space called Aparelha Luiza. For her, seeking a space of happiness requires confronting "the hemorrhages and violence that still occur. And I take them on through my very existence, as a trans Black woman these violences are in my body. So I make my body an instrument to negotiate my way to happiness." As a person subjected to constant harm, Erica expresses using the violence enacted against her as the means of transformation. Including Black trans women in the series makes the statement that they are included in the category of Black women and shows the multidimensionality of Black womanhood.

While these videos would not necessarily be considered representative, they do present a group of young women who fall outside of the mainstream images of Afro-Brazilian women. The existence of Black women in creative work is not unprecedented. Actresses such as Zezé Motta and Ruth de Souza and singers such as Adyel Silva, among many others, have forged paths in the creative arts in the past and made way for contemporary Black women to pursue such work. Yet the image of these young Black women pushes past the dominant images of Black women as service workers, subordinates, and sexual objects. What emerges is an image of entrepreneurial young people deploying their talent to sustain themselves. They appear as creative agents working for the next advertising opportunity, organizing tours and shows, and pursuing publicity for themselves.

Concluding Remarks

Although the lugar de fala, or place of speaking, is a metaphorical term that insists on the ability of different groups to speak for themselves, the *Afronta!* series, filmed and produced by Juliana Vicente, gives visual expression to the term. In each interview there is a unique backdrop and chair in which the interviewee sits. For example, Xenia França, a singer and songwriter from Bahia, sits in a plush leather chair. The cushion that she sits on has a rip in the seam, exposing the foam interior, which gives off a worn look. The grayish green wall that provides the background has exposed brick and color fading away in different areas. Various objects are assembled against the wall, including a green plant perched on large cement blocks and two large wooden blocks with round lightbulbs illuminated. Abstract art hangs at the top of the wall. França wears black pants, a shirt with a light brown and black pattern, and black sneakers with white soles. Like all the interviewees, she sits in the chair, facing the camera, recounting her life story and sharing her thoughts. Each unique setting distinguishes one interview from another, yet the continuity in the setup links them as a coherent project. The interviewees speak in a space of deliberate simplicity, but the backdrops communicate their artistic orientation. The backdrops are not distracting and force the viewer to focus on the interviewee and their words.

The *Afronta!* videos focus on the interviewee speaking and communicate the imperative for Afro-Brazilians to tell their own stories and experiences. Each speaker recalls their life experiences and recounts different moments in their journey of producing creative work. In that many young cultural workers in Brazil are represented as white, young Black women speak from a place of constant erasure and thus must constantly mark their presence. Their life stories delineate the multiplicity of their experiences but also root them in experiences of anti-Black racism, perseverance, creative talent, and enslaved ancestry as the particular place from which they speak.

Works Cited

Araújo, Joel Zito. 2000. *A negação do Brasil: O negro na telenovela brasileira*. São Paulo: Editora Senac.

Caldwell, Kia Lilly. 2007. *Negras in Brazil: Re-Envisioning Black Women, Citizenship, and the Politics of Identity*. New Brunswick, NJ: Rutgers University Press.

Candido, Marcia Rangel, Cleissa Regina Martins, Raissa Rodrigues, and João Feres Júnior. 2017. "Raça e gênero no cinema brasileiro (1970–2016)." *Boletim GEMAA* 2: 1–5.
Candido, Marcia Rangel, and João Feres Júnior. 2019. "Representation and Stereotypes of Black Women in Brazilian Film." *Revista Estudos Feministas* (27) 2: 1–13.
Carvalho, Noel dos Santos. 2012. "O produtor e cineasta Zózimo Bulbul—O inventor do cinema begro brasileiro." *Revista Crioula* 12: 1–21.
Chanan, Michael. 2003. *Cuban Cinema*. Minneapolis: University of Minnesota Press.
Costa, Haroldo, ed. 2009. *Fala, Crioulo: O que é ser negro no Brazil* Rio de Janeiro: Editora Record.
Dennison, Stephanie. 2013. "Blonde Bombshell: Xuxa and Notions of Whiteness in Brazil." *Journal of Latin American Cultural Studies: Travesia* 22 (3): 287–304.
———. 2020. *Remapping Brazilian Film Culture in the Twenty-First Century*. New York: Routledge.
Ferreira, Ceiça. 2017. "Gaps in Communication and Film Studies in Brazil: Feminism (and the Intersection of Gender and Race) and Film Reception." *Matrizes Journal* (11) 3, 169–95.
Heise, Tatiana Signorelli. 2012. *Remaking Brazil: Contested National Identities in Contemporary Brazilian Cinema*. Cardiff: University of Wales Press.
Hirano, Luis Felipe Kojima. 2019. *Grande Otelo: Um intérprete do cinema e do racismo no Brasil*. Belo Horizonte: Editora UFMG.
Hordge-Freeman, Elizabeth. 2015. *The Color of Love: Racial Features, Stigma, and Socialization in Black Brazilian Families*. Austin: University of Texas Press.
Jarrín, Alvaro. 2017. *The Biopolitics of Beauty: Cosmetic Citizenship and Affective Capital in Brazil*. Oakland: University of California Press.
"Juliana Vicente—*Diálogos Ausentes* (2016)." Itaú Cultural (YouTube). https://www.youtube.com/watch?v=BsgJZOE-5bw.
Kulick, Don. 1998. *Travesti: Sex, Gender, and Culture Among Brazilian Transgendered Prostitutes*. Chicago: University of Chicago Press.
Mitchell, Jasmine. 2009. "Hip-Hop Feminist Politics in the Film Antonia." *Revista Eletrônica Literatura e Autoritarismo—Dossiê* (December), 79–88.
Paixão, Marcelo. 2004. "Waiting for the Sun: An Account of the (Precarious) Social Situation of the African Descendant Population in Contemporary Brazil." *Journal of Black Studies* (34) 6, 743–65.
Patai, Daphne. 1988. *Brazilian Women Speak: Contemporary Life Stories*. New Brunswick, NJ: Rutgers University Press.
Ribeiro, Djamila. 2017. *O que é lugar de fala?* Belo Horizonte: Letramento.
Rodrigues, João Carlos. 1988. *O negro brasileiro e o cinema*. Rio de Janeiro: Editora Globo: Fundação do Cinema Brasileiro-MINC.
Santhiago, Ricardo. 2009. *Solistas dissonantes: História (oral) de cantoras negras*. São Paulo: Letra e voz.

Saraiva, Adriana. 2017. "População chega a 202,5 milhões, com menos brancos e mais pardos e pretos." Agência IGBE Notícias. https://agenciadenoticias.ibge.gov.br/agencia-noticias/2012-agencia-de-noticias/noticias/18282-populacao-chega-a-205-5-milhoes-com-menos-brancos-e-mais-pardos-e-pretos.

Simpson, Amelia. 1993. *Xuxa: The Mega-Marketing of Race, Gender, and Modernity*. Philadelphia: Temple University Press.

Souza, Edileuza Penha de, and Elen Ramos dos Santos. 2016. "*O dia de Jerusa*: Representações de gênero, identidade, memórias e afetos." *Gênero* (17) 1, 67–81.

Sovik, Liv. 2004. "We Are Family: Whiteness in the Brazilian Media." *Journal of Latin American Cultural Studies* (13) 3, 315–25.

Stam, Robert. 1997. *Tropical Multiculturalism: A Comparative History of Race in Brazilian Cinema and Culture*. Durham, NC: Duke University Press.

Telles, Edward E. 2006. *Race in Another America: The Significance of Skin Color in Brazil*. Princeton: Princeton University Press.

Vicente, Juliana, dir. *Afronta!* 2018; web series. Accessed February 10, 2020. http://tvpreta.com.br/.

Warren, Jonathan. 2017. "The Racist and Antiracist Traditions in 21st Century Brazilian Cinema." *Revista Tempos e Espaços em Educação* (10) 21, 17–28.

Chapter 11

Interview with Mari Corrêa

MARI CORRÊA (MC) AND GUSTAVO PROCOPIO FURTADO (GF)[1]

Figure 11.1. Mari Corrêa. (Photo credit: Thays Bittar)

Though Mari Corrêa is relatively unknown in the world of Brazilian cinema, for the past two and a half decades, she has produced outstanding work in the area of documentary filmmaking with Indigenous people. Born and raised in Brazil, Corrêa was trained in documentary filmmaking in France at the Ateliers Varan, an organization inspired by and founded with the support of the notable visual anthropologist Jean Rouch (1917–2004). A seminal figure in the cinéma vérité tradition and in the development of participatory and reflexive approaches to visual ethnography, Rouch's work blurred the lines between fiction and reality and confounded questions of documentary authorship and authority, as illustrated by *Moi un noir* (*I, a Black man*, 1958), *Cronique d'un eté* (*Chronicle of a Summer*, 1961), and *Jaguar* (1967). These characteristics would inform Corrêa's formation at the Ateliers Varan, where she became an instructor for several years during a period that she also worked as professional editor for documentary films and television programs. During the 1990s, Corrêa became increasingly involved in filmmaking projects in Brazil, especially projects focused on Indigenous people and perspectives in the Parque Indígena do Xingu, the vast Indigenous reservation created by the Villas-Bôas brothers in 1960, home to sixteen distinct ethnic groups. Her first film made in Brazil, *O corpo e os espíritos* (*Xingu, body and soul*, 1996), deals with the interaction between Western medicine and Shamanism in the Xingu. Corrêa's documentary style and her specific talents as a filmmaker become evident in this film. Hers is not an argumentative or informative form of documentary making nor is it an observational form of visual ethnography interested in capturing the Indigenous image. Rather, Corrêa's documentary approach promotes dialogic and reflexive participation, giving ample room for the musings of participants, such as Douglas and Prepuri, a health worker and a Caiabí shaman, the protagonists of *O corpo e os espíritos*.

In 1998 Corrêa joined Video nas Aldeias (VNA), the Indigenous filmmaking group that was started in 1987 by Vincent Carelli and Virginia Valadão. From its origins to the time of Corrêa's joining, VNA's purpose was to place video in the service of Indigenous people by producing audiovisual materials at their request. The footage produced was left with the communities themselves—though a few films for non-Indigenous publics were also produced, partly as a way to publicize and secure financial support to the group's work. Bringing her Atelier Varan experience to bear on the project, Corrêa was instrumental in transforming VNA into an Indigenous filmmaking school. Functioning through participatory filmmaking workshops held in Indigenous villages, Correâ's approach also generated coauthored participatory films, notably *Pirinop: Meu primeiro contato* (*Pirinop: My First Contact*, 2007). In this remarkable film, the Ikpeng people reflect on their recent history, from their memories of traditional life and their near demise during the 1950s when the group was diminished and weakened by wars with neighboring tribes, conflicts with white prospectors, and epidemic disease, to their at once traumatic and arguably lifesaving relocation to the Parque Indígena do Xingu (Xingu Indigenous Park) in 1964. While the park is home for the Ikpeng youth, such as Karané Ikpeng (who codirects the film), it is experienced by the village elders as a place of nostalgic exile. Putting in evidence, much of the potential of Corrêa's approach to the making of *Pirinop* is a participatory event that produces what it records. The making of the film was a catalyst for retellings of the past from multiple perspectives and for an intergenerational transmission of knowledge and memory. In accordance with VNA practices, the Ikpeng community viewed rushes of the film during its making, as well as early ethnographic films about the Ikpeng's first contact. This process of viewing feeds into their own remembering of the past, which escalates into village-wide reenactments of their past experiences as well as debates about the possibilities for their future, including the possibility of returning to their original homeland, outside the Xingu.

After parting ways with VNA in 2008, Corrêa founded the Instituto Catitu, which, in some important ways, continues her work with VNA but places greater emphasis on the participation of Indigenous women and on forms of knowledge and experience that belong to the feminine sphere in the Indigenous world. In her film *Quentura* (*Heat*, 2018), this is beautifully illustrated in the portrayal of cultivation of cassava plants in the upper Rio Negro. The women tend to the preservation and continuing cultivation of 280 distinct varieties of cassava as well as to an oral tradition related to the hierarchical society formed by the plants, which is as complex as the human society. Covering major aspects of Corrêa's trajectory, this interview consists of lightly edited excerpts from recorded conversations that occurred on three separate occasions. The first part was recorded on two occasions during Corrêa's visit to Duke University for the Amazon Frontiers conference in April 2018. The latter part of the interview was during my visit to the Instituto Catitu, in the city of São Paulo, in June of the same year.

GF: What was your first experience working with Indigenous people in Brazil?

MC: My first contact with Indigenous communities occurred in the Parque Indígena do Xingu in 1992. At the time, a friend who was a gynecologist working there told me about his experiences with Indigenous women, which was his first experience working with another culture—a culture that had distinct understandings of health and sickness as well as of the body. This really fascinated me. I contacted the group with which he was working, the Projeto Xingu of the Universidade Federal de São Paulo (São Paulo Federal University), a group that had been working in the Xingu for a long time, and proposed the idea of making a documentary about the theme. They agreed and took me with them for a first visit so that I could start the research for the film, but on that occasion they told me not to bring a camera. I went empty handed, except for notebook and pen. At the time, the Projeto Xingu was having one of their first workshops to train Indigenous people to work as health professionals. There were many young Indigenous people participating, the majority men but also a few women, representing many distinct Indigenous groups from the Xingu. At one point during the workshop, the physician Douglas Rodrigues, who coordinates the Projeto Xingu, asked me to take their VHS video camera and film the workshop, which they were never able to do during the workshops as they were too engrossed by the workshop's activities. I filmed parts of the workshop as well as testimonials and interviews with the participants and, when I returned to São Paulo, I quickly edited the material and returned it to Douglas and his colleagues. They loved it and this established a productive partnership between us, which allowed me to start making my own film on the relationship between traditional and Western medicines. I wanted to explore the film through a set of characters. On the one hand, there were the health professionals from the Projeto Xingu. On the other, I wanted to find an Indigenous shaman who was respected among the various Indigenous groups of the Xingu. It was then that I met Prepuri, an elderly and widely respected shaman from the Kayabi people. We felt an affinity from the moment we met. I explained to him the idea for the film and he promptly agreed to participate. Later he explained to me that his desire to be part of the film resulted from the fact that he was reaching the end of his life (he must have been around eighty years old at the time) and hoped to leave behind some kind of testimony. He observed that his own people were losing interest in their traditional culture and less willing to perform rituals, celebrations, and songs, and that he was one of the few surviving people who still held a vast knowledge about that culture and tradition. At that time, he was working on preparing his son to become a shaman. My camera and I were useful to him.

The process of making this film lasted about four years, during which time I traveled many times to the Xingu, sometimes staying with the medical team and sometimes staying with Prepuri at his village. He was enthusiastic about the making of the film. When I visited, I would place my hammock next to his. Sometimes he would wake me up at four in the morning to record his shamanic work. He loved to talk and had an incredible life story. The Kayabi people are not originally from the Xingu but from another area that had been invaded by rubber tappers. They were taken to the Xingu by the Villas-Boas brothers. Only part of the Kayabi people accepted the Villa-Boas' plan to relocate to the Xingu, and that group was led by Prepuri. Before leaving, he collected seeds from the plants they most valued in order to cultivate them in the Xingu—a gesture that suggests his awareness that this was likely a permanent move, without return. During these four years, I accompanied much of his everyday life and work as a shaman.

Given the topic of the film, there were some sad and difficult moments. I remember one moment that was particularly difficult and that called into question my presence and the presence of the camera. It took place in a FUNAI post in the Xingu, a place where there was a landing strip and a health center. Patients in serious condition would often be taken there as the post had a radio and the possibility of flying them out to a hospital. I was there when an elderly man in serious condition was brought in, I think he was in a coma. It was the weekend and there was no one to fly him out to the hospital. He stayed in the infirmary, receiving medical treatment and connected to IV tubes. At that time Prepuri was not available and another shaman was called in to tend to the man. The scene that followed was emblematic of the film that I was making as this man was cared [for], throughout that night, by a shaman as well as by health professionals. But given his condition I was also troubled about my place there. Should I film what was occurring? What right did I have to film it—to film this man who was visibly on the verge of death? I did the logical thing: I went to his family to ask if I could film the scene. The dying man's son, with whom I am still friends, was very calm about it: "Of course you can film, Mari!" At that point, I had already been visiting the Xingu regularly for four years and I was no longer an outsider. In the end, it's a simple scene: From the doorway, I filmed the man who was tended to by the shaman and by the nurse, who occasionally checked on him. The next day he left by plane to go to the hospital, where he passed away shortly after.

GF: You lived in France at the time?

MC: Yes. I was able to make this film because at the time I was already an established editor of documentary films and television programs there. Using my own money, I would fly to Brazil and work alone in the production of the film, doing my own camera work. I learned to do everything on my own. It was my first film as a director and it would be difficult to get the support of a producer. But I was able to produce most of the film myself.

Towards the end of the filming process, I returned to France and started looking for a producer to help me finish the project. Eventually I contacted Yves Billon, who agreed enthusiastically to produce the film as he had himself already filmed in the Xingu and worked with the Ikpeng people, whom I didn't know at the time. Yves helped me to finish the film, though I edited it myself. When I finished, I returned to the Xingu with the film to show to the health professionals who participated in it as well as to Prepuri. I remember gathering in front of a TV set with Prepuri and his family to watch the film. I was very anxious. As the film started, Prepuri suddenly stood up and I nearly panicked thinking that he would just walk away. Instead, he just got closer to the television, leaning on his staff, and watched the entire film standing up very near the TV, I imagine to see better. He loved the film. The film was bought by a French TV network and came out in 1996.

This film was my introduction to the Indigenous world and to the Xingu. As I accompanied the medical team during the production, I became acquainted with many different Indigenous communities in the Xingu. During the four years of production of *O corpo e os espíritos*, I continued my work as an editor and as a filmmaking instructor in the Ateliers Varan, in France. At that time, also, Séverin Blanchet, one of the founders of Ateliers Varan, invited me to participate in a filmmaking workshop with the Kanak people in New Caledonia. The workshop crew included Séverin Blanchet, myself, and Martin Maden, a Papuan filmmaker from New Guinea who had passed through the training of Ateliers Varan and helped create a cooperative of filmmakers in New Guinea. They went before me to start the workshop in the northern part of New Caledonia, where there are many communities of the Kanak, an Indigenous people who have an oral traditional culture. I joined in the second phase of the workshop, which was attended mostly by young Kanaks. The Kanak lived in a sort of veiled apartheid and were the targets of much prejudice and discrimination from the white population. The filmmaking workshop helped lift the self-esteem of the communities involved by creating a dialogue between generations and stimulating the curiosity of Kanak youth for their own culture, approximating them to the older generation, the primary holders of the group's oral tradition and knowledge. The experience was cathartic. It was then that I realized the full potential of the camera and of this particular form of filmmaking, which involves collaboration with communities who are brought into the very process of image production. It became clear to me that I wanted to bring this practice to Brazil.

GF: When did you join VNA?

MC: In 1997, Vincent Carelli called me in Paris to talk about the idea of training Indigenous filmmakers.

GF: Up to that point, VNA was not a school of cinema, even though Indigenous people did produce images.

MC: Right, the VNA work was inspired by Andrea Tonacci's "interpovos" idea, which consisted in using film as a form of communication among Indigenous groups. I had already heard about VNA because the brother of Séverin Blanchet, Vincent Blanchet, was friends with Vincent Carelli, and he told me that I should meet Vincent and perhaps work with him. Actually, before the 1997 phone call, I had contacted and met with Carelli during a visit in São Paulo. Then, Carelli told me that the work of Ateliers Varan was very different from the work of VNA because the VNA did not have the goal of training Indigenous filmmakers. The audiovisual recordings they produced were meant only for internal use, that is, for the use of Indigenous people themselves and not for the outside public. At that point there were already a few people like Caime Waiassé, Divino Tserewahú, and Kasiripinã Waiãpi who were doing a lot of camera work. Though some Indigenous people were taught to use the camera, however, the initial goal of VNA was not to train them to become filmmakers and directors. My first meeting with Vincent in São Paulo did not result in anything. I went back to my work in France. When he called me sometime later in Paris to invite me to join VNA, I was in the middle of editing my second feature-length film and could not join them. They held the VNA's first filmmaking workshop in the Xingu without me. We only worked together for the first time in 1998 in the state of Acre. As part of a larger workshop by the Comissão Pró-Índio do Acre (Pro-Indigenous Community of the State of Acre), Vincent led a workshop on animation and I led a video workshop. Though the workshop was short and involved people from many different communities, it went really well and served to test my workshop method, inspired [by] ten years of experience working with the Ateliers Varan. We agreed to give continuity to the workshop by working separately with each of the groups that had participated. The following year we worked with the Ashaninka.

GF: Many remarkable films in the VNA catalog are centered on Indigenous women. Carelli's *A festa da moça* (*The girl's celebration*, 1987), the group's inaugural film, focuses on a Nambikwara coming of age celebration for girls. Tserewahu's *Pi'onhitsi mulheres Xavante sem nome* (*Unnamed Xavante women*, 2009), by Tiago Campos Torres and the Xavante filmmaker Divino Tserewahu, one of the first Indigenous filmmakers to emerge from VNA, also focuses on a female-centered Indigenous celebration. *As hiper mulheres* (*The Hyperwomen*, 2012), by Carlos Fausto, Takumã Kuikuro, and Leonardo Sette, is similarly centered on women. It is notable, though, that these films are made entirely by male producers and that VNA has seemingly trained very few women in filmmaking. Could you comment on this and on the place of women in VNA?

MC: I think that indigenists of a generation before mine were very macho. The indigenist and "sertanista" culture was impregnated with masculine values. The VNA is not born from the culture of that earlier period, and it's important to note that women have always played important roles in the VNA. Virginia Valadão was one of the founders. After her, Dominique Gallois also became involved. Each of them had vital importance in the development of the project. Their importance has been downplayed in the way the VNA's story is typically told. I know you were talking about films, the products of VNA work, but this is related to the place women have occupied within the group. They appear as supporting cast and this casting is patriarchal. In the reports I saw after becoming part of VNA, Virginia and Dominique are given titles like "adjunct coordinator" and "assistant coordinator"—despite their importance and qualifications. There have been little and only passing acknowledgements of their actual importance. In my case, after I left VNA, even my bio on the site was modified. In the revised bio, I became a mere "collaborator" of the training of Indigenous filmmakers rather than the person that actually gave that training program its body, method, and direction. I think this has to do with the priorities of the VNA and a tendency to reduce the significance of women's contributions.

There was also a discourse that has now gone out of style but that was strong at the time, which posited that we should not interfere with the feminine sphere of Indigenous life because this would destabilize the communities.

GF: This claim was made in relation to women's participation in the workshops?

MC: Right. This was also a very common argument from leaders of NGOs [nongovernmental organizations] in response to the questions about gender inclusion posed by agencies of international cooperation. Because the international agencies that were responsible for financing NGOs are often from countries that value gender equity, there were questions regarding women's participation. The reports produced by NGOs often did not include a single female voice or presence and featured nothing designed specifically for women. The argument to justify that was that the attempt to stimulate women's engagement in areas that were not within their traditional sphere would amount to a disturbance in the organization of Indigenous society and gender relations. This notion prevailed for a long time, and when I joined VNA it was very strong still. In reality there was very little interest in questions and issues related to the feminine universe on the part of researchers and of the men who were leading the indigenist organization. Their main Indigenous interlocutors were also male. Thus, feminine perspectives were neglected for a long time.

Returning to the films specifically, I never had thought in the terms you propose. Is it necessary for a film about women to be made by women? I am not sure how to answer this. The production team for the film that I just finished [*Quentura* (2018)] included only two people, me and a camera person, Vinicius Berger. I am positive that the fact that he is a man made no difference in this film. Because of the way he behaves and his personality, the women we interacted with were completely at ease with him, as if he wasn't there. It wasn't that they were ignoring him but that his being there did not establish a masculine attitude of opposition or cause any inhibition. This impressed me. I can work with men without their presence interfering with my goal of making films focused on women. Of course, it depends on what kind of film I am making. In other situations, I would certainly choose to work with a women-only crew. This would be the case for a film I hope to make about maternity. I can't imagine discussing such an intimate topic in women's lives in the presence of men.

In many films made with Indigenous people, women's perception and even their presence may end up in the background, even if they are supposed to be the main characters, as in the films you mentioned. I think if such films had been made by women directors or by male directors who were committed to approaching their topics from women's perspectives, the result would have been different. There is also the fact that the universe of Indigenous women is more elusive and harder to access and film than the masculine. When I was making my last film, I was thinking about how much easier it is to film men and male cultural practices and forms of knowledge. Men are also more prone to speaking than Indigenous women. To film women, you have to carefully draw them out. It takes more time to approach their world.

GF: Regarding the workshops and the participation of women, my impression is that for many years only men participated in the workshops. It's not that women weren't allowed but that they did not in fact participate. Is this impression correct?

MC: Yes.

GF: Why didn't they participate?

MC: For many years, while I was in the VNA, we always did workshops by invitation—usually the invitation from the community's leadership. We would never offer ourselves and we would arrive in a situation that was somewhat already structured by the expectations of our hosts. I always brought up the issue of having designated spaces for women in the workshops. I would announce that there were spaces reserved for women, independently of the number of men participating so that it wouldn't seem like women and men were competing for the same spots. Still, Indigenous women would not come. The only exception was Natuyu Txicão, a very smart twelve-year-old Ikpeng girl. I don't know exactly what happened but she had the approval of her parents to participate. It's a story that maybe I should investigate and understand better. I never talked to her parents about this but their support was unusual. No one seemed to encourage women to participate. Natuyu had a very strong personality, though, and managed to impose herself despite being undermined by some of the men around her. A lot of this undermining is done in a joking tone—a joking depreciation of women that men know how to do exceptionally well and that sabotages women's self-esteem. You know, through mockery, ideas like "You are not good at this," "You will never be good at this," and "This is not for women" are communicated. Natuyu was able to face this. She was like a little tractor, unstoppable. When we would go to festivals and screenings, little Natuyu would come and be the only girl in large groups of men. For many years she was the only one. It was hard to know why, or what was in the minds of Indigenous women regarding the workshops without speaking directly to them in their language, without the mediation of men. I remember one time that almost made me give up entirely. We were starting a first workshop in an Indigenous community and I insisted, as always, that there were still spots reserved for women. One young woman came but she was being practically dragged by force by her brother or some relative of hers. "Look, here is one," he said. She was extremely embarrassed and I felt that her torture was my fault. Of course, she didn't stay. There was resistance to women's participation. The view was, "If women do these workshops and become filmmakers, they will go out of the community, have boyfriends and kids outside the community." Women needed to be held back.

When I created the Catitu Institute, one of my goals was to deal with these past experiences. I wanted to rethink the workshops and do work especially focused on women. I believed that there had to be a way to deal with this situation so that women might participate. Also, having worked for many years in the Xingu, I was realizing that things were changing. Women were participating more in general. They were attending school, speaking Portuguese, and becoming more visible. Like us, Indigenous men and women were fascinated with their cell phones. It's a different generation. It's not that any of them communicated to me that they wanted to make videos. But I thought that young women in this new moment were more likely to be interested in working with video, and I proposed having workshops exclusively for them. Given that when Indigenous men and women are together the men always take the roles of protagonists, who speak and expose themselves more, leaving women in the background (with a few exceptions), the best option [was] to do workshops with women only so that they could feel freer to express themselves without constantly negotiating with men. I don't think they enjoy having to dispute spaces and compete with men. I took advantage of a women-focused meeting that was occurring in the lower Xingu, organized by a health group. During the meeting, I proposed this idea to an assembly of Indigenous women. They embraced the idea at once. As I had taken cameras with me, we were able to do a mini-workshop right there. The assembly chose four women to participate and, to my great surprise, two of them were mothers with young children. I realized how much things had changed. The discourse that held women back used to include the argument that women were occupied with the care of children and their families. Thus, when you see a woman holding a child on her lap supported by the assembly to participate in the workshop, you realize that things are changing. Whatever the men might think, it was clear that for the women, having a child was not a reason not to participate, even if it might pose some difficulties. That mini-workshop was the first experiment in our program and we went on to make a few more workshops with Indigenous women.

The first village that we held a workshop in after this initial experience was the same village that I had worked with Prepuri, for my first film. I already felt at home there. People knew me well and trusted me. It's also a place where there were no men who were already working with video. There was no need for the women to compete over space. At that workshop I wanted to deconstruct the idea that the person who makes the film is the person who is behind the camera—or even that they had to be necessarily young or technologically savvy. I think that a filmmaker is a storyteller, and the best storytellers in Indigenous societies are the elders, not the young. Though these storytellers are often filmed, they rarely participate in the creation and direction of films. Typically, young Indigenous people are the ones who are trained in filmmaking and they seek out the elders as characters. I wanted the older women to come to the space behind the camera and to participate in the making of films. I invited Tata Amaral to teach this workshop with me. She is great and a very generous and positive person. And Tata never does the camera work herself. It was perfect. I had a living example of what I was talking about. It helped to demystify the film equipment. In the first part of the workshop, we didn't even touch any gear. It was focused instead on storytelling. It was incredible to see Indigenous women who are not from the technological generation, who are not even from the literacy generation, participating in the making of a film. There was also a fortuitous coincidence: when we arrived at the village for the workshop, we found out that the village's men had left on an expedition. It was a women's village. Freed from their husbands, they were able to focus completely on the workshop. This was an indescribable experience. In the end, they made a film based on a traditional lullaby. The film is titled *A história da cutia e do macaco* (*The story of the agouti and the monkey*, 2012) and is available on Vimeo. It's a story of an agouti who, while her husband is away searching for food, has an affair with a monkey. She becomes pregnant with the monkey's baby and hides this from her husband until she gives birth to a little monkey.

GF: What is the reaction of the men to these workshops exclusively for women?

MC: I think that they feel jealous. But to be fair the reaction is very diverse. Some men are very supportive, some are indifferent, and some are against it. Some families forbid them to participate for diverse reasons or excuses, from the reasons I already mentioned ("If you do this you will have romantic relationships and kids away from the community") or due to the jealousy of husbands, which is very common. Or sometimes they forbid them from participating just to demonstrate power over them—without a reason. The women who are more willful and obstinate learn to negotiate their freedom. Objectively speaking, it is much harder for women than for men to participate in the workshops and work on films. The fact is that they carry the burden of child-rearing and have more obligations in the home. It's much easier for men to pick up and leave at a moment's notice to do whatever they want outside the community. Of course, they have obligations too, like providing food to their homes in one way or another. But they can leave. The reality for women is quite different. The responsibility for children makes it difficult for them to undertake any professional activity. The community is also more critical, vigilant, and demanding of them than of men. And then, if they do not continue working on films after participating in a workshop, there are the recurring reprimands: "I told you, see? They don't stick to things. They don't take it seriously."

GF: One of the issues that emerge from the films you produce with VNA and the Catitu Institute is the issue of authorship. Many films confound traditional understanding of authorship—of who controls and directs the film. Can you discuss this?

MC: In the last workshop I did in the Xingu, there were a few Ikpeng participants who had worked with me in *Pirinop*. The workshop included people with a lot of experience making films as well as beginners. As the topic of authorship of the films has been generating a lot of discussions in the Xingu, I thought that it would be an important topic to discuss. We began the workshop talking about the West's legal and conceptual understanding of authorship, which is centered on the ownership of the idea. But when one of the elders tells an old story, or a myth, is he the owner or author of the story? Other people tell the same story as well. He is the author of his version of the story. Without arriving at definitive answers, we discussed these questions to open a range of possibilities for the meaning of authorship. As the Ikpeng who worked with me in *Pirinop* were there, we talked about the ways in which that film was signed. There are two versions of that film, each signed differently. In reality, though, the film has many authors, the first of which was Kumaré's father, who launched the film's theme by telling us about their first contact with the Villas-Bôas brothers when he was a kid. He owns his story and he is the one who brought up and instigated the topic. I have the impression that he led us to make a film about this. There are also many scenes in the film that were directed by the elders in the Ikpeng village, like the reenactment of the flight of the airplane, which was like a catharsis. They were acting but they were also reliving that moment. I remember one of them, Tomé, who said that he would not participate in the reenactment, but when the plane flew over the village and dropped gifts, he joined the reenactment scene wearing nothing but his underwear! It was a real event. In a moment like this, there is nothing "directed" in the classical sense of the term. It was directed in that we worked to create the conditions for things to happen. But the specific way in which things happened was out of our control and full of improvisations.

GF: Could I ask you about the significance of environmental issues in your work? In a sense, questions of the environment are always important in Indigenous films—there are always issues related to territory or water, etc. But environmental issues seem to be becoming more pronounced in your recent work, like *Para onde foram as andorinhas?* [*Where Did the Swallows go?* 2015] and *Quentura* [*Heat*, 2018].

MC: I think that my recent focus on the impact of climate change is circumstantial. *Para onde foram as andorinhas?*, for instance, was a commissioned film. In reality I don't know how to make films commissioned by institutions: I always invest myself in the project. But *Para onde foram as andorinhas?* was made at the request of Paulo Junqueira, from the Instituto Socioambiental, who had planned to go to the COP 21 [the United Nations Climate Change Conference, which was held in Paris in 2015] accompanied by an Indigenous group. Though they did not have the resources to bring a large delegation, somehow they wanted to bring the voices and experiences of Indigenous people, especially people that were "roots," members of Indigenous communities that don't usually travel or speak to the outside world. Junqueira wanted to bring these inside voices to the outside through film. I was seduced by this idea. And this is not a topic that I am knowledgeable about or that was part of my agenda. Of course this issue is inevitably part of our world—we read every day about it, but it was not one my personal interests. Yet I was seduced by the idea because the film's intention was not just to record people speaking about the environment but to capture the experience of the environment, the way people perceive the changing world around them, especially older Indigenous people who have observed climatic changes over a longer period of time and who have a great deal of knowledge about the earth and the environment. The idea was to make a film without specialists or white people and to allow for a different and rarely heard kind of speaker to communicate their experiences through the film. The situation in the Xingu is quite delicate, with the devastation of the environment around them and the impact of toxic agrochemicals in their territory, which is being studied by scientists but is still not well understood. I hadn't even realized how serious the situation was until I started making that film. I shot the film in 2015, which was an extraordinarily hot year. It was unbelievable, I had never felt so hot. We couldn't leave the water of the river. There were a lot of forest fires.

When we started making the film, we held a roundtable with a group of Indigenous elders to decide with whom we were going to work. There were no women in this roundtable, however. We thought about a couple of possible women participants, but the film had a tight schedule as the COP 21 was in November. I made the film in two trips to the Xingu and in neither occasion were the women I was hoping to include available. After making the film, I was left with questions about the perspective of women on the environment. Do they perceive and experience climate change differently? In a sense this is not gender specific—anyone could observe and comment on the same phenomena, even young people. But women inhabit a specific universe. They don't hunt, for instance. In hunting, men must witness changes that women do not. What do women perceive in their specific domain, in their field of knowledge? Is there something that we could only learn from the perspective of women? I was left with the desire to make a film to explore these questions, which were really open questions rather than hypotheses. The opportunity to do this film came from RCA–Rede de Cooperação Amazônica [Amazonian Cooperation Network], which brings together a large group of Indigenous and indigenist organizations. Luís Donisete, the coordinator of RCA, called me in the end of 2016 to tell me that they had resources available to fund a project connected to climate change, and I suggested making a film focused on the perspectives of Amazonian Indigenous women. That resulted in *Quentura*.

It's a bit early to talk about *Quentura*, which I just finished. It has had limited viewership so far. It has circulated mostly among Indigenous communities. But the reactions from the people to whom I sent the film is telling. People realize how important it is to have women as protagonists of Indigenous films. Beyond the importance of what they say about their world, it is crucial to give them a place from which they can be heard. There is a lot of pleasure in doing this kind of work as the women are very enthusiastic about participating and sharing their knowledge. This is a new moment in which there is a real and widespread interest in hearing what Indigenous women, who have long been silenced or ignored, have to say. There is a lot of work to be done in this area—work that will get done. It's great to be part of this process. I see my contribution as a soft form of militancy. Militancy itself—taking to the streets or making openly militant films—is not part of my profile. But what I can do is tease things out and bring them to the surface, as I do in *Quentura*. What impressed me most was the depth of their knowledge in their own areas of expertise. For instance, in the upper Rio Negro there is an elaborate knowledge of traditional agriculture that involves the cultivation of myriad types of cassava. The upper Rio Negro is an area where Indigenous people have been living under the influence of Salesian priests for centuries. The Salesians have shaped the people of the region in the ways that they wanted. Some Indigenous languages have gone extinct and every community has its church and chapel. The bells toll on Sundays and the local people, who are very religious, attend mass. Yet when you engage them in a conversation, something different emerges, like the notion that cassava plants are people [*mandioca é gente*]. The world of cassava plants is a hierarchized society that mirrors the social world of the upper Rio Negro. How does this mix with a Catholic view of the world? Cassava plants are people? This is not part of the Christian worldview. Once women start to speak about their universe, you realize that beneath the layer of Catholic acculturation, these Indigenous concepts survive. In spite of everything, women preserve an Indigenous worldview of their own domain.

Note

1. Translation to English and preface by Gustavo Procopio Furtado.

Chapter 12

Interview with Paula Sacchetta

PAULA SACCHETTA (PS) AND REBECCA J. ATENCIO (RA)[1]

Figure 12.1. Paula Sacchetta. (Photo credit: Carine Wallauer)

Born in 1988 (the same year Brazil promulgated its latest constitution), Paula Sacchetta debuted as documentary filmmaker in 2013 with *Verdade 12.528* (*Truth 12.528*) about Brazil's National Truth Commission. Her feature-length film about sexual harassment and assault in Brazil, *Precisamos falar do assédio* (*Faces of Harassment*), was launched in September 2016, shortly after it premiered at the Brasília Film Festival; it has also aired multiple times on Canal Brasil since March 2017 and has since been picked up by Amazon Prime. She also directed the short documentary *Quanto mais presos, maior o lucro* (*The More Prisoners, the Greater the Profit*, 2014), winner of the Human Rights Journalism Award, in addition to web documentaries for *The Guardian* as well as for Al Jazeera's AJ+ channel. Her television directing credits include directing two documentary miniseries: *Eu, preso* (*I, a prisoner*, 2019) (with André Bomfim) and *Famílias* (*Families*, 2019) about LGBTQ+ youth in the periphery. Trained as a journalist, she won the Vladimir Herzog human rights prize in the journalism category for her reporting on the Brazilian National Truth Commission in 2012.[2]

RA: To start off, do you identify as a feminist filmmaker, and if so, what does that mean to you?

PS: Yes, I do consider myself a feminist and there's no way to separate that from my practice as a documentarian. I believe that making documentaries is political, always. A way of being [*ser e estar*] in the political world. I can't separate what I do as a documentarian from what I believe and who I am.

Now, I am a feminist filmmaker, documentarian, but that doesn't mean that I make films only about subjects considered feminist. It's more how I position myself in my work, that I do so in a feminist way. You and I are here in this interview to talk mostly about one of my films, *Precisamos falar do assédio*, but I've made others that relate to feminism in one way or another. In August [2019] my new television series will be aired about the Brazilian prison system. There are eight episodes, and it's called *Eu, preso*. We portray Brazil's prison system through profiles of incarcerated individuals. Two of the episodes are dedicated solely to women because you can't talk about incarceration without talking about women. I have a kind of feminist radar that shows up in one way or another throughout my work as a documentarian. And so, that's what identifying as a feminist filmmaker means to me: having that radar on all the time, no matter what I'm working on, even if I'm working on a project that is not just about women's issues. I look for women's issues within whatever topic I'm working on. It means looking at the society I live in—a society that is *machista*, that is patriarchal, that is the fruit of a horrible rape culture—and at how power works, especially men's power over women. My work talks a lot about the body, too.

So, for me being a feminist documentarian means taking care to always approach whatever topic I'm working on through the gender relations that structure our society. If I, Paula, as a woman documentarian, believe in the documentary as a tool for social transformation, then all this has to be present in what I do.

RA: There's been a lot of discussion about a so-called fourth wave of feminism.

PS: Yes, my film *Faces of Harassment* wouldn't exist without it.

RA: One of the main characteristics of this fourth wave is that it is unfolding in large part on social media, on the Internet; it's taking new forms. The idea that we are in a new feminist moment is very much in the air right now. I was wondering if and how you relate to that.

PS: This fourth wave of feminism—what we call the Primavera Feminista in Brazil—has awakened for many women something that we were all feeling but hadn't been able to name until quite recently. And this awakening has taken place online, especially on social media. I'm thirty years old, and all of this started about five years ago or so—around 2014 or 2015. Shortly thereafter I went around to schools screening my film and meeting young girls. Even though they're only fourteen, fifteen, sixteen years old, they're light-years ahead of me [snapping her fingers multiple times]. They're much farther along in thinking about this topic than I was at their age, and it's all because of social media, the fourth wave. And of course, the issue was already in the air, so to speak, not just because so many feminists have been talking about it and taking action but because people in general have been talking about it. It's the issue of the moment and it's been everywhere on social media through movements like #MeToo and hashtags like #PrimeiroAssédio [#FirstAssault]. It's also gotten a lot of attention in the film world, too. For example, several women spoke out about it at the Berlin and Cannes Film Festivals.

Precisamos falar do assédio came out of this context; it wouldn't exist if it weren't for this wave. My film was the fruit of what happened here in late 2015, early 2016. Around that time, there was a cooking show that aired in Brazil called *MasterChef Junior* featuring contestants who were around twelve years old, that is to say, children. The night the show premiered, one of the girls' names became a trending topic on Twitter, which was inundated with tweets saying the most offensive things about her body. Things like, "It's not pedophilia if she consents," and much, much worse—all about a twelve-year-old girl! The next day an NGO called Think Olga launched a social media campaign around the hashtag #PrimeiroAssédio [in which women posted their own personal stories describing the first time they were sexually harassed or assaulted in order to draw attention to an epidemic of male sexual aggression toward young girls in Brazil].

As I witnessed all this unfold on Facebook, I was shocked to read the most awful accounts of violence by women who were writing about being sexually assaulted at four, five, six, twelve, thirteen years old. Most shocking of all was reading the accounts of my closest friends, women I'd known since I was twelve or fourteen years old—as I mentioned, I'm thirty years old now—and who were opening up about things that they'd never even told me before. It dawned on me that these kinds of things weren't being talked about even amongst the closest of friends. I even heard a story from my own mother that she never told me before! It was an incredibly powerful experience because we begin to recognize our own pain in other women's stories, and in recognizing that pain we were empowered to come together and say "no," and to speak what had been unspeakable so that it is no longer unspeakable. That's why my film is called *Precisamos falar do assédio*, because the film was born out of this context.

RA: I'm glad you brought up the title because I was hoping you could say a bit more about it. As you know, the Portuguese term *assédio* can mean both harassment and assault, which are two very different things in English. There seems to be an ambiguity there, which comes across most clearly through the women themselves when they wonder out loud if their stories are relevant to the project. So, I'm really posing two questions here, one being about how you framed the project in first presenting it to the women who participated in the filming, and the other being why you chose this specific term for the title.

PS: People are always asking me in debates and screenings why I chose the word *assédio* for the title. I wanted the documentary to talk about all kinds of violence against women, ranging from catcalling on the street to rape to physical aggression, all the way to femicide (although of course our ability to grapple with femicide was limited because we were working with survivor testimonies and by definition there are no survivors of femicide). The point is that I wanted the film to represent as diverse a range of experiences as possible.

Speaking for myself, I hate going out into the street and being catcalled; for me, catcalling is a form of violence. But there are some women who hate it as much as I do, who feel violated by it, but who wouldn't feel comfortable calling it violence, per se. So, with this in mind, I chose the term *assédio* (assault) precisely because it is so elastic: it is the broadest possible container that encompasses the entire spectrum of what women experience. This was important to me because I wanted any and all women to feel invited to enter the recording van and share their stories. There is a woman who appears in the film and starts off by saying something like, "But my story is about being raped. Does rape count as assédio? Can I still participate?" We left that part in. It was a deliberate decision we made during the editing process—and look, we had thirteen hours of footage that we needed to squeeze into only eighty minutes. I could have cut out that part, but I didn't precisely because I wanted to problematize my choice of the word *assédio* by showing all the messiness and confusion it generated. And the answer to the woman's question was that of course we wanted her to participate.

And there's one more observation I want to make about the title. The decision to use the term *assédio* was meant, above all, as an allusion to everything that was happening at the time. As I said before, we made the film while there was this whole #PrimeiroAssédio hashtag campaign going on in Brazil. That's why I thought the phrase *Precisamos falar do assédio* would make a very effective title. #PrimeiroAssédio, Precisamos falar do assédio: they sound a lot alike, right? It implies that the documentary is a continuation of the anti-harassment campaign; the film's whole purpose is to keep propelling things forward. Not to mention that there's also a real sense of urgency—a call to action—implied in the verb *precisamos*; it means we need to do this. When the film was chosen for a film festival in France and for distribution in the United States by Women Make Movies, we started thinking about what to call it in English. It's always really hard to translate film titles into other languages, but in this case, it was especially difficult. The literal translation of Precisamos falar do assédio into English is a real mouthful: "We need to talk about harassment." It sounds nothing like a hashtag, right? All the appeal is lost. So that's why we took the English word *harassment*—which is the translation of *assédio*—and combined it with the idea of faces, the faces on the screen of women telling their stories.³ For the French and Spanish titles, we simply translated from the English: *Visages du harcèlement, Rostros del acoso.*

RA: What was the process and logic selecting and ordering the twenty-six testimonies that appear in the film?

PS: We ended up with about thirteen hours of raw material. There were 140 testimonies total, twenty-six of which appear in the documentary. We filmed in March and the documentary came out in September, meaning that we finished all the editing within six months—it was really hectic. I ended up getting really sick at the time because dealing with such testimonies was so stressful.

I could have made a film that was 100 percent about rape, but that's not what I wanted to do. I had to choose what to include, and I wanted as many different kinds of experiences as possible, and also to show the different ways women react to those experiences. For instance, there is one woman in the film who recounts catching a Peeping Tom watching her while she was in the shower, and after it happens, she locks the front door behind her and never sets foot in that house ever again. Her story shows the extent to which the male gaze can be violent for women; she felt so exposed that she started having panic attacks. When she tried to tell people what happened, they brushed her off saying things like, "Big deal, he didn't even touch you." So we wanted to compile the testimonies in such a way that would subtly call attention to the many ways that women experience sexual violation. It can take any form, it can happen anywhere, and the aggressor can be anyone: a friend, a father, a husband, a boyfriend, a stranger, someone in a bar. That's really what I wanted to show: this is what women have to contend with all the time just because they're women.

Figuring out how all the testimonies fit together, what order to put them in, was a very complex process. The hardest part was the ending—we must have tried fifteen different endings before the final cut. The ending encapsulates the message of the film, so I had a lot of factors to keep in mind. For one thing, we couldn't end with a testimony of a woman wearing a mask since that would be like saying, "We need to talk about assault, but we need to wear a mask to do it." No, we need to talk about assault, we need to show our faces and say what it is we have to say. For another thing, we didn't want to end on a testimony like the one where the woman wearing the blue mask says, "I'm just a shell of my former self because of what happened to me." We wanted to end in a way that said something different, so we chose the testimony of a woman, Fernanda, who talks about how her mother eventually came around to the idea that assault is a serious problem after having initially resisted it. It's very symbolic. It's like saying: if you speak out, if you challenge assault, if you confront it, if we collectively speak out, people will start to get why this is a big deal. That's the whole point of sending this documentary out into the world, so that's why the documentary ends with that particular testimony.

And another thing: 140 testimonies might seem like a lot, but when you look at the statistics out there about gender-based violence from a mathematical perspective, you see that what we collected was only a drop in the bucket. When you think about the way we went about collecting the testimonies, it ended up being a random sample based on whoever showed up wherever we happened to be on a given day. Now, if you look at our 140 women, you'll see that they correspond exactly with Brazilian statistics—they match up perfectly. For instance, what are we women most afraid of? We're afraid that we're going to go out into the street at night, some guy is going to point a gun at our head, force us into a dark alley, and rape us. That kind of rape by a stranger in a dark alley constitutes less than 7 percent of all rapes in Brazil. So, where does rape happen and who is doing the raping? It happens at home, at work; it's a friend, an acquaintance, a father. A film with ten rapes by strangers in dark alleys doesn't match the reality of what's going on in Brazil. These were important things for me to take into account so that I wouldn't make a documentary that was totally disconnected from reality. The same thing goes for the masks. Out of the 140 women who gave their testimony, one-third chose to wear masks or disguise themselves in some way, so we wanted to maintain this same proportion with the twenty-six women who appear in the film. In other words, we took all kinds of things into account. For me, the montage process in filmmaking involves a lot of forethought. It's demanding and exhausting, but there also comes a point when somehow all of the pieces magically start falling into place. . . . It's very carefully thought out, but there's also a lot of intuition that goes into it. The ordering of the testimonies was dictated by both logic and intuition.

RA: As a spectator, I found many of the testimonies excruciating to watch. The documentary takes an emotional toll.

PS: Yes, of course. We open with a testimony by a woman who is anxious—you can tell from her body language—but who manages to hold it together, whereas the second woman who appears in the film is in a state of utter despair and anguish. In other words, we tried to alternate between getting into the heavy stuff and giving viewers a breather [*pegar pesado, dar uma respirada*]. Because when I watch the film, I truly think to myself: Wow, why am I putting people through all this? These eighty minutes are excruciating! The stories really affect the viewers. So, of course, we thought a lot about how spectators should receive each testimony and tried to give them breathers in between because otherwise the documentary would be all violence and barbarity. We had to find a way to create some minimal balance in communicating our message so that the viewer will watch the documentary all the way through to the end. I want people to watch the whole thing.

RA: I was really struck by the extent to which you gave women control over the process of telling their stories on camera, the prime example being the masks that you made available to anyone who wanted to conceal her face while taping. Where did the idea for the masks come from?

PS: The story behind the masks is the following: I wanted to give women the opportunity to speak without showing their faces, but I wasn't sure about the best way to do that. I thought to myself, maybe I could promise to obscure their identities in postproduction, like they do on television. But how can I expect them to trust me to actually follow through with that promise? These women didn't know me at all. I wanted to find some way for them to physically disguise themselves so that I wouldn't have their image on film at all if they didn't want me to—that way they would be more comfortable and know that it really was a safe space for them to speak. The only way to make that happen was to find some way to cover their faces, and that's where the idea of the masks came from. I sent out a call on Facebook—something like, "Calling all women artists who make masks, send me images of your work"—and received submissions of every kind of mask imaginable: masks made of papier mâché, clay, plastic, etc. And one of the women who sent in her work was a really amazing artist named Juliana Souza, who makes masks out of fabrics that are really expressive. A very important characteristic of her masks is that they had mouth holes, which solved two of my biggest dilemmas at once: they didn't muffle the women's voices (one of our major technical concerns) and the opening was just large enough to give the sense that there is an actual girl or woman behind the mask without compromising her identity. It also provided access to body language that otherwise would have been invisible: a woman might bite her lip while speaking or she might look down, for example. The masks allowed us to capture those cues and showed that there was an actual person behind there, which I thought was really important.

The process Ju [Juliana Souza, the mask artist] and I went through to design the masks was super intense. We watched every single movie we could find on the internet about violence against women on Netflix, etc. Films like *Brave Miss World*, about a woman crowned Miss Israel who was raped six weeks before winning the title of Miss World, and *The Hunting Ground*, about rape culture in US colleges and universities. We took screen shots of the women's faces as they told their stories until we had a catalog of their expressions. We pored over this catalog and started to identify the emotions we were seeing. We noticed that of the many emotions we observed, the four most frequent were shame, fear, anger, and sadness. (Actually, guilt came up a lot too, but we didn't want to make a mask representing guilt because that would just reinforce victim blaming, as if the woman were concealing her face to hide her guilt. No, she might feel guilty, but she isn't guilty of anything. When a woman is the victim of sexual violence, it's not her fault.) Anyway, for each emotion Ju studied how the women's eyes looked, how their mouths looked, whether they became flushed or not, and then used these observations as the basis for designing the four masks. So that's the story behind the masks.

When the women showed up at the van to record their testimonies, we explained how the process worked, that the idea was for each woman to speak for about five minutes, etc., and also that we had masks available in case anyone wanted to conceal her face. For those who didn't want to show their faces, we explained what each mask represented and they got to choose the one they wanted. But there was one woman who was an exception, who we ended up filming in the dark to hide her face. In her case we had to figure out an alternative to the masks because when I explained what they represented she turned to me and said that she couldn't choose just one mask because what she was feeling was a painful combination of the four emotions the different masks represented. So I told her, "Look, I can dim the light in front of your face instead. I'm going to be honest with you, though: I don't know if I'll end up using your testimony in the film or on the website because it won't fit with the other testimonies or the overall aesthetic of the documentary. But go ahead and record your testimony if you want. I just can't tell you what's going to happen with it." She said that was fine, that she wanted to go through with it. So, that's what we did. Later, when I watched her testimony during the editing I realized that she was the only participant who talked about being assaulted by her own father. It was important to include that in the documentary, so that's what I did, leaving it the way it was.

RA: Speaking of revealing and concealing, we catch a few fleeting glimpses of you in the documentary as you're adjusting equipment and talking with participants.

PS: Right. I do appear on camera in the film, but we wanted to limit my appearances so that you only see me in small doses. The women were always alone in the van while they were recording their testimonies. Nobody was watching or listening to them, which meant that we had no idea what they were saying while they were inside. The only times you see me in the documentary are when a woman is entering or leaving the van, but even those moments were often really intense.

Something we realized in the process of editing the documentary was that whenever we tried to add some cinematic element to the film, it never worked. For example, we tried to add a soundtrack, but it didn't work at all, and I'm like, What am I trying to do here, add some sad piano music to make people cry even harder? No matter what we tried to add, nothing worked. That's why the documentary came out so raw. It's really a raw, rough, bare film, which got us thinking about the possibility of including some of my interactions with the women in the documentary. Since it was already so raw, rough, and bare, it felt right to expose some of the process of making the film, and my interactions with the women are a big part of that process. For me, whether or not to include glimpses of those interactions in the documentary was a very delicate question. The women were acutely aware of being filmed while they were giving their testimonies, of course, but a few of them may not have realized that the camera was running the whole time they were inside the van, including before and after their testimonies, when they were supposedly "off record." I couldn't just include those parts without the participants' input, so I did a test screening for the featured women to show them what we were hoping to do with that "off record" footage. It turned out they were all fine with it. In retrospect, I realized that those intervals when we weren't officially recording were actually some of the most intimate moments in the documentary, when they blurted things out, asked questions, apologized for having said a certain thing or for speaking a certain way. These interludes add another dimension to the women's testimonies as the only instances where any kind of interlocution occurs, since the testimonies themselves don't involve interviews or interlocution of any kind.

RA: What was your experience like on the distribution end of things?

PS: Finding distribution for any kind of documentary is really hard in Brazil, and getting a major distributor to take on a documentary about a topic like sexual violence against women is practically impossible. Nobody wants to distribute something like that, much less finance producing it in the first place. It's really, really tough. There are some alternative ways to distribute films, though. For example, in my case we distributed the film ourselves, via our production company [Mira Films]. And it was incredible because we were able to screen the documentary in venues all over Brazil. We're talking tiny venues for the most part, but it did reach even small towns in states like Ceará. It made the rounds, and there were theaters where it was showing for multiple weeks, . . . so mostly the documentary got this kind of *distribuição de formiguinhas* [microdistribution, literally "distribution by tiny ants"]. Eventually the film was picked up by an incredible organization in the United States called Women Make Movies, which is distributing it in the alternative and educational circuits in the US and Canada. The documentary has been screened in various universities, and after that the organization was able to sell it to Al Jazeera. Once it started having some success, another organization here in Brazil became interested and wanted to distribute it, which led to it airing on television in Colombia, for example. It has kept spreading from there, and now it's available via VideoCamp, which is a really cool platform that distributes content. It's great since I'm not permitted to make the documentary available on the Internet due to a contract we signed when we sold the film to a channel called CanalBrasil. The documentary is on CanalBrasil (subject to when they schedule it to air), it's on NetNow (where you can pay to watch it on demand), and it's on VideoCamp where you can arrange to show it to students for educational purposes (it's for groups rather than for individual viewers). It's even on Amazon Prime now. So, even though it's not showing in theaters, it's still reaching lots of different places. All kinds of groups are accessing it, especially schools. I think it's great because I personally would never have the time to send copies to every teacher who wanted to show it to their students. It's a very democratic way to distribute films.

RA: One thing you've said in several interviews is that you wanted this film to take the conversations happening online to the streets. It seems that the reverse is also true: you took the testimonies you collected in the streets of Rio and São Paulo back online, and in fact *Precisamos Falar do Assédio* is very much a transmedia project. How do you understand the relationship between these two very different spaces, the street and the Internet?

PS: What most struck me when women began posting under the hashtag #PrimeiroAssédio was that there were no faces, no voices to go with the many, many testimonies that I was reading. When I said that I wanted to take the conversations happening online into the streets, what I meant was something along those lines. For one thing, I wanted to give voices and faces to all the stories that up until that point were just a bunch of words typed in an impersonal tweet or Facebook post. For another thing, I wanted the same kinds of conversations that were happening primarily online via social media to start happening in the real world as well. When the film was launched, we did screenings all over town, including public, outdoor screenings that you could literally see from the street. The van was parked in the street; we collected the testimonies on the street to draw the attention of people who wouldn't necessarily have paid attention otherwise. Instead of seeing it on Facebook, now they were passing by it on their way to work or school.

In terms of what a documentary can do that a hashtag campaign can't, I'd say that in this case the hashtag campaign was out in the open, but people didn't necessarily experience it in a public context because usually they were sitting in their houses reading the stories on their laptops or on their cellphones, so in that sense you could say the hashtag campaign was a relatively intimate phenomenon. The documentary was different because it was made for the purpose of generating public debates. It was screened in public precisely so that people could watch and discuss it together. It's not something you watch alone: you watch it with other women who have had similar experiences and maybe some guys who've been affected in one way or another. In other words, the emphasis was on stimulating interaction and dialogue between people.

Our original idea was to invite women viewers to record their testimonies to post on our companion website, but that didn't really work out the way we anticipated. I thought we'd be flooded with testimonies, but no. The van we used as a mobile recording studio turned out to be a crucial factor in our ability to get women to share their stories, probably because it was enclosed and private. The women felt safe and protected in there. The deluge of online testimonies that I was expecting never materialized. But even though we didn't end up getting as many recorded testimonies from viewers as I thought we would, the website itself still got a lot of traffic. In fact, it's gotten a ton of hits.

So the documentary wasn't originally conceived as a transmedia project; it became one along the way. How did that come about? Well, we made a film called *Precisamos falar do assédio*, or rather we launched a campaign that culminated in a documentary called *Precisamos falar do assédio*. In making the film we took thirteen hours of footage and edited it down to eighty minutes. And I said to myself, I can't collect 140 testimonies only to use pieces of twenty-six of them and leave the rest on the cutting room floor. We wanted all of the voices to be heard, but we weren't about to turn all of the footage into a thirteen-hour film! So, we needed another container for the material that we couldn't use in the documentary. The documentary also became a transmedia project by virtue of the digital world we're living in. For example, viewers themselves started sharing individual clips from our website, or the website itself, on social media. The project has stayed alive in that sense.

The transmedia phenomenon is super new in Brazil; we don't really have much of a tradition of transmedia projects, so *Precisamos falar do assédio* was innovative in that respect.

RA: One thing we haven't touched upon yet is what it's like trying to produce a film in Brazil as a woman director. What kinds of obstacles have you had to contend with in your career so far?

PS: If distributing a film as a woman is hard, imagine how tough it is to make one! I was recently hired to teach a course on documentaries . . . and one of the things they asked me to do was to organize a cine club (movie club) that sponsors monthly film screenings to accompany my classes. So I created the club and we started watching the films I selected: four documentaries, all directed by men. I thought to myself, great job, Paula, you of all people picked all male directors. When that happened I did some soul-searching, trying to figure out why I did that. And I concluded that it was because we [Brazilian women directors] have never had the chance to occupy these spaces before. It was hardly imaginable for a woman to direct any kind of film much less a documentary. All this prompted me to compile a list of women documentarians and their works to remind myself of the blunder I'd committed [*o absurdo que fiz*].

The official history of the Brazilian documentary is like this: man, man, man, man, pretty much all of whom are white and old these days. If you look at which director is getting all the funding, it's the guy who's made his name in the industry and already has a bunch of films—it's even worse than ever due to the horrid political climate we're living under right now. Nobody wants to give women directors a chance. No one is going to fund a woman director, much less a young woman director; the industry is even less supportive of young women directors who are Black. What we saw happen with public policies for funding filmmaking over the last several years—and by this I mean the Lula and Dilma governments—was absolutely incredible. Brazil was sending so many awesome films to international film festivals and the industry was exploding with filmmakers from outside the Rio–São Paulo axis, so many young women started directing films and TV series. Now all of that wonderful progress in decentralizing the industry is being reversed. It may not be totally over yet, but it's definitely coming to an end because of all the funding cuts. We need public policies to guarantee space for the young women who are producing films that are really amazing; the only thing we're all lacking is opportunity.

And it's like I was saying before, if distributing a film is hard as a woman documentarian, it's even harder producing one. Take, for example a new TV show I was working on recently that's on the Brazilian prison system. I mean, it's absolutely nuts. Sometimes I spend sixteen hours a day filming inside the penitentiary, which takes a hell of a lot of energy. It's physically and emotionally grueling, but that's just a fraction of what I have to contend with. For example, one time I spent a long day filming after which I found myself having to convince the soundtrack guy to go ahead with some editing I had asked him to do. I almost lost it with the guy. I told him, "Dude, stop for a second and think about whether you'd second guess one of my male colleagues." He would never question my male colleagues' authority the way he did mine. He treats me like I'm an idiot simply because he's not used to having a woman for a boss. The guys aren't used to having a woman call the shots. It never ends. It's so tiresome—exhausting, really. If there are fewer young women directing right now it's because of this kind of exhaustion. After fighting for so long, sometimes you just want to say, Fine, whatever, I'll just channel my energy into something else. It's a battle. Actually, I now try to just hire women as much as possible because I'm tired of having to deal with it. If you pay attention to the credits at the end of *Precisamos falar do assédio*, the names are almost all men even though it's a film about violence against women. So now whenever I can I want to give these opportunities to women because that way I don't have to constantly try to prove myself.

Which reminds me: I was just reading the list of nominees for the Gramado Film Festival, which were announced today, and I noticed that there were zero films directed by women. How is it even possible for a festival curator to do something like that in 2019? It's so frustrating.

RA: It's all the more impressive, then, that you've managed to produce so many films and TV series already. Is there a common thread that runs through your work?

PS: There's a common thread in the sense that I always make films on social themes related to human rights. I believe in the documentary as a weapon for transforming the world, so I always make films about topics that touch me, about things that are wrong with the world and that need to be changed. And to change something the first step is awareness. I remember when I went to screen my documentary about the National Truth Commission at a cursinho popular (a college test prep course) for low-income student in the periphery, in Capão Redondo, we screened it in a school gym to an audience of three hundred students on a Saturday afternoon. It was a little chaotic because there were so many people and the projection was fairly low quality—the projector we were using wasn't very good and the sound was a little off. But when the film ended, I asked the students if they had any questions, and all their hands went up! There was one girl who raised her hand and asked, "Now that I know about this, what can I do?"

So that's what I mean. I don't know if there's really a common thread to my work, but if I can generate that same kind of response—to raise people's awareness about injustices and inequalities and the things that are wrong with this world so that they then want to change things—then I think that is my role.

Notes

1. Translation to English and preface by Rebecca J. Atencio.
2. This interview has been edited for brevity and coherence. It took place on July 15, 2019.
3. The English title of the film is *Faces of Harassment*.

Contributors

Rebecca J. Atencio is associate professor of Portuguese and gender and sexuality studies at Tulane University. Her research focuses on the intersections between cultural production and human rights in Brazil. Her first book, *Memory's Turn: Reckoning with Dictatorship in Brazil* (2014), looks at synergies between Brazilian artistic-cultural production and transitional justice mechanisms. It received the Alfred Thomas Book Prize from the Southeastern Council of Latin American Studies and honorable mention from the Brazilian Studies Association. She's currently completing a second book examining feminist cultural expression in the form of alternative newspapers, grrrl music and zines, folk poetry, and documentary film. She has published articles in the *Luso-Brazilian Review*, *Hispania*, *Current History*, *Revista Anistia*, and other journals, in addition to essays in various edited volumes. Since 2019, she has served as Brazilian literature editor for the *Luso-Brazilian Review*.

Daniela Verztman Bagdadi is a German-Brazilian researcher and producer. She has a BA in communication sciences (Federal University of Rio de Janeiro), a postgraduate degree in filmmaking (Darcy Ribeiro Film School), and an MA in transcultural studies (Universität Heidelberg). She has worked for film and television productions as well as at research institutes and international organizations, such as the United Nations. Currently based in Berlin, she works at Deutsche Welle.

Jack A. Draper III is associate professor of Portuguese at the University of Missouri. His primary research field is Brazilian cultural studies, with particular emphases in cinema and popular culture. He is author of *Saudade in Brazilian Cinema: The History of an Emotion on Film* (2017) and *Forró* *and Redemptive Regionalism from the Brazilian Northeast: Popular Music in a Culture of Migration* (2010). He also translated the first critical edition in English of Mario Filho's *The Black Man in Brazilian Soccer* (2021). In his 2017 monograph, and in a variety of scholarly articles and chapters over the past decade, he has analyzed post–World War II Brazilian cinema in terms of its representations of emotion, gender, youth (children and adolescents), popular culture, genre (horror in particular), race, social class, built space, regional and rural Brazil, memory, history, democracy, and dictatorship.

Gustavo Procopio Furtado is associate professor of romance studies and art, art history, and visual studies at Duke University. His articles on Latin American cinema have appeared in several journals and anthologies, such as *New Cinemas: Journal of Contemporary Film, Journal of Latin American Cultural Studies, Revista Cine Documental,* and *Latin American Documentary Film in the New Millennium* (2016). His book, *Documentary Filmmaking in Contemporary Brazil: Cinematic Archives of the Present* (2019), won the 2019 Antonio Candido Prize for Best Book in the Humanities (awarded by the Brazil section of the Latin American Studies Association).

Reighan Gillam is an assistant professor in the Department of Anthropology at the University of Southern California. Her research examines the ways in which Afro-Brazilian media producers foment anti-racist visual politics through their image creations. She examines this subject in her book *Visualizing Black Lives: Ownership and Control in Afro-Brazilian Media* (2022).

Paula Halperin is associate professor of history and cinema studies and is the director of the School of Film and Media Studies at SUNY Purchase. Her research integrates media, history, and the public sphere in Brazil during the twentieth century. She has published a range of essays on cinema, television, race, gender, and the process of "being Brazilian." Her articles have been published in academic journals in the United States, Brazil, and Argentina. She is currently finishing her manuscript on historical imagination and popular cinema in 1970s and 1980s Brazil and Argentina. She also writes film criticism for websites and blogs.

Leslie L. Marsh is chair and professor of Spanish and Latin American culture in the Department of World Languages and Cultures at Georgia State University (Atlanta). She specializes in Latin American film and media studies, focusing on Brazil and more broadly on questions of citizenship. She is the author of the books *Brazilian Women's Filmmaking: From Dictatorship to Democracy* (2012) and *Branding Brazil: Transforming Citizenship on Screen* (2021). She coedited the volume *The Middle Class in Emerging Societies: Consumers, Lifestyles and Markets* (2015) with Hongmei Li (Miami University, Ohio). She is currently working on a monograph titled "Black Cinema in Brazil: Rethinking Authorship and Agency" for which she was recently awarded an NEH grant. She also codirects a series on Latin American cinema for SUNY Press with Dr. Ignacio (Nacho) Sánchez Prado (Washington University, St. Louis).

Cacilda M. Rêgo is professor of Portuguese and Brazilian cultural studies in the Department of World Languages and Cultures at Utah State University. She specializes in Brazilian media with a special focus on film and television. Her publications include two coedited volumes: *New Trends in Argentine and Brazilian Cinema* with Carolina Rocha (2011) and *Migration in Lusophone Cinema* with Marcus Brasileiro (2014).

María Mercedes Vázquez Vázquez is a lecturer and honorary assistant professor at the School of Modern Languages and Cultures of the University of Hong Kong. Her research centers on how class, gender, and race affect contemporary cinematic representations and unequal opportunities for film production. Representative publications include her monograph *The Question of Class in Contemporary Latin American Cinema* (2018) and contributions to collective volumes such as *The Precarious in the Cinemas of the Americas* (2018), *Brazil in Twenty-First Century Popular Media: Culture, Politics, and Nationalism on the World Stage* (2014), and *Jameson and Film Theory: Marxism, Allegory, and Geopolitics in World Cinema* (2022).

Index

À deriva (*Adrift*), 144
A felicidade delas (*Their happiness*), 59
A festa da moça (*The girl's celebration*), 240
A fórmula (*The formula*), 58
A história da cutia e do macaco (*The story of the agouti and the monkey*), 245
A hora da estrela (*The Hour of the Star*), 21, 50
A meia noite levarei a sua alma (*At midnight I'll take your soul*), 63
A sombra do pai (*The father's shadow*), 53, 63
As boas maneiras (*Good manners*), 52, 63
As minas do rap (*The women of rap*), 224
Abolição (*Abolition*), 222
Abreu, Gilda de, 34
Acquaria, 26
Afroflix (platform), 33, 61, 205, 206, 212
Afronta! (*Face it!*), 12, 218, 219, 224
Alfazema (*Lavender*), 33
Alma no olho (*Soul in the eye*), 205, 222
Almeida, Gabriela Amaral, 53, 56, 57, 63
Alvarez, Iasmin, 74

Alves, Paula, 22
Amaral, Suzana, 50, 165
Amaral, Tata, 18, 21, 26, 94, 221
Amaral, Tetê, 35
Amor Maldito (*Damned love*), 40, 66, 199, 205, 222
Ana Carolina, 21, 165
ancestralidade, 204
Ancine (Agência Nacional do Cinema), 7, 10, 19, 23, 29, 30, 38, 39, 40, 41, 47, 54, 59, 60, 65, 67, 71, 94, 97, 102, 103, 202, 213
Andrade, Malu, 86, 90, 94, 201
Andrade, Oswald, 210
Antônia, 26, 221
Aqualoucos (*Aquacrazy*), 55
Arraial do Cabo (*Village on the cape*), 164
Associação de Profissionais do Audiovidual Negro (Professional Association of Black Filmmakers), 204
Até o fim (*To the end*), 66
Avenida Brasil (*Brazil Avenue*), 57
Azoulay, Ariella, 95

Babás (*Nannies*), 141
Babenco, Hector, 25
Bandeira, Eliane, 165
Beauvoir, Simone, 73

Berger, Vinicius, 241
Blindness, 32
Bloch, Bruno, 54
Bodansky, Laís, 18, 22, 55, 57, 94, 201, 205
Bolognesi, Luiz, 205
Bombril, 210
Bomfim, André, 252
Borges, Cavi, 66
Bossay, Claudia, 4
Brasil, Samantha, 90, 92
Brasília, um dia em fevereiro (*Brasilia, a day in February*), 166, 168, 170, 173
Brava gente brasileira (*Brave new land*), 50
Brave Miss World, 259
Braz, Fil, 27
Bróder (*Brother*), 222
Bulbul, Zózimo, 204, 205, 222
Burke, Tarana, 95
Butler, Judith, 2, 74

Cabíria Festival; Cabíria Prêmio de Roteiro (Cabíria Script Prize), 52, 84, 92
Cabral, Inês, 165
Café com canela (*Coffee with cinnamon*), 66
Caffé, Eliana, 18
Camargo, Maria, 58
Campo Grande, 10, 11, 139, 140, 148, 149–156, 158
Campos, Franciele, 75, 87
Camurati, Carla, 18, 55, 56
Candido, Marcia Rangel, 199
Caputo, Stela Guedes, 204
Carandiru, 25
Cardoso, Isabel, 85, 90, 93
Cardozo, Maria, 74, 86
Carelli, Vincent, 234, 239, 240

Carlota Joaquina, Princesa do Brasil (*Carlota Joaquina, princess of Brazil*), 18, 50, 55, 65
Carneiro, Mario, 164
Carneiro, Sueli, 218
Carrossel: o filme (*Carousel, the Film*), 55
Cartel Adélia (Adélia's Cartel), 75, 87, 92
Carvalho, José (Roteiraria), 54
Carvalho, Viviane Valim (Roteiraria), 54
Carvalho, Walter, 26
Casa grande (*Big house*), 220
Castells, Manuel, 89
Catani, Vânia, 104
Cazuza: O tempo não pára (*Cazuza: Time doesn't stop*), 26
Celeste & Estrela, 22
Central do Brasil (*Central station*), 50, 150, 155, 158
Chanan, Michael, 219
chanchadas (light comedies), 61
Chega de fiu fiu (*Enough with catcalling*), 10, 116, 129–136
Chega de saudade (*The ballroom*), 22
Choueiti, Marc, 198
Cidade de Deus (*City of God*), 22, 58
Cidade dos homens (*City of men*), 22, 25
Cine Clube Mulheres do Brasil/ Women's Cinema Club, 92
cine testimonio, 219
cinema de autor/auteur cinema, 3, 4, 23, 30, 31, 34, 49, 55, 64
cinema de autor vs. *cinema de produtor*, 54
cinema média/"middle cinema," 59
Cinema Novo, 49, 205, 209, 210, 213, 222
Cobb, Shelley, 30, 31

Coletivo das Diretoras de Fotografia do Brasil (Collective of Women Cinematographers [DAFB]), 84
Coletivo Mangaba/Mangaba Collective, 84
Coletivo Vermelha/Red Collective, 85, 92
Collins, Patricia Hill, 218
Como era gostoso meu francês (*How tasty was my little Frenchman*), 210
Copacabana, 55
Cordeiro, Filippo, 54
Cores e Botas (*Colors and boots*), 223
Corrêa, Mari, 12, 233–249
Costa, Haroldo, 218
Costa, Petra, 3, 5, 11, 19, 39, 41, 64, 102, 183–194
Coutinho, Eduardo, 105, 164
Crenshaw, Kimberlé, 5, 75, 130, 137
Criativas: Oficina de Roteiro Audiovisual para Jovens Mulheres (Creatives: Screenwriting Workshop for Young Women), 92
Cuklanz, Lisa M., 120

D'Amato, Cris, 23, 26, 62
Da Rin, Silvio, 31
Daniel Filho, 23, 57
Dark water, 32
De, Jeferson, 222
De Lauretis, Teresa, 210
De Souza, Ruth, 224, 228
Demange, Luana, 63
Democracia em vertigem (*The edge of democracy*), 11, 19, 39, 64, 184, 185, 186, 191
Dennison, Stephanie, 21, 22
Desi, 102, 106, 107
Dhalia, Heitor, 144
Diálogos Ausentes (*Absent dialogues*), 217

Dimantas, Melanie, 50, 55, 56, 59
Dogma Feijoada, 222
Domésticas/Domestics, 157
Donoghue, Courtney Brannon, 27
Doutores da alegria—o filme (*Doctors of joy—the film*), 22
dramaturgo visual/visual dramatist, 57
Durval Discos (*Durval Records*), 50, 62
Dutra, Marco, 63

É proibido fumar (*Smoke gets in your eyes*), 62
Ela Na Tela/Her on Screen (film festival), 85, 92
Elekô, 212
Elena, 184, 185, 186, 190
Ely-Harper, Kerreen, 2
Elviras—Coletivo de Mulheres Críticas de Cinema (Elvira's Women Film Critics Collective), 84, 90
Embrafilme (Empresa Brasileira de Filme), 17, 35, 50
Empoderadas (*Empowered women*), 61
Escola Afroflix de Imagens (Afroflix School of Images), 205
Esmeralda, Carla, 50, 51
Estatuto da Igualdade Racial (Statute of Racial Equality), 200
Eu, preso (*I, a prisoner*), 252
Eu, tu, eles (*Me, you, them*), 50
Eustáquio, José, 22
Exilados (*Exiles*), 39

Facebook, 10, 32, 35, 73, 75, 76, 78, 80, 82, 84, 85, 87, 88, 89, 90, 91, 92, 93, 94, 95, 96, 110, 115, 122, 129, 136, 254, 258, 262
Falcão, Adriana, 56, 58, 62
Farias, Juliana, 115, 116, 117, 123, 129, 134

Fartura (*Abundance*), 211
Fausto, Carlos, 240
feminism, 2, 3, 73, 94, 252–253
Ferreira, Viviane, 33, 60, 199, 204, 206, 213, 222
Festival Palmares de Cinema (Palmares Cinema Festival), 222
Festival de Roteiro Audiovisual (ROTA Screenplay Festival), 52
Festival de Roteiro Audiovisual de Porto Alegre (Porto Alegre Screenplay Festival [FRAPA]), 52
Festival do Roteiro de Língua Portuguesa (Portuguese Language Screenplay Festival [GUIÕES]), 52
Festival Internacional de Cinema de Realizadoras (International Film Festival of Women Directors [FINCAR]), 35, 74, 86
Fidalgo, Sabrina, 33, 34
Film Fatale collective, 85
Filmmakers Festival [FINCAR]), 74
Filhos do carnival (*Sons of Carnival*), 55
FitzSimons, Trish, 3
Ford, Sam, 92
Förster, Annette, 72
Fotopoulou, Aristea, 94
França, Marlene, 36
Frazão, Fernanda, 10, 116, 129, 130, 134, 135, 138
Freitas, Iole de, 165
Friedman, Elisabeth J., 89
Fujinaga, Thais, 59
Furtado, Gustavo Procopio, 24, 36
Fuser, Marina Costin, 94
Futuro Junho (*Future June*), 161, 163, 166, 170, 174, 175

Gaijin, 21
Gaitán, Paula, 36
Gallois, Dominique, 240

Garcia, Susana, 26, 27, 28, 39
Gardenberg, Monique, 26
Globo Filmes, 8, 19, 20, 25, 26, 27, 28, 29, 36, 39, 40, 42, 61, 102, 103
Globo TV Network, 8, 20, 22, 26, 27, 28, 36, 57, 58, 59, 61, 66, 72
globochanchadas (light comedies produced by Globo TV), 26, 61
Green, Joshua, 92
Gutiérrez-Albilla, Julián Daniel, 20, 21
Gutman, Eunice, 165

Hannerz, Ulf, 92
Haraway, Donna, 10, 148, 158
Hart, Stephen, 200
Heise, Tatiana, 221
High art, 32
Hinke, Marcos, 54
Hirszman, Leon, 205
Holanda, Karla, 22, 165
Hollanda, Heloisa Buarque de, 22

Ilha (*Island*), 66
Iluminados, 22
International Film Festival Rotterdam (IFFR), 202
Ivanov, Débora, 94, 103, 202, 213

Jabor, Arnaldo, 164
Jehá, Regina, 165
Jenkens, Henry, 92
Johnson, Randal, 21
Juízo (*Judgment*), 64, 102, 163, 171, 174
Justiça (*Justice*), 64, 102, 104, 109, 163, 170, 171, 174

Kamanchek Lemos, Amanda, 10, 116, 129, 134, 135, 138
Katz, Ana, 25
Kbela, 11, 60, 199, 202, 206, 207, 208, 209, 210, 211, 212

Kilomba, Grada, 75
kinnovation, 139, 140, 142, 148, 149, 150, 156
Kogut, Sandra, 10, 36, 39, 153, 156, 157, 158
Koster, Henry, 149
Kuikuru, Takumã, 240
Kulick, Don, 228

La ciénaga (*The swamp*), 144
La mujer sin cabeza (*The headless woman*), 144, 145
Las viudas de los jueves (*The widows of Thursdays*), 144
Leal, Cristina, 22
Leão, Mariza, 31, 55
Lei do Audiovisual/Audiovisual Law, 18, 26, 29, 35, 36, 40
Lei Rouanet/Rouanet Law, 17, 35, 36, 37, 188
Lei Sarney/Sarney Law, 17
Leone, Caroline, 25, 52
Lessa, Bia, 31
Linha de passe (*Passing line*), 22
Lins, Consuelo, 141, 157
Lixo extraordinário (*Waste land*), 58
lugar de fala (place of speaking), 3, 5, 12, 187, 218, 219
Lund, Kátia, 22, 25, 32, 172, 173
Lusvarghi, Luiza, 22
Luz, Carmen, 206

Machado, Roberto Pinheiro, 28
Mãe Beata, 204, 205
Magalhães, Ana Maria, 18
Maia, Karoline, 157
Malhação, viva a diferença (*Slander, long live difference*), 61
Maldonado, Sofia, 58
Manela, Beatriz, 52
Manifesto Antropófago (Cannibalist manifesto), 210

Mascaro, Gabriel, 157
Matoso, Chico, 49
Mar de Rosas (*Sea of roses*), 21
Marins, José Mojica (aka Zé do Caixão/Coffin Joe), 63
Marsh, Leslie L., 22, 72, 142
Martel, Lucrecia, 2, 104, 144
Martin, Courtney, 89
Martin, Deborah, 21
Martinelli, Mirella, 21
Martins, Renata, 61
Mascaro, Gabriel, 157
Master chef junior, 115, 117, 254
Mata-me, por favor (*Kill me please*), 104
Matos, Carolina, 74
Matos, Vânia, 52
McIntosh, Heather, 120
Meirelles, Fernando, 22, 25, 32, 106
Mello, Selton, 57, 104
Mesel, Kátia, 165
Meu passado me condena (*My past condemns me*), 62
Minh-Ha, Trinh T., 205
Minha mãe é uma peça (*My mother is a character*), 26
Minha mãe é uma peça 2 (*My mother is a character 2*), 26
Minha mãe é uma peça 3 (*My mother is a character 3*), 26, 27
Minha vida em Marte (*My life on Mars*), 26, 39
Mister Brau, 58
Mitchell, Jasmine, 221
Moraes, Everlane, 33
Moraes, Flávia, 26
Moreira Salles, João, 23
Morro dos Prazeres (*Hill of pleasures*), 102, 109, 163, 171, 172, 173
Mostra das Minas (Women's Film Exhibition), 74
Mostra de Filme de Tiradentes (Tiradentes Film Festival), 54

Motta, Zezé, 228
Mourão, Mara, 22
Mulheres do Audiovisual Brasil/ Women in the Audiovisual Industry in Brazil, 86
Mulvey, Laura, 208
Munerato, Elice, 20, 22
Murat, Julia, 39
Murat, Lúcia, 18, 22, 25, 35, 50, 65, 94
Mutum, 153
Muylaert, Anna, 6, 10, 18, 50, 51, 55, 57, 58, 62, 65, 94, 142, 157, 158

Não toque em meu companheiro (Don't touch my fellow worker), 179
Nagib, Lúcia, 3, 4, 13, 21, 23, 29, 30, 31, 40, 44, 181
Nair, Pavati, 20, 21
Nascimento, Beatriz, 218
Nascimento, Denise Britz do, 22
Naves, Ludmila, 58, 59, 62
Nicácio, Glenda, 66
Neto, Aristides Monteiro, 84, 99
Nogueira, Marília, 52
Nogueira, Mirna, 53, 54
Notícias de uma guerra particular (News from a personal war), 172

O animal cordial (The friendly beast), 63
O corpo e os espíritos (Xingu, body and soul), 234, 238
O dia de Jerusa (Jerusa's day), 60, 199, 213, 222
O doutrinador (The awakener), 55
O mecanismo (The mechanism), 58
O outro lado da rua (The other side of the street), 66
Ó pai ó (Look at this), 26
O palhaço (The clown), 57
O processo (The trial), 11, 25, 64, 102, 104, 105, 106, 107, 110, 169, 175, 176, 177, 178, 179
O rastro (The trace we leave behind), 52
O sonho Bollywoodiano (Bollywood dream), 39
On the Road, 32
Os heróis trapalhões: Uma aventura na selva (The bumbling heroes: An adventure in the forest), 62
Os saltimbancos trapalhões (The bumbling acrobats), 62
Os Trapalhões (The Bumbling Ones), 62, 66
Olhos azuis (Blue eyes), 66
Olhos de Ressaca (Undertow eyes), 11, 184, 186
Oliveira, Janaína, 198, 200, 206, 213
Oliveira, Maria Helena Darcy de, 20, 22
Olmo e a gaivota (Olmo and the seagull), 184, 185
Onisciente (Omniscient), 59, 63
Opinião Pública (Public opinion), 164
Opressão (Oppression), 21

Padilha, José, 25, 58, 172, 173
Pape, Lygia, 165
Para onde foram as andorinhas? (Where did the swallows go?), 246, 247
Passoni, Moara, 3
Paro, Iana, 85, 93
Patai, Daphne, 218, 225
Paula, Betse de, 22
Paulo Gustavo, 27, 28
Pécora, Luisa, 32, 33, 34, 92
Peirano, María-Paz, 4
Pela janela (A window to Rosália), 25, 52
Pellegrino, Antônia, 104
Pellenz, André, 26
Perez, Glória, 58
Peso da massa, leveza do pão (Weight of the dough, lightness of the bread), 39

Passos, Mailsa, 204
Pessoa, Ana, 22
Pieper, Katherine, 198
Piñeyro, Marcelo, 144
Pirinop: Meu primeiro contato (Pirinop: My first contact), 235, 246
Praça Paris (Paris Square), 25
Precisamos falar do assédio (Faces of harassment), 8, 10, 13, 116–129, 135, 252, 253, 254, 255, 262, 263, 265
Preta Portê Filmes, 60, 200, 217, 223, 224
Prêmio Diadorim/Diadorim Award, 52
Prêmio Resgate do Cinema Brasileiro (Brazilian Cinema Rescue Award), 17
Primavera das mulheres (Women's spring), 104
Primeiro tratamento (First treatment podcast), 54
Projeto Cine Tela Brasil (Project Cinema Brazil), 205

Quase dois irmãos (Almost brothers), 22
Que horas ela volta (The second mother), 10, 11, 51, 62, 103, 139, 140–151, 153, 154, 156, 187
Quentura (Heat), 234, 241, 246, 248

Rainha (Queen), 34
Ramos, Maria Augusta, 7, 10, 11, 25, 36, 39, 64, 101–112, 161–180
Randall, Rachel, 157
realizador, 48
Renov, Michael, 2
Rezende, Julia, 55, 56, 58, 62
Rezende, Priscila, 210
Rezende, Sérgio, 31, 55
Ribeiro, Ana Paula Alves, 212
Ribeiro, Djamila, 5, 12, 129, 130, 218

Rio, a day in August, 170
Rist, Peter, 21
Roberts-Camps, Traci, 21, 22, 37
Rocha, Glauber, 205
Rodrigues, Carol, 51, 53, 55, 57, 59, 60, 61, 63
Rodrigues, César, 16
Rodrigues, João Carlos, 220
Rojas, Juliana, 51, 52, 58, 63
Roland, Dany, 31
Rosa, Ary, 66
Rosa, Sabrina, 66
Rouch, Jean, 234

Sacchetta, Paula, 8, 10, 12, 13, 116, 117, 120, 121, 126, 129, 251–265
sala de roteiro (a writers' room), 55
Salles, Walter, 22, 23, 30, 32, 150, 158, 172, 173
Salles Gomes, Paulo Emílio, 164
Sampaio, Adélia, 40, 66, 78, 81, 87, 199, 205, 222
San Martín, Patricia Torres, 20, 44
Santhiago, Ricardo, 218
Santiago, Lilián Solá, 206
Santos, Érica Ramos Sarmet dos, 87
Santos, Nelson Pereira dos, 210
Saraceni, Paulo César, 164
Sarno, Geraldo, 164
Schwarcz, Lilia Moritz, 141
Se eu fosse você (If I Were You), 57, 58, 62
Se eu fosse você 2 (If I Were You 2), 58
Seca (Drought), 174, 179
Seiger, Beatriz, 39
Sette, Leonardo, 240
Shaw, Deborah, 2, 14, 21, 200
Shu, Maria, 59
Silva, Adyel, 228
Silva, Camila Vieira, 22
Silveira, Anita Rocha da, 104
Sinfonia da necrópole (Necropolis symphony), 63

Smith, Stacey L., 198
Soarez, Elena, 50, 55, 56, 57, 58, 63, 65
Solberg, Helena, 165
Somos Mais que 30 (We Are More than 30), 84
SOS: Mulheres ao mar (SOS: Women to the sea), 26
SOS: Mulheres ao mar 2 (SOS: Women to the sea 2), 26, 62, 66
Souza, Jaqueline, 54
Souza, Juliana, 120, 121, 258, 259
Souza, Ruth de, 224, 228
Spcine, 85, 86, 103, 201, 202
Stam, Robert, 21, 220
Sueño Florianópolis (Florianópolis dream), 25, 39
Sundance Institute; Sundance Screenwriters Lab, 50, 51, 53

Tedesco, Marina Cavalcanti, 22, 87
Tejle, Ellen, 85, 94
Terra estrangeira (Foreign land), 30
Terrores urbanos (Urban horrors), 63
Thayná, Yasmin, 11, 12, 33, 60, 197–212, 226
The Constant Gardener, 32
The Hunting Ground, 259
The Motorcycle Diaries, 32
The Two Popes, 32
Think Olga, 115, 116, 117, 123, 129, 130, 134, 135, 137, 254
Thomas, Daniela, 22, 23, 30, 32, 187
Tim Maia, 104
Torres, Tiago Campos, 240
Trabalho cansa (Hard labor), 63
Trautman, Tereza, 62

Três Verões (Three summers), 156
Tropa de elite (Elite squad), 25, 172
Tropa de elite 2 (Elite squad 2), 25, 172
Tserewahu, Divino, 240
Tweets, 115, 117, 134, 254
Txicão, Natuyu, 242, 243

Um Passaporte Húngaro (A Hungarian passport), 39

Valadão, Virginia, 234, 240
Valenti, Vanessa, 89
Vamos fazer um brinde (Let's make a toast), 66
Van Dick, José, 89
VAV Vitrine do Audiovisual (VAV Audiovisual Showcase), 54
Vazante (Wetland), 187
Veiga, Ana Maria, 210
Vicente, Juliana, 12, 200, 206, 217–229
Video nas Aldeias (VNA), 234
Viñoles, Mariana, 39
Viramundo (World turning), 164

Werneck, Jurema, 218
Werneck, Sandra, 18, 26, 31, 165
White, Patricia, 36
Wursch, Yoya, 62

Xuxa em o mistério da feiurinha (Xuxa and the mystery of the little ugly princess), 26

Yamazaki, Tizuka, 18, 21, 26

Zama, 104